DEMOCRACY UNDER ATTACK

FALSE PROMISES, CORRUPTION AND SOCIAL KHAOS. A PATH TOWARDS TYRANNY

DEMOCRACY UNDER ATTACK: FALSE PROMISES, CORRUPTION AND SOCIAL KHAOS. A PATH TOWARDS TYRANNY: I am going to paraphrase an idea from Alexis de Tocqueville 1805-1859 **(1),** where he warns that "a book is written so that we have timely warnings of how Freedom is lost and not lose it. One should not write to escape despotism or dictatorship. I must note that De Tocqueville fell short in referring to despotism and not predicting the modern dictatorship in which not only oppression plays a role, but also a more serious element is added and that is that everyone in the new oppression would have been able to decide to fall voluntarily. in it or that has been captured by an ideological process of indoctrination. At this point it would be too late and we would not be able to get out of the worst possible political system ever created; It would not be as simple as killing the despot, because in every mind of every individual there would be a captive or indoctrinated despot. Additionally, this modern dictatorship will have interposed so many ideological barriers, so many unfulfilled promises, and will have concentrated unimaginable economic and political powers between the oppressed society and its freedom that resistance would be useless. Yes... A trap in which deep down lies the promise of equality.

We can always decide our future and our future; We are on time... and, it is not tomorrow, it is now.

The threat is subtle, but so vast and enormous that it can only be resolved with everyone's participation.

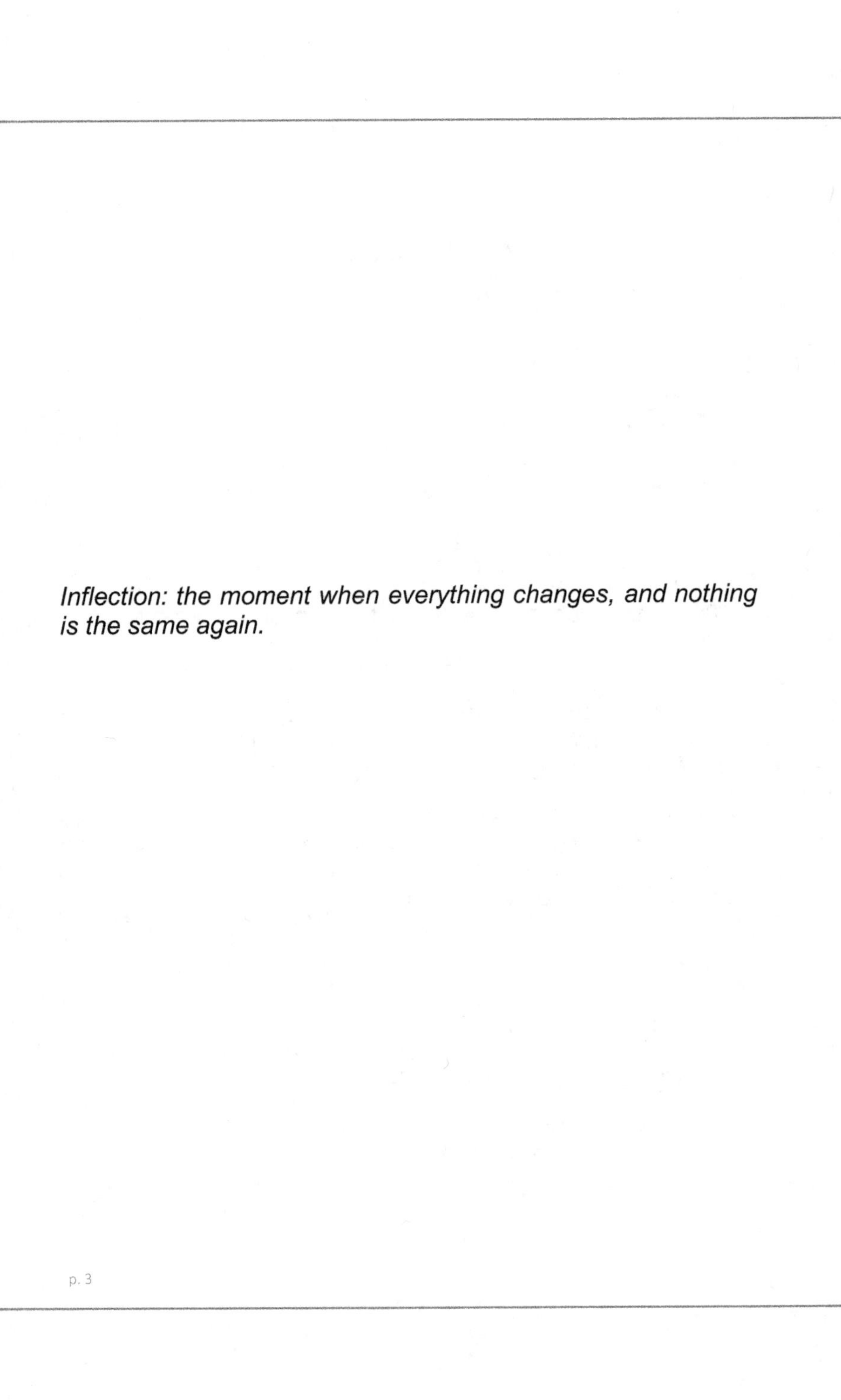

Inflection: the moment when everything changes, and nothing is the same again.

INDEX

PREFACE

Democracy, a concept rooted in human history, has been constantly tested throughout its evolution. Since its inception, democracy has emerged to establish rules, order, and limits for those who guide the destiny of human communities. However, in this scenario of shared decisions, the innate inclination of human nature towards unbridled power and control has become evident. This constant struggle for power, combined with the social unrest generated by the manipulation of political groups in the second half of the 20th century, which fostered social exclusion and the commodification of basic services and fundamental rights, has paved the way for currents of radical left come to power through democratic means.

The fundamental dilemma we face is that, regardless of their political orientation, once political groups come to power, the promises of advancement and progress often vanish into thin air. Democratic institutions, eroded by deep-rooted corruption, have left fertile ground for any political group to take up the banner of change in search of improving the living conditions of their fellow citizens and eradicating corruption. However, reality shows us that this ambition rarely materializes.

Citizen trust in democratic institutions is essential for the success of any government, regardless of its orientation. Unfortunately, over decades, this fertile soil has been contaminated by regulations and laws that benefit elites close to power and have facilitated the growth of corrupt acts. Widespread distrust in these institutions has paved the way for political groups on the far left or right to seize power, all promising change, renewal and equity, sometimes even proposing radical changes in the way countries are run.

This book, is the second installment of the series that began with "The Rise of the Left in Latin America in the Age of Unrest", invites us to explore the historical background of Marxism. It helps us understand that this option, whether presented directly and violently or indirectly and progressively, inexorably leads to the concentration of power and, ultimately, tyranny.

As we delve into these pages, we will explore the complexities of democracy, the struggle for freedom and power, and the challenges that democratic institutions face in the search for a system that truly serves citizens. This book is a reflection on the current state of democracy in the world, an invitation to reflection and, we hope, a call to action to preserve and strengthen the foundations of a just and equitable society.
Roberto Perea.

FOREWORD

The idealists against the pragmatists (2) (realism), in their struggle, keep societies in suspense; Even worse, in certain circumstances, they decide to throw it into the abyss.

Recent history shows us a clear intellectual confrontation between a group that we could call the pragmatists against the idealists. For the most part, both groups are encouraged by the honest belief that they are doing the right thing and that they are right. This same certainty of feeling like bearers of the truth is what unleashes the darkest acts and extremism on both sides.

These confrontations move to the economic, political, social level, and from time to time to the physical level and they try to resolve them through the extermination of the opponent.

After the fall of the Berlin Wall, unanimity did not prevail, the task - against poverty - was halfway done: the developed countries continued to be pragmatic and followed their path of economic inclusion, well-being, and prosperity with very few changes. On the other hand, in Latin America they did not understand the signs that there was no absolute winner, they did not see the alarms. The intoxication of absolute power increased the already existing inequalities and exclusions; They call this extreme situation neoliberalism; We call it: discomfort.

What strategy could take advantage of the discomfort to reverse a state of strategic loss into one of tactical gain, positions that could put you back in an offensive position and eventually reverse the situation?

The first and fourth parts of this book are about this slow, progressive and systematic strategy, how parts of history are taken, from each thinker, how they take advantage of triumphalism, understand and use resentment, exclusion, rage and hatred, turning them into a political tool. Those who confront each other are human beings, where the desire for absolute power could be what animates them the most; Among their blind fighting options could be throwing society into the abyss.

Spontaneous economic relations that generate inequalities versus the redesign of them that collide with the free development of human beings.

Idealism does not exist in the animal world and as a general method, the animal world resolves any contradiction based on the preservation of the species and solves it in a relatively natural way: the law of the fittest and strongest. It would also be said that animals are subject to laws; man can choose.

In the initial stages of society, of civilization, structures replicated from the animal world prevailed: hierarchical and the power of the strongest that fulfilled their purpose, preserving the species. However, concepts, some born of human design and others not, such as cooperation and solidarity allowed small related tribal societies to achieve developments in the sense of general well-being; They were the glimpses of idealism.

When the size of the population infers a certain degree of complexity to tribal social relations, a new element emerges on the scene that complicates the matter even more: successful spontaneous processes begin to occur in exchange that improve individual well-being and, by extension, The general; what is successful is immediately copied by other individuals. We are governed by the same laws that organize the animal world: they reward the fittest, not having any type of consideration for the least fit. We already know the result of successful economic exchange: they allow you to accumulate wealth and initiate the inequalities of the free market that will accompany us for the rest of history. However, from idealism and "ought to be", there will be solutions that come from "human design" with the aim of solving spontaneously generated problems of inequality. We all know the results - they do not lead to the sustained well-being of society - and in most cases it complicates or distances other achievements of society such as freedom. Many of these "improvements" collide with human nature and the force of their goodness forces them to be installed under duress: the confrontation is born between "good idealists" who could end in tyranny and pragmatists who achieve well-being at the cost of inequalities that encourage the resentment.

However, societies choose their path for themselves and by doing so spontaneously, in freedom, they do not care about inequalities, they choose what works, what is natural to them: in Latin America they chose the family businesses, the micros, the small businesses. Despite this, they are ready to be forced to follow another path; a path designed without inequalities, but which brings them closer to the poverty from which they are fleeing, and the tyranny barely overcome 250 years ago.

INTRODUCTION

This book is written to be read by the left, the right, unionists, socialists, liberals, economists, non-economists, and anyone devoid of doctrines and in full use of pragmatism that allows them to see reality.

Part of the information for its development arose from unfinished discussions on certain topics within the INFLEXION Thinking Tank made up of my colleagues Roberto Perea and Carlos Ruiz. Special tribute to fellow founder Hector Aillón RIP.

This book has required continuous research and invaluable input from close people who understand my desire to go further and have opened a door for me in their everyday places: I talk about the Cuban friends in exile who allowed me access to the island. , not as a tourist but as another Cuban: talking to people, eating what they ate, getting on the buses, taking collective taxis, drinking rum in places only for Cubans; live the day-to-day.

I must give special thanks to my unionist friends, both those indoctrinated by socialism and those who are not. That's the kind of people I value: people with consistent convictions (good or bad, in my opinion, but consistent). I arrived at places that could be the envy of any social or economic researcher, places so remote to speak with each type of people so different, with such disparate interests, that sometimes I am assailed by the fear cast by the impossibility of the meaning "tower of Babel"; of everything that this can mean in terms of irreconcilable opinions.

I would like to be able to thank you all, but you understand that there are unspeakable places, situations, and characters for the simple reason that they would carry their guilt and situations that must be overcome; I remind you that some warned me: don't mention me... thank you all... thank you...

I hope that your doubts are resolved by these writings and that you are prepared in case there is something that you do not want to hear; However, I consider it a sign of responsibility towards future generations.

I just hope that one day we all have a place, a space within well-being in this country.

There are several purposes that encourage me to write this second book; All of these aspects are in one way, or another linked to the first book: THE RISE OF THE LEFT IN LATIN AMERICA IN THE FULL ERA OF UNREST. This first book exposes how unrest is installed in an environment, apparently, of defeat in which "history is over." This context is openly taken advantage of by the counterpart with a proposal that accentuates exclusion to seek unlimited economic and political power. Military regimes were no longer necessary; Now it was an economic siege that only benefited big business through the kidnapping of rights (health, education, pensions) for its own benefit. This second book studies in detail the deployment of the left's strategy that is doctrinally installed using the state; It reveals its goal, which is none other than the search for power without limits. The interests of society resist between both forces and ultimately show their robustness. Both groups forget, leaving aside that the true excluded people have already opted for a third path: starting their small businesses making use of their freedom and their right not to let themselves die of hunger. In both books, the need for the development of a third volume is outlined in which the economic path taken by this larger percentage of the population can be expanded.

Economic topics are treated as stories and in some cases with graphics so that they are accessible to all audiences.

The first purpose is personal and is to resolve the feeling of frustration that has repeatedly accompanied me in all the discussions in which I have tried to explain the greatest challenge that freedom in Latin America has faced in modern times. The reasons for which I have declared myself unable to make myself understood due to lack of arguments to transcend from the irrational to the rational universe. Additionally, the events triggered are diverse, dispersed and extended over time; However, they are methodical, systematic and I repeat, deeply irrational; This last aspect is what makes it difficult to specify its seriousness, and to understand -know how to read between the lines- from rational thought.

All this clarification will be in the first part, however, due to the dense nature of the topic, I see it necessary to give it an analysis from a sociological and productive point of view, almost a materialist one (economic activity determines all other tasks); and a deep historical sense. So we see it necessary to clarify where the terms equality, freedom, despotism and tyranny come from; For this reason we will begin by explaining how humanity frees itself from despotism and tyranny following the passion of seeking equality and along the way we find the feeling of freedom (you have or you don't have freedom and you have to feel it); Equality and freedom continue to this day in the form of opposing political movements. We will analyze the bases, pillars, and incentives to produce value and wealth of each economic scheme that we review. We will develop new tools to emphasize the fundamentals of incentives in an economic system; The reader must put special effort into understanding these old concepts, underestimated by economists, however they are considered the new objectives of the successful strategy, demonstrating that if these sensitive points are attacked the economy of a country will not be able to recover, in fact the damage is so deep and complex that it puts society…civilization at risk.

We will qualify and establish a test of tyranny in each society analyzed to subsequently understand the seriousness of the current threat to freedom and the resurgence of tyranny - we believe that it is a natural tendency of humanity to tend towards tyranny - which only dresses in different clothes in history. We will define in history - with the help of Viscount de Tocqueville, Marx, Engels, Proudhon, Foucault, Sartre, Derrida, Von Mises, Hayek, Friedman and others - the parts of a strategy from those who plot in silence hoping to explode, even those who methodically and systematically understand the hidden forces in society to unleash passions and impose their criteria (we call on the reader to be patient and later, and in the conclusion of the first part, unite the pieces that are scattered throughout history and come together with a force capable of destroying a society); Additionally, you must understand how it is possible to carry out a strategy of this caliber completely unnoticed and the most important contribution is that you can establish an effective counter strategy. We must be clear that history has a spontaneous way of becoming and human design is opposed to it - human design seeks to correct what the free performance of history generates, such as inequality, for example - and clashes with human nature, responding to this with coercion, oppression and tyranny.

No less important is the identification of groups susceptible to being instrumentalized against a system and leading to its destruction. It would not be fair if we did not also identify the counterpart, the groups that can be the salvation of the current economic system and of civilization itself as we know it. The common thread of the first part is equality and its development in history will call on idealists to plot under schemes of coercion to impose a "better" world free of inequalities; We will observe the development of modern left-wing political movements. We will return to this thread in the fourth part to analyze this winning strategy already in power and its effect on liberal democracy.

In the second part we will continue with the thread of Freedom from the point of its absolute loss: slavery. New elements will emerge, such as the freedom that exists in the United States, where property, inclusion, and the weapons to defend it come served on the same platter. We must be able to add these new ingredients and compare them to what we are finding that occurs in Latin America. Another aspect in this part is to understand what ancient slavery consists of, considering its main concepts: remuneration for work, food, life itself, the right to defend oneself, the denial of property and weapons. They must be able to compare, based on concepts, the slave system with the modern economic-political systems that have emerged since the 18th century and are perfected and adapted to the present. It must be understood that there is nothing new in the systems proposed in the modern and postmodern era - things are changed so that everything remains the same - they simply improve and strengthen the concepts, good or bad, that have worked. It is essential to deduce how slavery is made legal, sometimes by force of use and custom, which is finally reflected in the laws, to be enforced by force of arms.

In the first and second parts we will develop the second purpose, but perhaps the most important: and that is that only the appearance of freedom begins to tear us out of poverty (it is freedom and only it): **All the forces of initiative and creativity of the being human were hidden in slavery and servitude; Only when Freedom was installed was talent unleashed and all those productive forces were unleashed, generating value and wealth like never before in the history of humanity, lifting large sectors out of poverty that for more than 20 centuries had known nothing but poverty. survival and extreme poverty.** Only in this way, by removing the constraints on freedom, was such progress achieved in the well-being of the population. The other aspect linked to this second purpose is how the measure of freedom also measures the degree of well-being of the people. Hayek already said it: Any reduction in freedom reduces the rates of progress of civilization.

The third purpose is to expose from its core, a proposal that in its deployment shows to be successful in criticizing the current system and in taking advantage of the existing unrest, it is successful in overthrowing the bases of an existing economic model and establishing itself in power, but , failed to create new value and wealth; The sum of destruction of what exists plus failure to produce new value leaves the economy completely helpless, unable to feed and maintain the existing population.

The first and fourth parts of this book generate the information necessary to understand the new strategy of seizing power of the left and its scope; More than that, the risk in democratic terms of underestimating their purposes and their determination to impose what they consider should be our redemption and a better future for all of us.

I am concerned about the irresponsibility of the promoters of this strategy and their little attachment to the immediate consequences in terms of damage to the health of society. In another order of things, much more worrying is the naivety with which institutions are left alone to withstand such an attack against them; The most silent and strongest attack has been structured against the institutions of liberal democracy in Latin America.

For the fourth purpose we intend to establish some causes why economic development in Latin America is elusive; The methodology is the comparison between the liberal democracy - the United States of America - most successful in creating value and wealth with ours in Latin America. At the time, it should be possible to establish what one has and what the other suffers from. We alert the reader to the first and second parts where we analyze American society from two different points of view (in the first part pursuing Equality and in the second part from the point of view of freedom with private property and individual capacity to defend it). The reader must be clear about all this previous baggage to insert the cultural theme of corruption, of economic exclusion in Latin America to understand the differences with the American model.

Finally, we will return to the analyzes carried out in the first two parts, to see in the fourth part where the proposals and measures of the new apparently directionless governments really point: their purpose is to destroy the bases, the pillars, and the incentives of our economy. Next, we will look at its effects on well-being, on general progress and how the reduction in income of the entire society in general is guaranteed.

The fifth purpose is to demonstrate that, if individuals are left free to choose the path of their progress and well-being, they will choose free enterprise and entrepreneurship. Proposing otherwise is going against nature, it is also irresponsible and unscrupulous. The majority in Latin America has already chosen, has already opted for free enterprise; This is demonstrated by more than 70% of the population in Latin America that participates in the economy in the form of businesses run by ordinary people (family businesses, and microenterprises): they did not choose collectivization. It is their response to discomfort, to racial economic exclusion; It is a response in the form of work, effort, dreams, employment represented in the rummage, micro and family businesses: they are the expression of the people in economic freedom.

In the fifth and last part of the book, we will touch on the aspects mentioned in the previous paragraph; will prepare the themes of the third book. Consequently, we will make a proposal of what the new left should be from the current situation of most of the population that is in the rummage, family businesses, micros, and SMEs, very despite the exclusion. These majority sectors of the population have not been and will not be considered by the right, because they themselves despise rummaging, as much as those on the left despise the free enterprise intrinsic to the family businesses. We will outline what we consider a state of well-being for them, for those who cannot yet afford it, but who offer all their efforts to get ahead and one day soon be able to face and cover their own expenses.

It is important to note that we see ourselves as left-wing in the sense that we value the people's micro-businesses; We move away from the outdated models of the traditional left, which only lower the prosperity of the people and plunge them into the darkest and deepest poverty. The proposals, in the final chapter, represent the support that the people need to move from survival to well-being by virtue of the freedom that the people must choose their development and not to impose on them - as they intend - something that they consider to be fair, but that has not been requested.

When looking at family businesses and microenterprises, our proposal will establish the measures of what we consider should be done to support them, so that they can freely develop and consolidate all their creative potential of value and wealth; Its connection with large companies is vital to raising the income of society in general; so as not to start from scratch. This will demonstrate how wrong is the current policy of the right that ostracizes popular efforts and that of the left that attacks big business (ignoring the social value of private property, dragging society to hunger and scarcity). recognizes the value of small businesses due to their entrepreneurship and free enterprise component (he sees it as the fruit of the forbidden tree).

FIRST PART

EARLY WARNING: WHEN EQUALITY IS EASIER TO UNDERSTAND THAN FREEDOM

In the five units of the first part, we take a historical journey from the 18th, 19th, 20th and 21st centuries following the human passion for the search for Equality that has marked the steps of an entire current to the present day and to the detriment of freedom. This journey is necessary to develop tools from the simplest point (feudalism), that allow us to understand the type of attack that the economy and society itself receives today. We will follow the development and contributions of different currents to the most successful strategy deployed today in Latin America. The sixth unit will clarify the way in which human beings develop and strengthen concepts such as family, institutions, order, laws, the rule of law, property, and freedom. We will contrast this liberal vision of the family with the contributions of post-Marxism (postmodernism) - for comparative purposes that lead us to understand which aspects are prioritized in a strategy. Will this answer the reason why the school-family binomial is under attack?

1

THE STRUGGLE BETWEEN FREEDOM AND ITS COUNTERPART THAT GENERATES PASSIONS: EQUALITY

In this unit we go about Tocqueville's ideas expressed in his book: "Democracy in America". With historical sense we will go to confront the alarms that he already pointed out, with the situation that Ibero-America (3) is experiencing at this moment. We will look at the violent entry of liberal democracy (in the English and French revolutions) to wrest land ownership from feudal lords. The subsistence production that only the land provides in feudalism will be changed by the overflow of wealth never created with which capitalism erupts. We will discover the pillars, the bases and the incentives that support and move the feudal economy, as well as those of liberal democracy; Later we will run a tyranny test on both; you will have to compare. By having exposed the bases, pillars, and incentives in an economy, we will deduce the direct and indirect ways to destroy an economy; You will be amazed at how elemental and simple the attack could be. We will test your projection capacity to take these ideas from the 18th, 19th, and 20th centuries, frame them in the 21st century of the networks that potentiate and accelerate everything; will infer that the methodology used is a time bomb where any group could attack a society if it has the resources and convinced people. The tyranny test will help us discover if in the future any form of government, no matter how hidden, meets the requirements to be considered a potential tyranny and endangers freedom.

UNDERSTANDING THE EARLY WARNINGS OF TOCQUEVILLE IN THEIR HISTORICAL CONTEXT

To take Alexis de Tocqueville (1805-1859) is to take him in the 18th century in a feudal context in Europe, of upheaval in the political and social spectrum with a view to the democratic phenomenon that was taking place in America (4).

EQUALITY AS A SOCIAL CONSTRUCTION AND BECAUSE IT IS BUILT IN DESPOTISM

November 1648 put an end to the English Civil War that had pitted the forces of King Charles I against the parliamentary army under the command of Oliver Cromwell. The sovereign was deposed; He was arrested on charges of high treason against the people and exercise of tyrannical power. The king claimed that he was responsible for his actions only before God!

A single blow of the ax driven by the passion generated by class equality separated the head of the monarch, giving a blow to monarchical despotism; This is how democracy made its way. A similar process would happen to Louis XVI, guillotined in France in 1793 by the French Revolution.

Europe had experienced two transcendental processes (English and French revolutions) that would guide the direction of socio-political changes - said changes driven by two new concepts or ideas: Equality and freedom, which would establish the end of the feudal order and its fixed classes and immovable groups of aristocracy, clergy, and serfs - which would occur in the following centuries:

English Revolution

The first is the English revolution (1642-1688), where the final events that were unleashed were part of a chain of events that had been brewing to reduce the power of absolutism for the benefit of Parliament: Equality and freedom (5) and They were on the rise.

Equality and freedom only existed between equals, that is, within social classes; between classes there were insurmountable borders determined by privileges of blood, of birth; The rights as well as the ownership of the land were exclusive and hereditary: there was no equality between one class and another; much less freedom. The servants (servitude) were tied to the land; This means that they could be sold with it.

In the economic aspect, changes were already underway; It was noticeable in activities typical of cities such as commerce and exchange. Craft production was driven by incipient technological advances, however, they had to wait another century to get the true boost of the first industrial revolution with the application of steam and mechanization. These processes of creating value and wealth in a different way than what the land could generate, began to create mobility (6) - for the moment only economic - but which in its beginnings created what would be considered unprecedented in history: the social and political mobility.

It is necessary to understand that political and social changes occur when "real power" is lost by the ruling class.

Real power in the Middle Ages is given, first, by the prevailing paradigms: the lord who owned the land, the blood aristocracy and serfdom, concepts that were transferred to culture (way of life). Then, uses and customs generate laws that reproduce domination. Lastly, military strength – the most important job of royalty and aristocracy was to train daily in the military arts; These activities were prohibited to servitude - it was therefore the military component that enforced

the laws of servitude and subjection created by themselves; Any change was grounds for repression.

At this time, the new ideas (equality and freedom), although incipient, were part of the collective ideology as opposed to the legal framework of servitude.

The ownership of land as the only element to create value and wealth, to generate the well-being of the feudal lords, was under siege. It was besieged by a new economic class with a system that allowed the production of goods (shirts, belts, etc.) coupled with the possibility of trading; to exchange (mercantilism). This new system gave them the economic power to subdue feudalism, since their possibilities of creation and wealth multiplied by more than ten times compared to the original form that the land gave to the feudal lord. The die was cast: the blood rights of the monarchy and the aristocracy that allowed them to maintain their armies and vassalage had been overcome by the force of ideas (equality and freedom) and of a new wealth that free enterprise gave: was born the capitalism. Feudalism was collapsing.

All that was missing was the final blow that would come from the social and political changes that had to be made due to the force of history and that normally their vehicle is weapons and due pressure. This occurred in England two hundred years earlier than in revolutionary France in 1789.

French Revolution

The second is the French Revolution **(7)** (1789-1795) that consolidated the loss of power of absolutism, the progress of liberalism and the division of powers as we know them. The changes and advancement of equality not only occurred in mobility between social classes, but before the law. The law was already being configured as a separate expression and as an element of defense of the blood aristocracy and servitude against the authoritarian despotism of the king: I am the law and my power is given by God.

The fusion of the first and second articles of the Declaration of the Rights of Man and of the Citizen, 1789 **(8)** gives us light on the new meaning of freedom - freedom being understood as the uprooting of the land for the servant -, (which previously, it could be sold with the land) and equality: which already brought together two new concepts; mobility between classes plus Equality before the Law of the aristocracy, the serfs and the clergy. He declared the end of despotism: men are born and remain free and equal in rights. Such rights are liberty, property, security, and resistance to oppression.

As you can see, the search for Equality (9) has been a desire of society even more than the search and preservation of freedom; These are the dangers that loom over it.

Each of the seventeen articles of the Declaration of the Rights of Man and the Citizen is a death certificate to the privileges and blood rights that feudalism brought and added a new paradigm to the concept of equality (social mobility): equality before the law.

The process that occurred in France had characteristics very similar to the English ones, in which economic equality had been generated spontaneously in a process of exchange and mercantilism that allowed the creation of new classes and new wealth; The changes that sought socioeconomic equality occurred abruptly in the revolution.

PILLARS THAT SUPPORT THE FOUNDATIONS OF FEUDALISM
ANALOGY OF THE HOUSE TO EXPLAIN THE SYSTEM, DIFFERENTIATE A DIRECT ATTACK FROM AN INDIRECT ONE AND SHOW THE PILLARS OR BASES THAT SUPPORT THEM

The current account of the example of the French Revolution leads the reader to understand how an economic-political system is overthrown with a direct strategy, that is, with an armed uprising or a revolution directed against the forces that defend the established order. The holding classes are then dispossessed and a change in ownership occurs; Each change in ownership develops its own cultural structures and institutions that sustain and reproduce the new system. The reader should also be able to deduce a third aspect that results after implementing a revolution (direct or indirect strategy) that causes the perpetrator to be led to the temptation of **"Unlimited Power."**

So far, the reader has only perceived direct attacks and will need some instrument or new concept that allows him to deduce an indirect attack when we state it. The indirect attack is different and difficult to perceive; It will be necessary to identify it when we talk about post-Marxism (Postmodernism) and more specifically Antonio Gramsci.

Stating the pillars or bases that support the bases of each system that we are going to analyze, called feudalism, liberal democracy, and socialism, will help us in the task. This new perspective will allow us to connect elements that we directly associate with the bases of an economic institution, such as the ownership of productive elements, others related to what is done with the property to reproduce the system. There are others that are a little more difficult to relate to, such as what makes you use those means to produce, that is, incentives. The latter are the most important in cases in which an indirect strategy of destruction of the system is established.

The house analogy

Let's give an example, to understand this topic through analogies where a house will represent the system: for feudalism the house itself is the property of the land (origin of all wealth), the bases and pillars that support it are legitimacy (given by God), the power of institutions (church, class division, administrative systems, etc.), finally due obedience (usages and customs of servitude that become culture and laws); The house is protected by armed soldiers who force obedience.

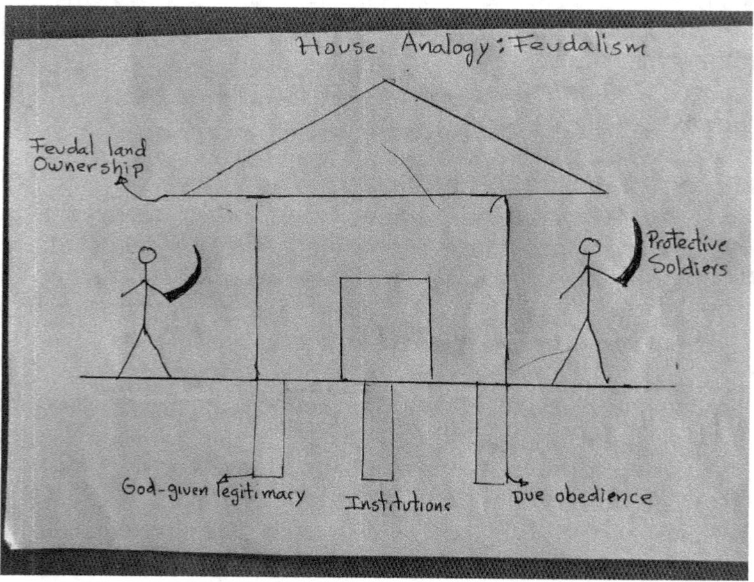

Direct attack on feudal property

The direct attacks on feudal property occurred first by militarily defeating the nobility who led the protective soldiers, and then going for the ownership of the land, that is, destroying the house and then removing the pillars or bases of feudalism to be replaced by those of liberal democracy. Everything in that order.

How the feudal system reproduces.

Feudal society was united by the weapons held by the nobility; These weapons subjugated and tied the people to the earth.

The way to reproduce this system was marriage between nobles that united the lands or wars that subjugated them; By subduing or gaining new lands, the people tied to it were also obtained, that is, new servitude was added.

PILLARS THAT SUPPORT THE FOUNDATIONS OF FEUDALISM:

FEUDALISM
Ownership of land: The land belongs to the Monarch and the Aristocracy.
Laws: Social classes are divided, and you cannot go from one class to the other.
Institutions: Inheritance (of lands, properties, and noble titles) occurs through the bloodline, only between Nobles, between classes.
Monopoly of force: by the monarch and the Nobles. Wide use of force towards the civilian population to maintain the status quo and due obedience.
God-given legitimacy.

Institutions: The Clergy and the church are part of the feudal power.
Concentration of powers in the nobility.
INCENTIVES: the first incentive was force and oppression exerted by the nobility. The nobility managed to increase the productivity of the land when it allowed serfs to keep part of what was produced on their land (partial ownership).

How the system is reproduced

The feudal system is maintained by the force of oppression, its reproduction does not occur through incentives as in capitalism, it occurs only through wars or marriages between monarchs that end in forcible annexations or unions of territories.

The revolutionary processes (French and English revolution) that occurred in feudalism - and that normally ended in tyrannicide - were precipitated by the presence of monarchs who multiplied all the feelings of discomfort of living without equality, the lack of freedom, the denial palpable access to well-being and the mistreatment received.

METER OF TYRANNY IN FEUDALISM

The tyranny meter is another conceptual construct that will allow us to evaluate and classify each political economic system in history and measure activity in power according to its proximity to tyranny and coercion against freedom. In principle, the zero point of tyranny should be taken in slavery, then moving on to the servitude of the Middle Ages; However, the serious concepts explained here that were born and have been developing for more than 10,000 years are only refined over time, reappearing with greater impact in modern political processes (there are concepts that were incipient in feudalism, but that were "purged" by the new, more modern aspiring tyrants). This is the reason that feudalism begins with a measure of 57, while measures of tyranny of 80 will be found in more modern political economic processes or systems.

Eighty (80) is the maximum tyranny meter of this Test and gives us an idea of oppression and how actually coercive or potentially harmful to freedom a system can be. Each factor has a maximum measure of evil according to the tyranny of five: it is more tyrannical the closer the factor is to five.

METER OF TYRANNY IN FEUDALISM

Power Factors or Actions	Tyrannical Rating from lowest to highest (1-2 Green. 3 Yellow. 4-5 Red, where 5 is maximum tyranny)	Observations
Use of force against the population	4	The servants had only their work tools (hoes, scythes, plows).
Executive power concentration	5	All powers in the Monarch.
Concentration of judicial power	5	All powers in the Monarch.
Legislative power concentration	5	All powers in the Monarch.

Possibility of getting out of the tyrant through tyrannicide	2	There are many historical records of the people getting rid of a tyrant.
Use of indoctrination in Society	2	Indoctrination is a modern process. Bodies in feudalism were tyrannized, however, minds remained free.
Dissidents may be expelled	3	Exile was considered one of the greatest punishments in ancient times along with the death penalty.
Possibility of individual and collective organization	4	That Freedom existed for the Aristocracy.
Possibility of putting -from the authority- the population one against the other	1	There was class division, and they were cohesive within. Pitting civilians against each other is a modern phenomenon.
Possibility of developing some type of property that allows one to defend oneself from the State.	2	Owning the land was wealth and this belonged to the nobles and the king; Any manual work was considered common, impure (that is why the free market, and the bourgeoisie could emerge). You could not have land (only Blood

		Nobles and Titles), but other activities could be developed.
Possibility of losing life	4	In many cases the life of servitude could be disposed of.
Freedom Meter	5	Only the aristocrat, royalty and clergy are free; The easement is tied to the land and can be sold with it.
Equality Meter	5	They are equal between classes, that is, the noble is Equal to the Noble, but Class Equality or transgressing class boundaries was never allowed. They were social, economic, and political boundaries and were inherited by blood. They were the bases of the feudal system.
Possibilities of receiving compensation for your work	3	Feudalism achieved those five days of work went to the lord and two days to the serf.
Possibility to choose your job	3	The job is assigned to you by the feudal lord. Later in Burgos, it was already possible to choose a job.
Religious freedom	4	Religion was part of the system of oppression.

Measurement of Tyranny in the feudal system: 57 out of 80 the maximum.

THE AMERICAN PROCESS: PROPERTY, EQUALITY AND FREEDOM

Independence of the United States (1776)

Alexis De Tocqueville carefully studied the entire process that occurred in North America and the special characteristics of democracy in that part of the Anglo-Saxon world.

He encountered peculiarities, such as that feudalism, with its privileges and class rights, could never be established in America; A revolution was not needed for something that never existed. From its beginnings, it was very difficult for the English Crown to transfer the feudal administration system and land property laws (it was not possible to establish the blood rights of the traditional social classes, to grant the English aristocracy the properties of the Crown in pursuit of its colonial exploitation). The colonists did not allow it; - the explanation of this aspect is found in the second part of this book (10) - so, there were very special circumstances, and outside the prevailing law, in the management of the property, which allowed it to be created for the first time the "sense of American economic inclusion", which continues to this day: "the American dream". After unsuccessful attempts to establish the administration under the tutelage of the Lords, an experiment was carried out that gave the colonists the power represented by the ownership of the land, without succession through the bloodline: they found themselves one day with power and lands given for exploitation. The next revolutionary act for its time was the holding of elections, where settlers with land could vote. The property granted achieved equality, then the achievement of freedom occurred after the war of independence. Class equality (social and political) came with the first democratic election held among property-owning white men. In America, in its beginnings there was only freedom and inclusive equality for white men with property; It was not the time of women or black slaves.

Later, the process of inclusion (equality and freedom) with property continued in America, granting to the west the delivery of land to the new settlers who arrived in the new world.

This feeling of inclusion (equality and freedom) properly endures to this day and is what has made America great and has constituted the **American Dream.**

What do the English Revolution, the French Revolution, and American Independence have in common?

Taken from the book Why Countries Fail by Daron Acemoglu and James Robinson, page 18: "Others, like Great Britain and the United States, became rich because their citizens overthrew the elites who controlled power and created a Society in which Political powers were much more distributed, in which the government had to be accountable and respond to the citizens and the vast majority of the population could take advantage of economic opportunities."

We would only add that these countries, including France, chose liberal democracy as a path to economic development. The rest of the European countries, in which well-being is evident, copied this path.

PILLARS THAT SUPPORT THE FOUNDATIONS OF LIBERAL DEMOCRACY
ANALOGY OF THE HOUSE TO EXPLAIN THE SYSTEM, DIFFERENTIATE A DIRECT ATTACK FROM AN INDIRECT ONE AND SHOW THE PILLARS OR BASES THAT SUPPORT THEM

The house analogy

The analogy of the house will also be used here, updating some concepts of Liberalism.

We are going to represent the house as the private property of the means of production (now in capitalism the factories and companies are what give rise to all the wealth), the bases and pillars that support it are legitimacy (given democratically), the power of formal and informal institutions in addition to all the relationships that constitute the rule of law (family, patriarchy, social, economic, political, cultural and religious order). Legitimacy and the rule of law generate another basis, which is due obedience.

Additionally, indirect pillars of the system appear, we call them incentives, they are what make individuals reproduce the system, the desire for profit, individual and collective savings, investment, that you have for yourself what is produced in your work, that you can inherit your children. More and more pillars of the house appear based on incentives as free as the market is. Incentives are what make economic liberalism successful in the creation of value and wealth (poverty reduction). Understanding the concept of incentives is key to intuiting and deciphering an indirect attack that aims to slowly and unnoticed topple a mud giant. Returning to the house analogy, this house is necessarily, like all houses in all systems, protected by armed soldiers.

Direct or indirect attack on liberal democracy

In this unit we will be limited to observing the characteristics of democracy in the United States from the search for equality, to capture its singularities of freedom with property and weapons; In subsequent pages we will focus on the types of attack when we want to take down this system.

How the system is reproduced

In the free market, incentives are given that make people want to continue investing and therefore reproduce the system of value and wealth creation (poverty reduction): a businessman who can save and reinvest his profits as he freely wants, you can reinvest in your company or invest in other companies or other businesses. Continuing with the house analogy, we are going to find numerous houses under construction (as many more houses as the market is freer).

Apart from the three fundamental pillars (legitimacy, institutions, and due obedience) that we bring from feudalism, liberal democracy adds the rule of law and incentives. These last two, added to the possibilities that freedom has by releasing all the talents that humanity has restrained (slavery and servitude), generate a whole series of creative processes of wealth and value never felt before. If we transfer this to the house analogy, we will see houses under construction everywhere (this is the reason why we see businesses, companies, and ventures everywhere).

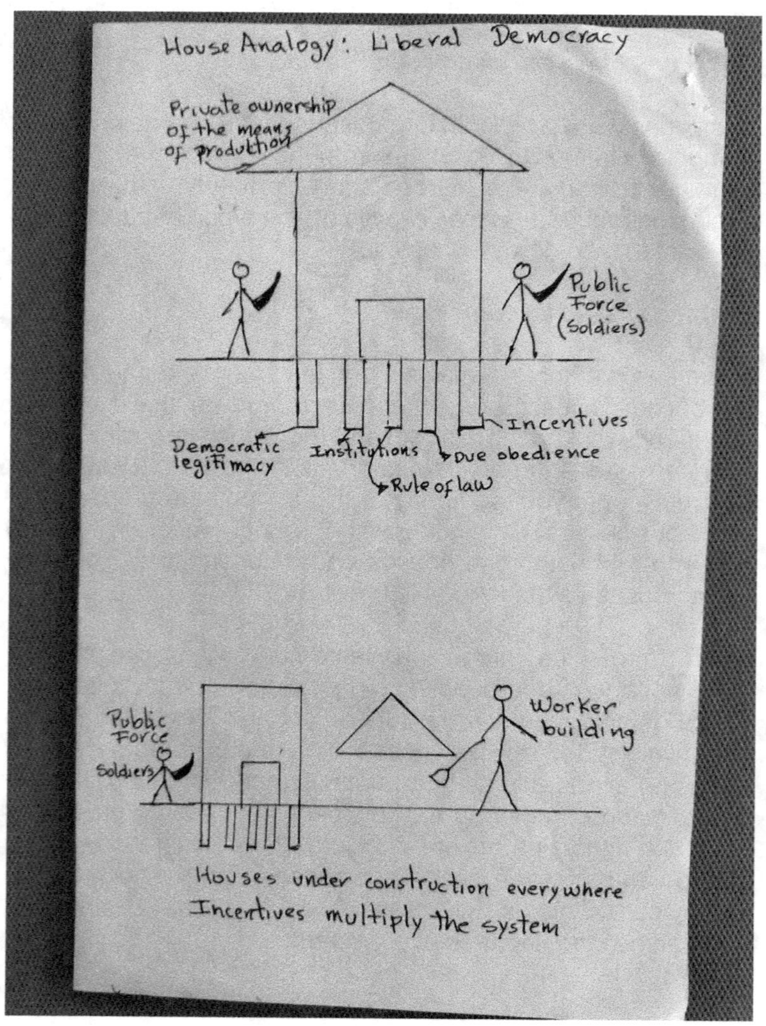

House Analogy: Liberal Democracy
Private ownership of the means of production
Public Force (Soldiers)
Incentives
Democratic legitimacy
Institutions
Due obedience
Rule of law
Public Force Soldiers
Worker building
Houses under construction everywhere
Incentives multiply the system

PILLARS THAT SUPPORT THE FOUNDATIONS OF LIBERAL DEMOCRACY:

LIBERAL DEMOCRACY
Private ownership of the means of production: Land is no longer the greatest generator of wealth. The land and the means of production are in private hands.
Class equality before the law.
Rule of law: they are the set of formal institutions (laws, prison system, family, etc.) and informal institutions (trust, security of payment in the exchange of a good) that enable social, political, economic, cultural, and social relations. religious practices occur in order, harmony, and transparency, enabling business culture. It starts from a fundamental premise in which in a free economy with the Rule of Law the dispersed and spontaneous knowledge of society can be better expressed in terms of wealth production, commerce, and exchange.
Wide social and economic mobility between classes given by the free market.
Inheritance is passed from parents to children by law.
Monopoly of force by the State: Use of force limited in the constitution.
Legitimacy given by the people: through one man one vote and enshrined in the Constitution.
Division of powers: Democracies are in principle weak so that they do not oppress the individual.
Strength of currency: as a means of payment, exchange, savings, valuation of goods.
Strength of new concepts: such as private and public savings that allow the investment and reproduction of capital.
INCENTIVES: are those that allow the system of creating value and wealth to reproduce. Example, private savings,

inheritance, having for yourself what is produced by your work, profit, freedom to buy and produce.

The unprecedented processes that were taking place in the United States and observed by Tocqueville, make us generate a meter of tyranny, which is the great threat that looms over all the advances in equality and freedom achieved:

METER OF TYRANNY IN DEMOCRACY

Power Factors or Actions	Tyrannical Rating from lowest to highest (1-2 Green. 3 Yellow. 4-5 Red, where 5 is maximum tyranny)	Observations
Use of force against the population	3	The cases are clear in the law.
Executive power concentration	2	The division of powers is instituted by the Constitution to preserve freedoms and prevent state oppression.
Concentration of judicial power	2	The division of powers is instituted by the Constitution to preserve freedoms and prevent state oppression.

Legislative power concentration	2	The division of powers is instituted by the Constitution to preserve freedoms and prevent state oppression.
Possibility of getting out of the tyrant through tyrannicide	1	It leaves each period by constitutional term.
Use of indoctrination in Society	2	Freedoms are promoted, including those of thought, however, the mass media can direct opinion. Even with the problems that the system brings, it is the best possible considering the tendency of human beings towards total control of power.
Dissidents may be expelled	1	The elimination of exile is one of the achievements of democracy in the face of feudalism. However, Communism reinstitutes it legally and informally.
Possibility of individual and collective organization	1	It is a strength and a right to live in Democracy. The model's detractors are also free to conspire against it.
Possibility of turning the population	3	It is not a custom and Democracy is instituted to govern for everyone; However, it can be done,

against each other		the communists repeatedly try to do so in their quest to undermine the foundations of Democracy and contravene the established order. Let us remember that it is a practice instituted since Karl Marx's Communist Manifesto.
Possibility of developing some type of property that allows one to defend oneself from the State.	1	Private property is a fundamental right in liberal democracy. The United States Constitution is not only designed to acquire as a symbol of power, but it allows it to be defended with weapons if the State turns against individuals.
Possibility of losing one's life by the state.	2	
Freedom Meter	2	Freedom is instituted in every written Constitution, however, according to Tocqueville, each person must feel it and seek it.
Equality Meter	1	Equality before the law is established as a right.
Possibilities of receiving compensation for your work	2	It has allowed the creation of working classes with very high incomes. There are problems, but it is the best path currently available.

Possibility to choose your job	2	Freedom to choose your job.
Religious freedom	1	Religious freedom.

Measurement of Tyranny in liberal democracy: 28 out of 80 the maximum. This is the system that is furthest from tyranny and allows the development of the individual.

The reader should already understand that humanity's passion is the search for equality and that in that search it finds the feeling of freedom. That what animates the leaders is the search for control, for total power, consequently, tyranny arises. You must be clear about how a direct attack on a society and an economy develops by virtue of the new tools that allow you to see its pillars, bases, and incentives. The look of democracy in America gives a renewed and unknown face of freedom: freedom with private property and weapons to defend it.

2

THE MOMENT WHEN THREATS TO FREEDOM BECOME REAL FOR TOCQUEVILLE: EQUALITY IS MORE IMPORTANT THAN FREEDOM

We will continue with Tocqueville's story as a methodology to identify the hidden dangers that democracy itself and the groups that besiege it bring: a society where equality is its objective places itself at the risk of tyranny; In contrast, a society inclined more towards freedom is susceptible to falling into anarchy. This unity is the second part of the conquest of equality and is the discovery of freedom. Immediately afterwards, only after having discovered it; freedom begins to be lost.

Alexis Henri Charles de Clérel, Viscount de Tocqueville belonged to the blood aristocracy; In fact, his parents almost died guillotined in the French Revolution, so he was a spectator of the beginnings of Democracy as it was shown in the documents after the budding revolution (Democracy as a form of government, with division of powers , focused on the rights and freedoms of the individual and equality before the law) and the economically inclusive Democracy that was developing in America and that allowed white men , initially without land, to be property owners and exercise the vote. However, Tocqueville took this for granted, he was seeing something more significant and profound than the form of government or equality before the law.

For Tocqueville, "Democracy is defined by the passion for equality"; He calls Democracy that place where there are no fixed classes, but all individuals can rise and fall; a place where everyone is alike. All this in contrast to the aristocratic feudal society - absolute monarchy (11) - where social classes could not be flanked. For him, the end of the aristocratic class society is already clear and clear, but it is not certain if the new Democracy is a guarantee of freedom: is the democratic society going to be free or despotic?

For Tocqueville, this passion for equality that dominates Democracy is revealed as a tendency in each case by the analyses: Equality is the passion that has guided each historical process in which aristocratic despotism has been eliminated and has led to Democracies in where freedom has begun to be felt. Freedom has been sustained thanks to laws protecting Individual Rights, the division of powers, culture, checks and balances. However, at this point it is not known if Equal Democracy is capable of preserving and harboring freedom or if despotism is going to return in other clothes.

If society's passion is equality, it will be somewhat homogeneous - the levels of "somewhat" will be easily measurable in degrees of oppression; in which nothing can be changed and assimilates them to societies without freedom: he predicted the characteristics of collectivist societies, reaching the extreme where even the way of applauding must coincide with the overwhelming support for the "Idea of the Great Leader"; situations that we have seen in China, North Korea, Cuba, Venezuela or the former Soviet Union.

Equality is more attractive because everyone understands it, it is intuitive, it happens spontaneously; Subsequently, the construction of the concept is given by reason: the clothing does not matter because we have the same pair of eyes, gender is also discardable as a difference, we have the same number of fingers. It is easier to direct the search for equality if we all see it (remember that at this time equality was eliminating hateful class privileges - social mobility - and equality before the law).

Freedom is a feeling, it is a non-transferable sensation, it is more complex to understand it; finally, it is culturally constructed for each town; and each people can say if they have it or not, if they feel it... but with the condition that we have to feel it daily to realize that at some point it was lost!

At this point, there are for Tocqueville these examples of societies and where Democracy could take them: where freedom is more important than equality, it could eventually result in anarchy; if the priority is equality before freedom, it will result in tyranny and despotism; Ultimately, a Society where the balance between equality and freedom can exist is desirable and stable.

THE SYMBOLS OF TYRANNY OR DESPOTISM IN DEMOCRACY: PROPHETIC DEFINITIONS.

Tyranny of One

Very based on the Napoleonic experience and the beginnings of post-revolution Democracy, in which the Emperor, Napoleon Bonaparte, monopolized the other powers, which felt unable to stop him, becoming an appendix of the first.

Tyranny of the Majority

This is one of the greatest challenges in Democracy and is to prevent the Executive, or even the Legislative, from constraining minorities until they silence and disappear. Minorities in free opposition could be a new government.

Tyranny of thought or public opinion

Exercised from public opinion and inhibit free expression. They destroy dissent because they tend to censor themselves or because they are overwhelmed by discrimination, dissident thought is compressed. The radical danger of this new variant of tyranny is that the majority sweeps away and inhibits to the point of repressing free expression.

Ideas, even if they are predominant in the majority (hegemonic), if they are not discussed, run the risk of becoming perverse vices or evil doctrines. The culture of the confrontation of ideas is what gives vitality to Democracy and freedom.

bureaucratic tyranny

When citizens become subjects and return themselves, of their own free will, to the fold of the despot and tyrant. They become subjects of tyranny.

This type of despotism is perhaps one of the most worrying, since it occurs in a situation in which the person, call himself a citizen, desires or wants to be.

The deep abyss of bureaucratic tyranny

This situation is reached in several ways. However, the one that drags the most is the person's disinterest in the political issue; Tocqueville called it Individualism at the time (12) whose meaning, at that time, was to be apathetic to politics: the fragmented society that is created takes care of its own private issues and forgets public affairs; public issues dangerously become "state issues"; The state is creating a "Golden Cage" and corruption appears in an entity that we have allowed to arise and that only feeds on our taxes.

The "career politician" has the same particular interest in our own things that separates us from politics in the "political thing" and his logic is to think about his own personal well-being and that of his electorate.

Another cause, but no less important, arises with the advent of the commercial era since the economic dimension appears in the spheres of the individual and this may be dedicated to the construction and enjoyment of the goods and services (new property) acquired through the market.

Others are those trying to participate in the economy; they do not achieve it or feel that they have achieved very little; They try again, but they don't succeed, until they finally give up and exclude themselves. They ignore society, becoming a threat: these people feel that they have nothing more to gain in this society and risk losing everything they have achieved so far.

A conflict arises between those who want to preserve the little they have achieved and who believe it is right versus those who want to change what they consider to be wrong but accept the possibility of losing everything in the process. This dichotomy between those who do not achieve it versus those who achieve little is what the heartless and ruthless opportunists take advantage of to dress up as redeemers and push Democracy into the void and return to tyranny and despotism.

How many are there who try and fail; How many those who achieve little? Who are they? Where are they? How fertile are these groups to utopian or redeeming ideas? What are their characteristics? Are they representative, are they a minority?

Because if they are the majority, the system is failed or is about to fail since a large group does not know or lacks the minimum requirements and conditions to be successful or at least stand out. However, this group, although it is not a majority percentage, represents a non-negligible threat to the rest of society, to progress and even to the very future of civilization.

Feudal monarchical despotism chained bodies and could even torture them, but minds were free. It was relatively easy to get out of the despot through tyrannicide, Tocqueville wanted to say. But if citizens make themselves subjects of tyranny, they self-imprison their minds and in each of them there is a tyrant who would eventually have to be killed to free them; The task of emancipation is no longer so simple.

There is another trick, somewhat natural, however, associated with the previous idea and it is that of the paternalistic state: a father who has chosen the path of keeping his offspring in his fold, contrary to emancipation and the sense of a father who brings them to life to be free; to face their own challenges. A state that seeks to transcend authority, protection of the social sphere, begins with the harmless workplace; From here one thing leads to another – as happens inexorably and cruelly in the development of every utopian idea, that a greater evil must be incurred to try to correct the previous lesser evil until oppression and dictatorship are inevitable-.The 20th century has witnessed many harmless proposals such as: "guaranteeing work"; but, to be able to do so, he would have to own all the means of production; This would not be enough because it might be necessary to regulate the labor market; The force of this last idea is so beneficent that it is not worth even obtaining consensus; We must force her to live her grace…this is the danger of a megalomaniacal leader with magical and fallacious thinking. The personality that accompanies this type of thinking is that of irresponsible do-gooders. Finally, a utopian society is only sustained by the force of oppression where its creators denote a deep contempt for the individual, for their capabilities and freedoms by trying to say that they should want; What should they work on? What should they eat?

Not everything is lost.

The democratic system, one person one vote, is not a guarantee of freedom. It can be as good or bad as the people behind that vote.

In fact, there are societies that hide tendencies that take them back to servitude.

The ability to make good decisions in modern society becomes uncertain, but the society in which we are going to live depends on that, whether we go towards Freedom or back to servitude depends on it.

Participation is key.

Alone we are weak, but together we are powerful. Tocqueville noted when he compared the associations given by aristocrats in Europe, in which, due to their high purchasing power, very few of them were enough to achieve their objectives; However, the culture of association found in America seemed very powerful in counteracting the power of the state and its ability to co-opt (in its sense of keeping) the activities and daily space of individuals on its way to authoritarianism and despotism. .

Citizens must participate; they have to make the administrative decisions of the state. Politics absorbs citizens, their rights, their freedoms, their lives.

Democracy must be one of contradictions, which generate small, gradual changes in which revolutions do not fit, always taken advantage of by opportunists and megalomaniacs.

Perfect and ideal social structures come with the temptation to use violence to implement them.

If Democracy does not punish one person, one vote, if it looks the other way, the space becomes nationalized. We must protect and encourage associative life, administrations and local control, freedom of the press, freedom in social networks, independent justice and all institutions that collude and conspire against state tyranny: a citizen commitment to public virtue, delivered to the interest of the country. This last proposal by Tocqueville is extracted from the depths of the social actions of the American - from what he observed with wonder while, on his trip to America - in which he compares the associative action of the American to solve any problem, versus the manifest request that they would make. almost all European citizens to the state; This request for state action comes from European culture and would be indifferent to whether it is still a tyrannical monarchical or democratic government.

This unit provides the identification of the two groups, among others, (those who do not achieve it or are not interested and the welfare state) that could put the Nobel Prize-winning Democracy and the recently discovered freedom at risk. It should be clear to the reader that living in Democracy is a great step, that currently there is no better system. It must also have been clear to you the multiplicity of new risks in Democracy (it is designed to be weak so that it does not oppress us); The effects of exercising or not exercising can lead again to tyranny and despotism. The defense of freedom must be permanent!

3

WHAT SYMBOLS OF TYRANNY OR DESPOTISM IN DEMOCRACY DID TOCQUEVILLE NOT MANAGE TO SEE?

Being in my country I saw that well-being was not for everyone; I felt the lie: well-being was manifested for a few. My first trip to a socialist-communist country was seeking to escape that lie. Already in that country my disappointment was total when the lie was maintained; It was worse, and well-being became elusive for everyone.

It took me a while to realize how lying was part of everything and I understood that the best system to live in would be one in which lies were difficult to say, difficult to maintain and where lies were not the creed of tyranny.
Boris Ackerman

The Count de Tocqueville will continue to accompany us until the beginning of this unit; We will leave it to him to resume the chronological journey with Karl Marx.
In this unit we will understand socialism-communism from the Dialectic itself instituted by Karl Marx: its proposals, such as its

exponents, which characterizes its leaders, its followers, the birth of indoctrination with the purpose of subduing minds (no longer only bodies are slaves; minds too) so that they allow tyranny to reside within them. After this, the test of tyranny will mark at maximum value with modern political systems that refine absolutist tyranny; They only take elements of history, purifying the most disastrous ones. Its pillars, bases and incentives are more idealistic and depend on "should be" more than on interest and human nature.

Many of the semblance of tyranny and the return to despotism mentioned by Tocqueville at the beginning of democracy are used today; Additionally, there are new ones that are more dangerous for freedom; Some, if not all, are used by would-be tyrants.

"Despotism was an inevitable evil sent by God" and in which usage and custom made them right. The nobleman considered his privileges to be legitimate and maintained for centuries an immutable legal order of misery for the servants. The serfs had assimilated servitude as their way of life, and they saw despotism as "natural."

Only when the despot became a tyrant were the minds freed from servitude (a way of life converted into law) and executed the tyrant; to fall again into another subtle, or different, despotism, but ultimately another tyranny: it was the only form of government that was known; It was what there was. The despot, in reaction to any uprising, could tie and torture the bodies of his servants, however, the minds remained free...this would change when humanity refined the worst methods of indoctrination possible with the birth of fascism and the consolidation of Marxism-Leninism. The mind is transmuted into the object of tyranny through indoctrination, creating one of the greatest threats that freedom has ever faced in the history of humanity.

Fascism

We are not going to analyze fascism in this book, despite its serious repercussions on the world order, its negative impact, and its participation in the death of millions of people during the Second World War. The reason is that its malicious appearance has been understood and it has almost been banned. His historical actions have been catastrophic, but fortunately short. In economic terms, fascism is pure interventionism that preserves ownership of the means of production in private hands but restricts their effects. The individual retained private ownership of the means of production but lost the ability to decide what to produce and how much to produce; everything was subject to the designs of the state. As for the profit, the owner kept part of it.

THE PROMISE OF EQUALITY IS CHANGED FOR THAT OF ELIMINATION OF EXPLOITATION: MARXISM

The conceptual changes that are going to be imposed and spread are of such magnitude and so overwhelming that it is necessary to contextualize them again to assimilate the reasons why broad sectors once again consent to the imposition of tyranny as necessary. The question arises: what kind of higher stages of well-being in society are they looking for to allow tyranny to mediate?

Sectors of the population inclined, according to Tocqueville, to execute and carry out Marxist ideas.

There are series of events or situations that sometimes come together to make others possible; In this case we talk about the population that participates in the economy:

There is a group that manages to generate a business network; In principle, they do well because they manage to appropriate resources in their processes of producing certain goods and services that satisfy needs. However, they converge in the sense that these citizens give up their private space to the state to be able to dedicate themselves to their economic activities. This group has a lot to lose with a change.

On the other hand, there is another group that tries; however, they do not have the skills required to be successful and they give up; They don't want to try anymore. There is a third group that will never try and will be on the sidelines of the process collecting the crumbs. These last two groups are the subjects that eventually come together to be the breeding ground, the trigger for the actions of these new ideas that loom over the horizon. Finally, there is another group that, without directly belonging to the latter, are **functional** to what is coming because it benefits them, they feel ideologically close, or they are going to be part of the leadership of the new change. These latter groups have much to gain when acts are generated that herald changes in ownership.

The new way of seeing the world and history: Marxist dialectics. So, his dialectical proposals are:

They define their antagonist by stating their problems. They define themselves as the contrast to the opposite. Marxist dialectics follows these principles: if you want to sell yourself well, define yourself through your opponent's problems using fallacies, paradoxes, comparisons that show what is bad about the other. Concepts are constructed negatively.

They create a sense of community by defining an adversary and excluding the rest, opposing groups, opposing society: something will come out of Khaos (21).

Finally, they offer a solution to a problem in terms of benefits; This is the reason why their proposals are so persuasive: **they explain the need for things, the benefit they would bring; never the how. Nobody wanted to be against this so good!**

After the stage of autosuggestion, of enjoyment, has passed; It is difficult for the individual to find the trap; What's more, he refuses to see it - everyone wants him to do well, and it is foolish to delay a little longer to see possible doubts that the intellect always raises. Many people already applaud (the force of hegemonic thinking; these people have previously been prepared, indoctrinated, forced, or paid). So many people couldn't be wrong. You took the shortcut that you will hardly be able to get out of.

They are redefined from historical materialism.

From the materialist point of view, each form of production generates its own legal tools and institutions (formal and informal) and consequently its own government that protects them.

High social sensitivity

Social and historical facts emotionally as opposed to another group who are practical and rational. However, what they are unmatched in because they handle it very well is in understanding how the human mind works, how it perceives reality.

The sensitive do not notice the inaccuracy of their arguments and their proposals suffer from the particularities and detail that the how must include, the more detail the how must include, as well as the repercussions our actions have on society, on the life and death of people. The best thing about this strategy is the way of counterattacking, of destroying the opponent: the practical and rational are attacked for their demonstrated lack of sensitivity towards social issues; this is used to use against him. Faced with an attack on the person themselves (such as this one in which they bare their inner self) the counterpart is left speechless, they become vulnerable to the attack and the weight of public opinion (but they are not the object of this study).

If, on the one hand, they are sensitive, they are also very careless - in the sense of being irresponsible - in the details and in the repercussions of their actions; On the other hand, they are quite stubborn and determined (guided by a greater good). The above must be understood that nothing is going to stop them, and they will try again and again because they are guided by the conviction of the "greater good." Let us also remember that Marxist dialectics is a process of discovery in action that invites us to move forward, reanalyze the strategy and execute again.

Another aspect that deeply marks their actions is their status as bureaucrats. For the most part they have been and are accustomed to the tranquility of a fixed salary, intending to transfer that to the rest of society; Obviously, they are unaware that most people are fighting for their daily lives and that their peace of mind is the anguish of many.

In terms of entrepreneurship, their sensitivity can be seen like this

Let's take the following for granted:
His idealistic halo added to his high sensitivity allows him to better capture reality, connecting with people's problems; They become part of it.

In general, the entrepreneur, as opposed to the sensitive person, can turn a business idea into a winner, he will look for the means, he will find someone to accompany him, he will save, he will go through difficult situations, but he will persevere. He will be able to build a great machine (we return to the analogies - the word great machine, in this paragraph, refers to a business or undertaking) full of gears: we can call that the ability to do business, to undertake; perhaps the entrepreneur cannot understand how the gears and pinions he has created work. However, the sensitive has a better reading of those gears and pinions than the same person who created them. What's more, he sees the gear being able to put a stick in it, to stop it and stop the machine; -This can be extended to stopping the entire capacity of an economy to create value and wealth through the only possible side, that of private entrepreneurship- (the bases, pillars, ISA -Ideological State Apparatuses; we will see them in this first part, unit four- , incentives are part of the gears and pinions that are inside businesses - called entrepreneurship -).

A question arises: why is indoctrination needed in this new stage of history? What is new that culture or usages and customs turned into laws can almost not compel?

The historical pattern of individuals in the creation of value and wealth is broken.

The processes of economic discovery (13) have occurred with small examples of individuals who carry out an activity in which they do well, obtain a benefit and others, depending on their capacity, try to copy something that they see as positive, creating a new industry or a new sector.

What concerns us for the topic of this book is the social characteristic that other individuals see other individuals being economically successful and copy those activities themselves; In this way the productive fabric is reproduced.

Marx's new proposal is going to break with that scheme, presenting an unprecedented framework in which private property and initiative are suppressed; forcibly collapses the entire free enterprise system that is being formed to leave everything related to property, the production of goods and services to the state. The private initiative of many individuals is replaced by a large investor - who cannot be copied - and a general plan. This approach requires the "conviction" of the masses (indoctrination), or paid followers or, failing that, the obligation (oppression) for them to do so.

"The how" (how they are going to do it) is never explained, nor the inconveniences of taking paths of human design that have never been tested in contrast to the natural and spontaneous order that an individual would take when he sees that another is doing well and only copies his actions; This natural and spontaneous way is how successful processes are configured and applied in society, with small tests as failures and then, depending on their success, they are replicated as many times as the market allows. The same system begins to inadvertently create the mechanisms that will make it perennial: they develop a series of events, which form patterns, these in turn are part of more complex structures and then the ideas are elaborated and installed in the collective imagination. These are the characteristics that keep a successful process running until another process emerges that has the strength to modify it: it is creative destruction. **Non-human spontaneous processes do not need to be directed centrally despite how complex and multitudinous they may seem.**

The new doctrine inserts this pernicious innovation of transmuting spontaneous processes - which are copied without any agreement between individuals - into processes of human design. The illustration on these points answers the initial questions; The type of profiles that are needed to promote Marxist revolutions is understood: you only need convinced and indoctrinated people (who do not understand the profound damage they do), who only follow the "general plan of the great leader", who push, unite and if necessary, force the processes.

This was the profile of people who served them before the advent of Marxism with the communist manifesto in 1848. To achieve this type of people, indoctrination is essential.

Marxism promises to eliminate exploitation.

For the first time the engine of revolutions in history, its driving force, its passion, its promise, is not equality (of classes and Equality before the law, which Democracy had achieved); Its objectives changed: Eliminate the exploitation of man by man that capitalism generates.

The objectives to be destroyed are the private property of the means of production with all the formal or informal institutions that allow and protect their actions, called: rule of law (which allows economic, social, and political relations to occur with order and transparency; that is, they allow business), culture, educational system, religion, division and structure of division of powers, etc. The contempt for the bases of Liberal Democracy is clear.

The concept of private property arose, according to Marxists, in the production process in which natural resources and the work of the proletarian are appropriated (objective theory of value or labor value) to produce a good and satisfy a need. In this context, private property came to destroy feudal property. Likewise, communism seeks to install collective property and destroy private property. For the first time in history, enormous economic, political, and social resources are concentrated in a single entity: the State. This concentration of resources is only comparable to the times when the monarchy reigned, but the fundamental difference is that capitalist industrialization had unleashed levels of production and wealth creation never imagined; At this point the size of the feudal monarchical state is not comparable to what the collective communist state inherited. So was tyranny.

"The exploitation of man by man" occurs in the process of profit - considered immoral - by seeking to maximize the utility of the businessman where this was only possible by stealing the work of the employee, said the Marxists. As the reader realizes, they despise wage labor that follows supply and demand, they despise the division of labor. Bourgeois labor relations were also about to end.

The salary promises, being faithful to their dialectical method, are extremely attractive: "that they earn everything they can earn so that they have the best possible life." They promise it after collectivization and the centralization of the means of production. When history is forced and forced to give birth to socialism-communism for the first time, we attend ecstatically and with great hope to see the unfulfilled promises and then the horror: the unfulfilled promises because the system does not allow any of its individuals to (who is not a party leader) has something additional to the survival salary (in addition to the salary, food aid and subsidies for basic services that are not enough for the entire population) and the horror that is felt when you sense what is coming next of the destruction of all knowledge of production, of the knowledge of exchange relations that history had accumulated in individuals and that had allowed the level of development, income, and well-being that civilization had until that moment. In full awareness and with knowledge of the consequences, a small fraction of the population drags a majority into facing a very feasible possibility of hunger and hopelessness; The cause is the elimination of private property in addition to all the relationships that are installed in culture, which allow the development of civilization as we know it. Ultimately, in the free market, what is exchanged is nothing more than property titles.

HOW TO IDENTIFY NEW PROPOSALS IN THE FUTURE THAT RETURN THE PATH OF SOCIALISM, AND WHICH INDEFECTIBLY LEAD US TO TYRANNY?

They must, to a greater or lesser extent, comply with the following concepts, most of which were outlined by Marx:

Why does Marxist doctrine despise and advocate for eliminating Liberal Democracy?

Because in Democracy only those who have property are free (which for Marx is a very small percentage) and it is already expropriated for the majority. His vision of private property: Private property of the means of production is what generates the exploitation of man by man.

Because profit is immoral, for them it is a theft of the worker's work.

Because its doctrine, due to the intrinsic dialectical method, is intransigent with other ideologies seeking the destruction of the opposite. It is the religion of the state, hence their fanaticism and intolerance.

Because their doctrine forces them to look for a just man who works for the common good; When they don't find it, they force it, as opposed to freedom.

Because they consider their doctrine universal law, like gravity.

What specifically does Marxism aim to eliminate?

Marxist doctrine is aimed at eliminating private property as the origin of the exploitation of one class by another; It will eliminate all the formal and informal institutions that allow free enterprise to germinate, develop and endure; among them: culture, social order, laws, religion, the rule of law (a set of regulations that facilitate social, economic, political and commercial relations to occur with order and transparency).

ANALOGY OF THE HOUSE TO EXPLAIN THE SYSTEM, DIFFERENTIATE A DIRECT ATTACK FROM AN INDIRECT ONE AND SHOW THE PILLARS OR BASES THAT SUPPORT THEM

What is the strategy for taking power? A direct attack.

The strategy for taking power, in pure Marxism, does not differ from what history already brought and which had been proven in the French Revolution; Innovation refers to the fact that it is systematic and directed: it is direct, violent (the one who best described it was Lenin in his writings) so much so that particularly for Latin America, guerrillas were orchestrated. After the armed forces that defended the system were defeated, the expropriation was quickly carried out; Finally, the third step is the destruction of culture, of the rule of law, of the bases of Liberal Democracy.

Using the analogy of the house - where the house is the private property of the means of production - the guards that protect it (military forces; first step) are directly attacked and defeated, then the house is demolished (expropriated). private ownership of the means of production; second step), extract all the bases and pillars of the house (liberal democracy; third step) to be replaced by other pillars typical of Marxism. Incentives are the collateral losses that occur when changing from private to public property; That is, there is no longer any utility for the investor or capitalist, there is no longer a total salary for the worker, etc. That said, private property is no longer the source of achieving the dreams of the individual as such.

It is important to understand the graph to follow the order of the steps of the Marxist-Leninist strategy:
First Step: Defeat Public force.   Second step: Expropriate private property of the means of production. Third Step: Destroy the bases and pillars.

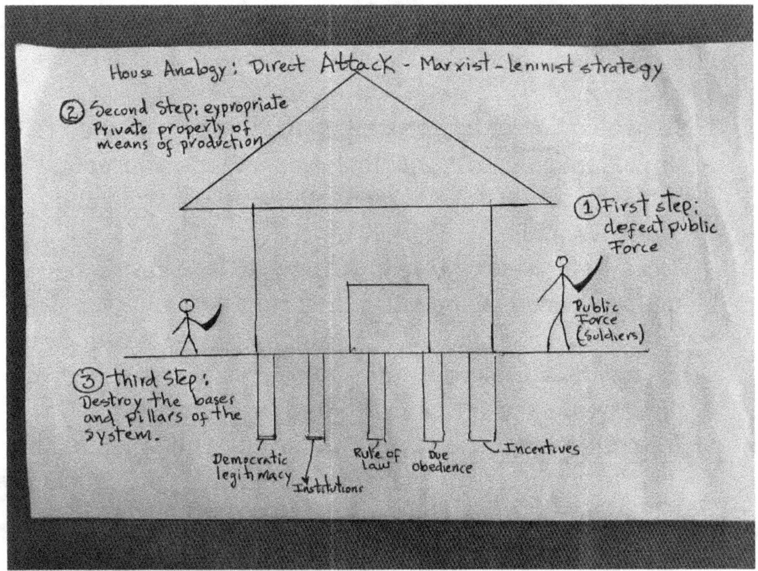

COMMUNIST MANIFESTO

We are going to present the ten postulates of the Communist Manifesto (14) of 1848, more as an illustration to identify whether future movements obey or continue to identify with Marxist doctrine (15). If this sentence is fulfilled: your actions could be as destructive, as they were in the past:

> ➢ Expropriation of land ownership and use of land rent for State expenses.
> ➢ Strong progressive taxes.
> ➢ Suppression of the right of inheritance.
> ➢ Confiscation of the property of all emigrants and seditionists.

- ➢ Centralization of credit in the hands of the State through a national Bank with state capital and exclusive monopoly.
- ➢ Centralization of transportation in the hands of the State.
- ➢ Multiplication of national factories, means of production, plowing and improvement of land according to a collective plan.
- ➢ Proclamation of the general duty to work, creation of industrial armies, mainly in the countryside.
- ➢ Articulation of agricultural and industrial farms; tendency to gradually erase the differences between the countryside and the city.
- ➢ Free public education for all children. Abolition of factory child labor in its current form. Unification of education with material production.

There are two aspects that he recycled from feudalism: the class division, where the first is the non-working bureaucracy and the workers; The second aspect is oppression, what was called vassalage in feudalism as the obligation to work without receiving adequate compensation; Marx renames it as: the obligation to work for everyone.

Not only did the last criterion not consider the human factor that will resist obligation and tyranny, but it included others that it took for granted and that, if not met, would make improvements in work environments impossible; such as, for example: "the bureaucrats and scholars are going to make it more pleasant, for this reason, there will be more free time", "those who work are the same ones who make the decisions, there will be more free time", those privileged in education will suggest improvements to do things better".

When things have reached this point, after including in the new economic recipes - on which the lives and future of millions of people will depend - components from previous eras and elements that are too naive and innocent, it is necessary to ask ourselves: what was done? equality and freedom?

Society retreated because this promise does not come immediately or guaranteed in laws or written in a political constitution (16), but rather after fulfilling a series of elements that would be under human judgment whether to fulfill them or not. Marx said: once the relations of production based on property and that create exploitation of one class by the other are suppressed; After this, class antagonism will be eliminated because they are all equal classes (17); The disappearance of the class struggle and its incompatibility will lead to the disappearance of political power (18) – we will migrate from socialism to stateless communism – and at that moment the free development of freedom will be for everyone.

Everyone will be equal and free, not like in capitalism or feudalism where a few were free and equal; here they will all be... a story that seduces, in the appropriate population group, subrogated the right to exercise class violence for a greater good. Huge blunders, dangerous naiveties: disaster was served.

The reality is that never in the history of humanity has a class conspired against itself; a self-inflicted disappearance will never happen, the opposite happens ; If it is allowed to be on top of another, it will reproduce, extend, increase oppression and domination: communist life without a state never arrived; The communist party never came out of power, it had power without limits.

What it did achieve was downward equality (the entire society in poverty, except the communist bureaucracy that became the new oligarchy) since it brought with it a decrease in income, once again bordering on poverty and indigence (see the explanation in the second part, unit six: because it impoverishes the population); By attacking the entire productive fabric based on private property, torpedoing the foundations of value and wealth creation (society's incentives) without proposing something functional in return, it plunged it into a downward spiral. Finally, he destroyed the best and released the worst of human beings. He destroyed the best, which is his ability to not let himself be defeated and move forward to achieve his life plan (a few who achieve it drag down the others who do not have the ability, do not achieve it or do not want to). He released the worst: laziness and disinterest in his future; just waiting for alms and pity.

The balance of dogmas (excerpts from the Communist Manifesto)

Marxist doctrine is intransigent and intolerant of other ideologies; We already know that this obeys the Marxist dialectical method that generates a content that disputes its reason with science: it is almost "science made knowledge"; this methodology and the content - which does not explain how, and which breaks with a spontaneous historical model in which wealth is created - that it transmits. The method, plus the message, only need an executor, they need a convinced man, seduced by the promise to carry out the necessary actions.

For the Marxist, the freedom expressed in laws that Democracy brought is only enjoyed by a minority, which is why they want to eliminate it.

For the Marxist, property has only been achieved by a small minority, it is already abolished for the majority, so they want to abolish it for that small percentage.

The promise is the elimination of exploitation to achieve equality, this is definitively downward in the income and general well-being of society. The communist utopia dragged work to levels of slavery never achieved: "they go to work for the well-being of everyone, including themselves."

Communism sees women doubly exploited, the first when they are the private property of the husband and the second when they are another instrument of production of the capitalist system.

For the communist, the concept of family is a privilege that only exists for the bourgeois; Once again they consider it abolished for most of the population.

The communists pass the nationalist concepts to supranationalism ones, considering the extension they make of the concept of exploitation of man by man in the productive process, to other matters that may not have a connection: The interests of the proletarians surpass the borders of the countries where they are exploited by the bourgeoisie and borders only serve for some nations to exploit others.

There is an important concept that is established from the beginning; It is like fighting – using the term combat in its meaning of eliminating – ideological rivals and their philosophical approaches, as well as other groups with which there are affinities on some issues but that do not fully agree with the method, however , are functional to the cause; These types of allies are kept as temporary allies: this fight is postponed.

For the pure Marxist, its primary objectives are clear: the elimination of private property and the institutions - formal and informal - that have allowed and make possible the relationships (commercial, social, economic, and political) - rule of law - in which there is commerce, free markets and the accumulation of wealth by the successful.

In its desire to eliminate property and institutionality, communism looks deeper by proposing to eliminate aspects that are more difficult to relate to exploitation such as morality, values and religion (in later pages we will see that post-Marxism (**Gramscian postmodernism**) takes up these aspects, placing them in the crosshairs of their strategy to propose that their destruction would mean removing the bases of the free market system for its reproduction - said strategy is still being executed - For this point they consider a historical story and order of things: when The communal property of primitive tribal socialism gave way to feudal property, at that time, the old polytheistic religious religions were also replaced by Christianity. Communism, in turn, with its new relations of production (19) will determine social changes necessary to guarantee its action and permanence. This historical determinism that wants to be imposed in this field forgets that religious, social, philosophical, and moral ideas have been gradually modified over time to accommodate their needs for a motherless birth. - to the extent that they need to replace something as strong as religious desire and faith in a superior being with faith in the state. It is definitive that Marx cut off all historical gradualisms; seeks the elimination of exploitation with revolution as a method.

There are many decisions, and they all have in common to cancel, eliminate or abolish. They seem like impeccable decisions - many virtuous ideas appear in the mind of the socialist leader, all guided by his morals and that strong determination to do good; However, they do not explain: how? His "Dialectic" training prevents him from seeing beyond the proposal and in his brain, there is a prohibition on interweaving all the repercussions that a utopian, wonderful, pharaonic idea that solves everything in one fell swoop can have - riddled with good intentions, but that had never occurred spontaneously in history; They all require that they must be executed, carried out under oppression. This path was a serious deviation from what it should be, so much so that in the end the results showed one of the greatest setbacks, back towards tyranny and despotism that humanity has ever given. That was in terms of Freedom, in economic terms it was a catastrophe; determined a drop in income and stagnation in the well-being of the population.

METER OF TYRANNY IN MARXISM

METER OF TYRANNY IN MARXISM

Power Factors or Actions	Tyrannical Rating from lowest to highest (1-2 Green. 3 Yellow. 4-5 Red, where 5 is maximum tyranny)	Observations
Use of force against the population	5	The only important thing is the Communist Party and its supporters. The others are disposable.
Executive power concentration	5	They concentrate all powers, faithful to their Dialectic, their dogma, and their method; And

		what is more serious, they reestablish the worship that existed in feudalism of the king, but this time to an all-powerful leader.
Concentration of judicial power	5	They concentrate all powers, faithful to their Dialectic, their dogma, and their method; And what is more serious, they reestablish the worship that existed in feudalism of the king, but this time to an all-powerful leader.
Legislative power concentration	5	They concentrate all powers, faithful to their Dialectic, their dogma, and their method; And what is more serious, they reestablish the worship that existed in feudalism of the king, but this time to an all-powerful leader.
Possibility of getting out of the tyrant through tyrannicide	5	It is almost zero. In this writing we consider that only an implosion of the system would allow it to end.
Use of indoctrination in Society	5	There is a tyrant in every mind. All types of indoctrination and threats to free thought

		are instituted by the State.
Dissidents may be expelled	5	It has been established since Karl Marx's Communist Manifesto.
Possibility of individual and collective organization	5	The communist only considers its existence, any association that does not originate in the state is declared an enemy.
Possibility of turning the population against each other	5	It has been established since Karl Marx's Communist Manifesto.
Possibility of developing some type of property that allows one to defend oneself from the State.	5	They despise private property as the main cause of exploitation and try to abolish and hinder it. It has been established since Karl Marx's Communist Manifesto.
Possibility of losing life	5	Dissidence is the worst thing for the communist. Persecution is instituted both by related civilians who receive benefits from the regime, and by the repressive apparatus of the state.
Freedom Meter	5	Only the communist bureaucrat is free. Freedom for citizens is

		defined in terms of oppression and what the leader decides.
Equality Meter	5	Everyone is equal in poverty. Communism has promised well-being that must be provided by the "Fair Socialist Worker" that they have always been looking for in human beings. They failed in every attempt, their utopian ideas clashed with human nature.
Possibilities of receiving compensation for your work	5	The concept of salary is destroyed: you must work as much as you can and receive as you need. They are societies that lose the incentive to work. The historical progress achieved in Liberal Democracies with respect to the remuneration of work is lost. They forget that the Human Being works for himself and his family, never for a stranger. That concept that existed in tribal societies, where everyone was related, is

		impossible to replicate in larger societies.
Possibility to choose your job	5	The job is assigned to you by the state.
Religious freedom	5	The state religion

Measurement of tyranny in the Marxist system (socialism-communism): 80 out of 80 the maximum.

It is necessary to mention that the score says that it is more tyrannical than the system (absolutism) in which the tyranny was born.

Tyranny in Marxism acquires an especially dangerous refinement because it has never reached such dimensions in history. For this reason, it is necessary to mention its potential and risks for society.

REFINEMENT OF TYRANNY IN MARXISM

He has managed to create a dialectical method that seduces, that bypasses the rationality of the individual, taking him from the origin of many problems, directly to a captivating solution; without going through the flats and problems that the rational analysis of the implementation discovers and in which a rocky path always arises. This method requires, to keep the leader's veneration high, a string of "charming ideas"; one after the other and all coming out of Aladdin's lamp (Marxist dialectic). This is given by the very nature of these ideas, in which the charm declines and requires another impulse. Finally, the goal of keeping your followers constantly and irresistibly seduced is achieved.

Tyranny is easy to maintain when a group charged with carrying out the Marxist project is delimited, a captivated group, which has received indoctrination in such a way that tyrants and the tyrannical way of life inhabit them; in such a way that they accept their mission of forcing it on others, generating the entire structure to prevent tyranny from decaying (social, cultural, political, religious aspects, etc.)

Marxist tyranny, even in Democracy, identifies a vulnerable social group that it makes the object of temporary benefits, indoctrinates them to install a tyrant in each of their minds, then launches them against the rest of the population in a violent manner. Normally this group is the least prepared intellectually, the one that has the least capacity to defend itself (the state becomes a father that will force its weakest children to stay in the nest; it will order to attack its weakest children). strong because they would eventually challenge him for power).

The other population group that does not resist tyrannical violence leaves the country, leaving everything behind. The country loses valuable people, all its knowledge and experience are lost. Tyranny has installed fear, persecution, the implacable threat. He perfected the exile in the most cruel and subtle way possible, by using the same citizens, pitting them against each other, knowing that this will make those who do not consider confrontation as the path and decide not to resist oppression give up their protest.

Marxist tyranny learns to strip the population of wealth and power, leaving them defenseless before them. It pursues private property and the capacity it generates in the defenseless individual, since it allows him to protect himself from state oppression.

Marxist tyranny has concentrated unimaginable economic, social, and political powers in a single entity: the state. That and the monopoly of force has managed to make the power concentrated by themselves impregnable.

In its blind desire to destroy private property and install another model, it destroys the business fabric: it ruins the system of food production, services, and simple processes that society has generated to improve well-being.

Marxist tyranny has destroyed the superstructure (culture, laws, equality before the law, rule of law, family, religion, etc.) that gave cohesion to society, to Liberal Democracy and allowed it to function.

Disaster is served in the hands of people endowed with infallibility and goodness - who consider that the end is so good that any means is worth it and loss of human life: the end justifies the means - who despise the Liberal Democratic system. This contempt leads them to implement Marx's ideas through armed revolutions, which reached their maximum expression with Lenin, and which will go to the base of the Liberal Democratic system, to expropriate private property. Immediately afterwards, they will destroy the institutions that support it, destroy class equality (equality before the law), the rule of law that supports liberal economic relations, culture, religion, order, and social relations, etc. They will ruin civilization as we know it and whose achievements have taken us to levels of freedom that humanity has never achieved. Liberal Democracy is not perfect, but it is the best achievement that human beings have acquired in terms of Freedom. It is a result of his innate imperfection and the crude tools he has had in the search for something so elusive, that you only know you have found it if you feel it and by the time you miss it, it may already be too late to get it back.

Marxist socialism and by extension communism came to consider its own disappearance due to its impossibility of reconciling its promise, its dialectical method of conceiving it with its subsequent need to force and oppress human beings to carry it out. He faced the individual's innate desire to resist and oppose anything carried out by force, despite how good it may seem, he faced his nature to help himself and his loved ones. However, it has been the most successful exercise of tyranny in human history. Only the implosion determined its end.

PILLARS THAT SUPPORT THE FOUNDATIONS OF SOCIALISM:

The direct pillars emerged from human design and not from a spontaneous generation of history. Pillars such as liberal incentives were replaced by tribal concepts of community work, by utopias of the socialist just man who will work for the common good and not for himself and his children. Everything was under oppression; After this did not work, violence followed.

PILLARS THAT SUPPORT THE FOUNDATIONS OF SOCIALISM:

SOCIALISM
The land and the means of production are in collective or state hands. Concentration of all economic power in the state.
Collective production plan. Vital minimum provided by the state. The differential salary by salary is eliminated.
The new social classes are the communist bureaucracy and the workers.

The rule of law is eliminated, and we move to new socialist legal relations.
Social and economic immobility. Everyone wins the same.
Inheritance is eliminated.
Monopoly of force by the state. Use of force at the discretion of the Communist Party and enshrined in the constitution. It implements innovative schemes of violence, repression and defense of the state carried out by armed civil groups. Refined indoctrination schemes.
Legitimacy given by force of arms. You do not decide to accept the legitimacy of the state; You are bound under penalty of persecution and death. There is no dissent or different thinking.
Concentration of unimaginable powers in the state.
Strength of the state as a generator of basic food and general well-being.
INCENTIVES. Socialist Maxim that instituted low productivity: from each according to their abilities and to each according to their needs. For Marx the incentive to produce is Moral. Superior morality: the Marxist appears in the Manifesto as morally infallible, with divine abilities to be the administrator of almost anything, good in his own right in contradiction to the bad bourgeois.

only mention the pillars of socialism, we will not explain how a direct or indirect attack occurs because in this writing we propose the idea that socialism-communism is impregnable - it is only possible to overthrow it through a self-implosion generated from the top by its leaders - after it has been installed. since it is protected by coercive oppression that is capable of being generated from the centralization of violence from the state apparatus, the concentration of all powers and the accumulation of unimaginable economic powers in a single entity.

What we will do is prepare the concepts of the next unit; The definition of socialism changes after each failure, it is rebuilt, it is invigorated (its flag: equality and its installation strategy are very powerful). So much so that the best preamble is to see how socialism is being explained to the new generations; it is imperative to analyze its transmutation.

We are going to use the definitions of the 1974 Nobel Prize winner in economics Friedrich Von Hayek. These have had subtle variations that respond to failed attempts to install it:

Socialism 1956: movement organized to deliberately and centrally plan the economic resources of all individuals, in which the state is the owner of all the means of production.

Socialism is a profound redistribution of income, that is, of income through taxes and the institutions of the welfare state. According to Frederic Hayek in 1976.

In the prelude to the 90s, long before his death in 1992, his conception of the term already added other nuances: Any systematic and deliberate attempt to want to organize, intervene and replace any area of human interactions; especially the moral traditions of society, interrupting the cultural evolution of institutions. It is intended to replace these moral schemes (which the history of humanity has taken thousands of years to develop and whose knowledge is dispersed throughout society) with others of human design, without assuming the impossibility that belongs to reason. human by not having all the necessary knowledge and not recognizing the existence of an implicit spontaneous order. Its definition already announced where the new indirect strategy would go: **Gramscian postmodernism.**

The reader in this unit should have become more familiar with the analogy of the house, with the strategy of direct attack, noticing that Liberalism adds more bases, pillars, and incentives. Marx transfers the direct attack used in feudalism making it systematic, premeditated. The reader must, from dialectics, understand the types of proposals, the profiles of the leaders and executors of the strategy (the same will be repeated in more modern times in Latin America); You must know how to interpret and understand that the tools contained in the communist manifesto are not a dead letter, that it has many followers who silently believe in this, that they are committed to carrying them out, that its doctrine encourages them to feel pious, because of this they go to be relentless.

The reader must also have noted, with concern, how the measures of tyranny increase as time approaches the present; The reason for this is explained by the fact that more modern movements learn to better use the tyrannical elements used in history.

You must have noticed that we have mentioned the word Gramscian postmodernism twice; The first time we associated it with neocommunism, neo-Marxism, post-Marxism. All these definitions have a high degree of accuracy. The second time mentioned was in Hayek's 1992 definition, which relates it to the attempt to reorganize through laws or imposition the social and moral codes of society to stop the reproduction of the free enterprise system; The latter is what will occupy us in the rest of the book.

4

NEW MOVEMENTS IN LATIN AMERICA: DEMOCRACY AT RISK AND OTHER SUBTLE ARDIES OF TYRANNY

A social formation that does not reproduce the conditions of production at the same time as it produces will not survive even a year.
Karl Marx

Every violent change in property is preceded by a revolution.
Ludwig von Mises

A few years ago, in the first semester of 2020, I entered university to study first year of law; The intention was none other than to verify and verify the extent to which functional leftist ideas were penetrating the minds of young people. Indeed, the teachers - with the exception of one who was a foreigner and another teacher who was old enough not to participate in the trap - warned or inadvertently repeated attacks on the system:

everything is wrong, and it is the fault of neoliberalism!
They had sown the ideas in fertile ground, all that was left was for the events to be unleashed!

It was an interesting discovery, there was a lack of more evidence to assume the indoctrination strategy in young people, but it was what I was looking for.

We will continue with the direct and continuous explanation of the idea that we had been developing. We will resume socialism communism where we left it, and we will transfer it from the fall of the Soviet Union to install it in Latin America. No person who was not a fanatic would defend Socialism at this time!
Europe and developed countries continued their pragmatism towards leftist ideas. In Latin America the conditions were conducive for everything to be different, emerging in the process the desire for total power: half work in poverty reduction, high rates of inequality, racial exclusion, legal corruption; in short, rampant unrest. Social justice, equity, equality are very powerful ideas to die for; the strategy had to be readjusted and readapted to it. Gramsci was reintroduced, to the Postmodernists, the direct attack that seeks to destroy private property was reconsidered by the indirect one.
Finally, a long, painful, but ultimately successful indirect attack strategy was chosen. However, due to its origin and background – the direct strategy conceives itself as inspiration within the dictatorship of the proletariat; The new indirect strategy has been tried to be hidden, its origin has been kept so hidden that it has not been given the proper baptism - this strategy (like all of them, including those on the right) can be pushed hard in order to lead to the loss of Freedom with the purpose of total power. If it seeks total power, when deployed, it entails the destruction of Liberal Democracy. We are saddened by the fact that an entire imperfect historical process depends on the strength of some institutions as much as on the tyrannical aspirations of the promoters.
Consequently, in units 4 and 5 of this first part we will review the new strategy in detail from the point of view of a group that seeks total

power. We will divide the analysis so that regarding this unit, number 4, we will recognize its potential in terms of its origin, its drivers, its objectives, as well as the possibilities of affecting the prevailing system. For this purpose, it will be good for us to see what the analogy of the house tells us, what the Tests that we have designed tell us, what the backward comparisons with socialism tell us, and forward, verifying that there are no tyrannical pretensions. In unit 5 we will see the deployment of the strategy, its actions, and tactics. We will end in unit 6 trying to understand the reason for the new objectives of the indirect strategy; For this we must demonstrate the importance of culture, school, family, order, and the rule of law within the functioning of the system.

This unity is fundamental due to the contribution and impact on the ideology of Gramsci and the postmodernists. We will approach this topic from two sides: the first, liberal, to which the reader is already accustomed, and the second from historical materialism (Marxism) - it will be announced when the writing becomes Marxist -. The reader will be able to contrast the differences: analyzes from Marxism lead to Louis Althusser's Ideological Apparatus of the State ISA, which are the same ones we have been seeing and which we call the formal and informal institutions of the rule of law.

How much have the scenarios and strategy changed in the last thirty years?

The scenarios have changed in our postmodern era, we no longer have the scenario of an ideology that proposes a direct war against the coercive power of the state to change the economic system and create a new society with other social standards, other values; That was something visible and palpable, there was something violent to face and the answer was obvious. Now the strategy was not seen, only its effects in which Western civilization itself as we know it was collapsing before our eyes. We are not prepared, there were no tools to counteract something that cannot be seen but is felt; just observe undaunted the slow but systematic debacle that generates small attacks, insignificant hostilities that corrode morals, laws, values. They wear down the pillars of society, these pillars fall little by little, the economy paralyzes, recedes, becomes immobilized, large sectors fall, society is terrified by small flashes of violence, sustained, without apparent direction, systematic that stop when They achieve their goal and the final blow comes with a very clear name of advance on Freedom: everything begins with subtle tricks, soon the tyranny is stripped naked and the loser this time may be the same civilization as we know it...

Next, we are going to review in detail all the contributions received in this new strategy, the orientation it takes and its scope (potential for change in society -liberal democracy- as we know it):

NOW IT IS INEQUALITY, WHICH AS PASSION DIRECTS HISTORY

In previous pages our guest, The Count de Tocqueville, warned us of the risks of a strategy permeated by the innate desire of human beings for total power and that mostly sought equality. This case is no exception, and its camouflaged nature gives it special gravity.

Tocqueville, planted at the beginning of Democracy, could never have foreseen the events to be unleashed today; He didn't even consider them.

Let's try to understand what happened, what changed; new actors continue to wave the flags of equality, well, we already know that it is a passion of humanity and a constant in recent history. However, there is a barely perceptible change, now it is the fight against Inequality caused by Neoliberalism!

Equality before the law, Freedom and again Inequality.

There were two processes that were occurring almost simultaneously in history and that gave the death certificate to feudalism. The first, Equality before the law recently achieved by history, immediately after defeating feudalism - as a class system after the French revolution - the second, which unleashed the newly acquired Freedom, spontaneous economic processes - which contained no direction human - based on free enterprise, and that germinated and spread giving people, in an apparently random way (business ability has no relation to how intelligent or pleasant the person is; or to their noble origins), the economic success as well as the inequality in their income - it was no longer due to a theme that you are born of blue blood - but that situation in the eyes of the new critical observers, was a new exploitation (socialist ideas were born) that multiplied in the extent to which the new model developed the Industrial Revolutions; Each time the exploitation was greater and a new class was formed that plundered the other. It was clearly immoral and unacceptable. These new ideas were being clothed in revealed truth, morality, infallibility, scientific and predestination. From the caves, through the crusades and touching the inquisition, every time human beings call upon morality and make the truth their own, difficult times come.

History once again provided a driving force that diluted the feeling of satiety that this new Equality could generate: it was being lost as soon as it was achieved. Do we wonder why they dilute so quickly? The reason could be because history itself is inexhaustible and provides its own sustenance. Another reason is that the actors refuse to disappear, or because the story, for it to happen, needs to have antagonists. In short, the system refines itself by being more perfect than we understand and adjusts itself to the extent of the events that are going to happen and the actors that are going to intervene, in more modern times, against Inequality.

Either way, we don't know; We can only infer from the evidence that can be observed, we know something about the method that has been followed until now and about the actors who are still an option for history and for the people, so that we analyze the repercussions of the actions of these new actors, in current and future events.

THE METHOD USED BY THE STORY ITSELF AND THE SENSE IN WHICH THE EVENTS OCCUR

That we would like more than to affirm and be able to verify that certain successful strategies deployed obey a Machiavellian brain with the capacity to execute conspiracy theories - we know that there is a certain obscene fascination of humanity for all this - that involve individuals, eras, societies, situations, violence, political results, economic catastrophes, etc. But no, we cannot affirm it. However, it is possible that we are underestimating the capacity of these events and of individuals to work in association, without any agreement, where individuals and their feelings are dragged towards the events that must be unleashed. We recognize that if there are certain individuals with the ability to add fuel to the fire and know which buttons to press to make certain events become their allies, come together, and contribute to their goals; in the same way that it seems that this series of events could have a life of its own. Now, what is quite plausible is that a person educated and versed in the subject of understanding how events occur systemically, their causes and effects, and after analyzing some specifically, can recreate it; that is, to generate them again as a laboratory and observe them and then use them systematically against a society, institution, or people.

How far does our individual interaction with events go? How far is the possibility of manipulating them?

For each person to answer these two questions, we must understand the logic of the processes - we are going to give a simple explanation - and the sense in which they occur and how they are perceived by human beings:

In short, in each event there are tangible events through the senses; We can see them, feel them, hear them, observe them. **These are the events that occur.**

Now, these events are isolated or are being repeated; They obey patterns (conscious or unconscious). **Here we are finding out systematicity and deliberation.**

We must find out if there is a relationship between the patterns and the obvious facts. **What forces trigger these patterns.**

These events could not occur if our morality did not allow it; let's change the word moral to a set of values; These events would not occur if our set of values did not tolerate them. **Here are the paradigms that define good and bad, acceptable, and unacceptable.**

An inquisitive question arises and even more disturbing than the previous two and extremely challenging: **is it possible to change the sense - which we saw in the previous paragraph - in which the events occur?**

I summarize the events in the sense that you want to change: first plant the ideas, the value system (Paradigms) and then some patterns and forces that lead to future events being triggered.

This was what was triggered by the change in strategy of the left: **first they needed an extensive work of indoctrination, which prepared the fertile ground for their ideas, an advance of positions where the morals and values of individuals were relaxed to allow certain events. that otherwise would have been impossible. Then take the culture (undermine the foundation) and the entire scaffolding will fall on its own.**

ANTONIO GRAMSCI (20) AND THE ENTIRE POSTMODERNIST CURRENT (21) (LOUIS ALTHUSSER) GAVE AN ANSWER TO THESE TWO UNKNOWNS:

The Marxist Preamble

Gramsci agreed with Marx that the exploitation of the capitalist system started from private property, as well as that the social structure, culture, values, laws, education, religion, sustain, feed and reproduce the productive scheme. . They also agreed with the need to tear them down.

The discussion expanded from the concepts left by Karl Marx around infrastructure (private ownership of the means of production) and superstructure:
   a) Legal-political superstructure (law and the state).
   b) Ideological superstructure (different ideologies, religious, moral, legal, political, etc.).

The graph of the superimposed blocks helps to understand the concept given by Marx, to advance to deeper ones.

<table>
<tr><td>IDEOLOGICAL   SUPERSTRUCTURE</td></tr>
<tr><td>LEGAL   SUPERSTRUCTURE</td></tr>
<tr><td>INFRASTRUCTURE: PRIVATE OWNERSHIP OF THE MEANS OF PRODUCTION</td></tr>
</table>

What happens in the economic base (infrastructure) determines what happens in the two floors above, that is, in the superstructure; Lenin would start from here to develop the direct violent attack.

The fundamental theory was that the superstructure – and in accordance with historical materialism – was determined by its base.
They develop a new unit of thought:
- 1) The superstructure has relative autonomy with respect to the base.
- 2) It is a reaction of the superstructure to the base.

Which in turn triggers the Marxist definition of the State as a machine of repression that allows it to remain in power with its repressive support forces: police, courts, prisons, army, etc.
The state is divided into:
- a) State Power: it is the objective of the political struggle of a certain class, its possession and conservation.

b) State apparatus: this can continue to operate for the previous classes, even though power is sedated. In democratic elections, state power is in session, but not the state apparatus that we call institutions.

Summary taken from Althusser of the Marxist theory of the state:

1) The state is the repressive apparatus of the state. 2) a distinction must be made between state power and the state apparatus (institutions). 3) the objective of the class struggle is the power of the state and the use of the state apparatus according to its class objectives. 4) the proletariat must take state power and develop in the subsequent stages a radical process, that of the destruction of the exploiting state (the goal is state power and control of the entire state apparatus).

From this point, two strategies of taking power take distance: a) the violent and direct Marxist-Leninist and b) the indirect **Gramscian postmodernist.**

The Gramscian contribution

Gramsci's great contribution is to establish that the power of the hegemonic class is not only sustained by the power of weapons, but that there is a legitimacy that intellectuals generate with the consensus where citizens decide to obey.

Consensus is achieved through institutions such as the church, schools, universities, unions, the family, science, journalists, art; In each of these there is an opinion leader who reproduces the dominant ideology, and it can also be ended. By reaching out to them, a new consensus can be achieved, and cultural hegemony achieved. Taking this into consideration, the events would be unleashed in a different way than the revolution, position by position would be taken within the state until the final takeover. The time it takes must be in accordance with the solidity of liberal institutions, but the values of society will be so undermined that they will allow the advancement of new actions and ideas that replace those that were previously hegemonic.

The fundamental difference with Marxism-Leninism is therefore that **Gramscian-Marxism proposes first to take the culture, that is, the teachers, the journalists, in general the intellectuals and opinion leaders. For Antonio Gramsci, the state is not only sustained by the force of arms, but also by its legitimacy and credibility.** The latter is the consensus created by intellectuals that makes individuals adhere to hegemonic ideas; that is, choose to obey the prevailing order; However, that is its Achilles heel, and its consensus can be ended and the order subverted.

If we appeal to the analogy of the house, Gramsci and Althusser reverse the order of the attack: first take the opinion leaders (including the most important ISA, the school) and then attack the bases of the system, its pillars, incentives, its institutions (family, church, patriarchy, etc.), culture in general, the rule of law and everything it generates in terms of trust, order; That is, all the aspects that allow and contribute to the system being sustained and reproduced. Eventually, private property and military forces will fall alone. (See graphic analogy of the house).

THE POSTMODERNIST CONTRIBUTION: THE CONSOLIDATION OF THE NEW STRATEGY

We must understand this current within the Marxist logic that tries to refocus the unfulfilled promises of Marx himself, what did not happen, revisionism looking for elements that could lead to the same goal: eliminate exploitation, eliminate classes, therefore eliminate inequality, and finally make man as free from economic relations as from other social and cultural predicaments.

Louis Althusser clarifies postmodernist concepts for us in his book: ideology and ideological apparatuses of the state (a Neo-Marxist vision). The reader should be prepared to learn that from here on we will resume the use of Marxist rhetoric and terminology (we will also mark the end).

Althusser's great contribution is the continuation of Gramsci's work in redefining the concepts of Ideological State Apparatus (IEA).

His great redefinition of the state is a prologue of where his contribution is directed: the state apparatus is not only repressive, but includes institutions of civil society: church, schools, unions, etc.

    a) State power.

    b) Repressive apparatus of the state: government, administration, army, police, courts, prisons, etc.

    c) Ideological State Apparatuses (ISA).

The repressive apparatus functions mainly under violence (repression); The ISA have the following characteristics:

    a) They operate mostly under ideology, but they also have some hidden pressure: the school expels you.

    b) The ISA are mostly private: school, family, religious, political party system, unions, media and press, cultural institutions, culture itself, etc.

    c) The ISA function as a dominant ideology, what unifies them is the ideology of the ruling class.

    d) If the ruling class has the power of the state and the repressive apparatus of the state, it must also manipulate the ISA.

    e) Without hegemony in the ISA, one cannot remain in power.

There is a principle outlined by Marx, but not delved into, in which the significance of this topic is seen:
Distinguish in the social revolution between the material upheaval of the economic conditions of production and the legal, political, religious, artistic, or philosophical forms in which men become aware of that conflict and carry it to the end.
This first principle is then deepened so much that it allows establishing a beachhead for the assault:
The ISA can be taken because they are rooted outside of ideology, in the infrastructure, in the relations of production (which are exploitative, Althusser notes). Then, the weapon of ideology can be turned against the classes in power.

THE FUNCTION OF THE ISA IS TO REPRODUCE PRODUCTION RELATIONSHIPS

How to overcome the monolithic structure of power plus repression plus ideology?
The reproduction of production relations is ensured by the exercise of state power in the apparatus of the repressive and ideological state. **However, Althusser clarifies, if the following is understood, it is possible to penetrate and leave without action the functions of reproducing the system:** a) all apparatuses function with repression and ideology. b) the repressive apparatus is a centralized and organized whole under a unity of command in the dominant classes. It contributes to ensuring by force (from the most brutal to simple laws, ordinances, or censorship) the political conditions of reproduction of the relations of production. c) The ISA are multiple, autonomous, decentralized and therefore susceptible to being taken in a limited or total way. These express the effects of class struggle. From the ISA the action of certain repressive apparatuses can be blocked.

Louis Althusser will place great emphasis on how the school and the family (in modern capitalism) receive the legacy of the church and the family (in the Middle Ages) as the most preponderant and important ISA, in a way that points out the path and priorities. in the deployment of the indirect strategy in Latin America. We will return to this aspect at the end in a chapter on the family.

For didactic reasons we are not going to continue with the Marxist approach and terms, but we will rename the ISA as we had identified them as culture, formal and informal institutions, laws, the rule of law, etc.

The puzzle of the new strategy is put together, consolidating the contribution of Gramsci and the postmodernists.

We are going to analyze some concepts that individually do not give us a meaning, but placed in the right place they greatly explain certain situations, what happens, is happening and could anticipate something of an uncertain future that could be unleashed in these unknown paths of postmodernism. either. Classical Marxism failed in its conception of the working class as the central engine of the great revolution - today's proletarian is just another bourgeois; is more concerned today with changing cars or refrigerators than embodying a liberating crusade - in its scientific character - revealed truth - alongside the concept of private property (given in history as a spontaneous process of appropriation or theft), Marx undervalued the role of culture in society, in civilization. Gramsci coined stronger ideas around the role of culture as the basis of the development of civilization than what Marx outlined. The superstructure referred to by Marx (culture and others) was much more powerful than the scope given by him.

Gramsci was ahead of his time; his contributions are taken up several generations after his death and in the midst of postmodernism that the last two generations of the population have experienced. The new contemporary context is the post-industrial, service economy, in which we experience the transfer of national to supranational sovereignty due to globalization - although this aspect is being reconsidered - and the Internet that brought with it the most profound change whose repercussions we are only trying to understand. understand and process. **The biggest change that the Internet brought us is that "the truth does not exist": the truth can be rewritten; Another change, but no less important, is that power brings truth.** The third substantial change is that other paradigms and ways of facing, enjoying, and obtaining the rewards of life can quickly be created. This is achieved by the immediate multiplier effect of the networks, an effect that a few years before could take years to produce through traditional means.

The other great contribution is that postmodernism proposes the rejection of the great concepts or categories that became "law sculpted in gold" in modernity: truth, logic, the subject, identity, gender, etc.

It rejects and there is no longer truth, nor logic, nor reality, identities do not exist, the subject does not exist, so that approaches can be made outside the scientific order, the logical order, adding new categories of the individual (friends), etc. It destroys the order that rationality had given to power and there is no longer a way to differentiate good from bad, to distinguish what is appropriate or not; In this situation everything is unpredictable, and anything can happen. It is valid to redo history and create a new story according to something planned. Stories that transform the truth are valid (there is no truth). They can be deconstructed (22) – as a text made up of words said Derrida – concepts and identities that have shaped Western culture, that have allowed development and civilization as we know it.

Foucault finds power and revolutionary potential in the small contradictions of society, you just have to look for them, unleash them and deconstruct them: If classical Marxism based, on the great class struggle and the proletarian, all the contradiction that it needed to generate to maintain society against one another; There is now power in countless small causes: man against woman (feminism); there is power in the exploitation of women (patriarchy); there is power in the heterosexual and the homosexual (LGTBQ+ movement); there is power in the defense of nature (environmentalism); there is potential in the contradiction of the criminal against society (The criminal has been constructed by the disciplinary system, there is power in removing laws and reducing sentences); There is power in the contradictions of the entire existing disciplinary system, be it schools, churches, prisons and all the systems that respond to the needs of the rule of law that the free market (capitalism) needs to reproduce.

It must be understood that the identification of these new micro power relations in all the contradictions of society, and that society itself has resolved them through rules, discipline, institutions (formal and informal), laws or legislation, unleashing them has the potential to destroy liberal democratic society itself. Additionally, due to the detail and level of damage that unleashing them from political power entails, it means the setback to all the social progress that has been achieved so far, that is, the setback of Western civilization as we know it.

In the end, truth is a construction of power and there is only the truth of power (according to Foucault).

Who benefits from the destruction of the truth? Which power will be strong enough to reinstall certain order? Is all this logical or is it a desperate act? Is something being deconstructed or, on the contrary, is something related to power being constructed? And if it is again the search for total power, are we talking about the all-embracing power of the state?

In the fourth part of this book, we will once again question the actions of this new philosophy from power.

Seeking the benefit of the doubt, we will baptize this new indirect strategy deployed as **Gramscian postmodernism;** It works independently of others that may be running at the same time.

Gramscian postmodernism is a strategy that renews and changes the old Marxist strategy of direct attack on the military forces to, after their defeat, expropriate private property of the means of production and create new values, incentives, and legislation in accordance with the new economic structure. **Gramscian postmodernism** deploys a series of attacks on the bases, pillars and incentives of society and the economy, by releasing the forces that lie hidden in the formal and informal institutions and laws that society itself has instituted to restrain them. The situation created prevents the reproduction of the system, annuls the rule of law, and generates a Kaos (23) that will precede the fall of private property and military forces; These will fall alone. **Gramscian postmodernism** receives contributions from Marx in its conception of the problem, it receives contributions from Gramsci and postmodernism, developing the cultural issue undervalued by Marx and others.

The capitalist dynamic has had an unforeseen effect within the fatalistic predictions that foreshadowed the collapse of the system due to the growing separation of businessmen and workers with increasing poverty. This did not happen; On the contrary, the middle class appeared that was not in the plans of any of the parties, the substantial improvement of well-being for large sectors of the population and the creation of an upper class within the workers advocates the total disappearance of socialism-communism; His reaction to such an existentialist threat has been **Gramscian postmodernism.** Socialism communism proved incapable of producing new wealth and led to the widespread impoverishment of the society where it was applied. This event poses a survival challenge for this ideology that is driven to seek new foci of revolutions, awakening the forces hidden in the small contradictions of society, destroying the formal and informal institutions that society itself has designed and that have allowed civilization. Such institutions are today under attack by **Gramscian postmodernism.**

As far as we have observed, Gramscian postmodernism is about the relaunching again and again of the successful strategy (based on dialectics) of seizing power in the face of the errors of liberal democracy and in the presence of unrest (non-forceful reduction of poverty, exclusion, corruption, lack of defense of the achievements achieved and inequality).
This relaunch is only new in the strategy of establishing itself, but it does not solve the fundamental problems in its implementation and consolidation, such as the generalized impoverishment of the population, death, the inability to produce new wealth, migration due to scarcity and hunger. The advance on freedom and the vicious circle closes again. In unit six of this same part we will explain how damage occurs in the business fabric.

A STRATEGY IN LATIN AMERICA DEPLOYED TO ELIMINATE INEQUALITY WITH HIDDEN OBJECTIVES AND POSSIBLE SIGHTS OF TYRANNY

Background in Latin America

We will briefly mention aspects that we touched on in the first book: THE RISE OF THE LEFT IN LATIN AMERICA IN THE

FULL ERA OF UNREST. In this book we refer to the chronology of certain events that culminate with the coming to power through democratic means of leftist groups that two or three decades ago were considered marginal and whose voting power was meager.

The unrest, exclusion (the social elevator does not work) and entrenched corruption throughout the political spectrum made a strategy possible that would transmute the scenario that was favorable to the dominant elite.

BACKGROUND OF DISCOMFORT IN LATIN AMERICA

HISTORY OF DISCOMFORT

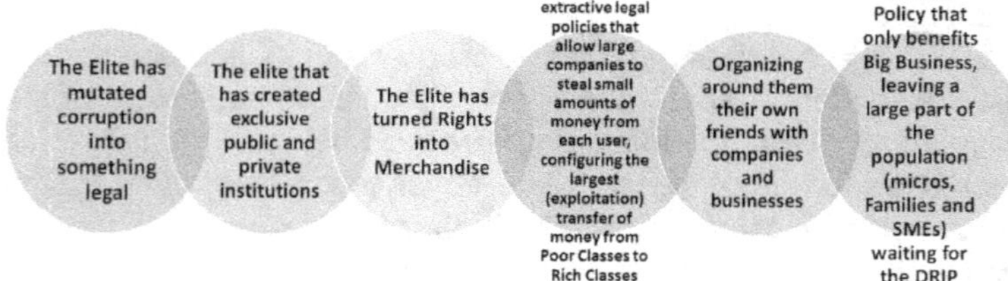

The unrest was the scenario in which the left stirred up inequality and resentment, demonstrations were held, violence was used to corner civil society, tactics were implemented that were repeated in each country, Neoliberalism was blamed, and change and anti-corruption promises were made.

We intend to demonstrate that some tactics only work within discomfort; If this is disabled, part of the malicious method would be disabled. Other tactics precede the deployment, having their own inertia, being functional because they fulfill a function, sharing sociological or philosophical modes or origins.

A NEW POTENTIALLY DESTABILIZING STRATEGY.

Naivety in politics and war is a capital sin:
We are facing a current built from belligerence and counterpower, with individuals trained in dialectics, violent confrontation, in the need for a single direction in antagonism to democracy - reconciling ideas - and in the duality of choosing between the potentiality of a strategy that can bring total power (and have another chance in history for more of the same) or recognize that there is something we do wrong and insert ourselves within the legal framework, respect democratic principles and work within established norms.

The other strategy: the elephant hidden in plain sight.

We are going to try to put the political strategy in a structure that can be easily understood; which is based on common aspects that all of them share; We will ask Chat GPT from OpenAI about these, but we will not stop to talk about concepts that have already been explained or exposed in the previous book, we will go on to establish that it is installed around the main idea of political strategy:

Parts of the strategy

-Current political analysis: we already know that the psychological profiles of the promoters of the strategy, due to their training, are the most sensitive to identifying the problems of the current system.

-Define the objectives: win elections, take power of the state and its repressive and ideological apparatus, influence public policies, promote a specific social change, establish a new economic-political system or all the above.

-Construction of the political platform: this is what is visible and where the gaze of supporters and detractors should be directed. An important part of the leaders in each country have admitted the influence of a progressive current (22); This is the visible way, so that we will present its doctrine in the references and bibliographic sources.

-Mobilization and support strategies: in this field they all work at the same time; From here we should be able to explain the astonishing growth from almost meager popularity and voting intention to overwhelmingly winning key elections.

-Preparation of the ground: indoctrination of young people well in advance, beginning at school (evidenced by Gramsci and Althusser), penetration of opinion leaders.

- Social movements demanding minorities: that permanently seek to attack institutions to remove limitations that nature has imposed on human beings; They are instrumentalized and become spiritual children of socialism and now of progressivism in the sense that, like those, they seek in social institutions the roots of the conditions given by nature and therefore removed from the action of man and aim to reform them by reforming nature itself (Von Mises): example feminism, patriarchy, etc.

- Legislation that exacerbates and attacks morality: Outside of power and from it; support and promote legislation that resurfaces all the contradictions that society has curbed with formal and informal institutions; even with laws.

- The normal marketing strategy of the new political party: this is the one that is the same as that of all other political parties and promotes progressive proposals (22). As a characteristic in Latin America, campaigns are inserted to exacerbate resentment, hatred, division and reverse payment as compensation for exclusion, as well as the **Gramscian postmodernist indirect strategy;** Both are the ones that are potentially most destabilizing; However, they agree that they are only functional within the discomfort; However, the discomfort has been deactivated... Both have been deactivated.

- The **Gramscian postmodernist** indirect strategy: this is the hidden one, which goes to the bases, pillars, and incentives of the system of liberal democracy (see graphic analogy of the house). From power it takes the form of legislation that advocates seeking shared well-being: redistributive and redistributive income policies are included here.

- The temptation of violent groups: before and after the seizure of power. The temptation is to instrumentalize any group that is excluded, discriminated against or that seeks vindications.

- The visible leaders of the strategy: This apparent lack of clarity and coherence is instigated by its leadership; It then forces us to ask and identify: who are the architects and executors? We see that they are the same ones who once brought us a violent strategy and proposed change with the oppression and tyranny of the entire society. A second question arises, which requires caution: have they only renounced the violent form, or have they also given up changing society (Democracy) and our way of life (Liberal)?
The answer to the first question may be: yes. The indirect strategy embodied by **Gramscian postmodernism** would

confirm this. To answer the second and third questions, we resort to verifying that the consequences of its implementation open the possibilities of ceding total power and with it the changes in the democratic lifestyle and in the liberal way of life (they despise our lifestyle).

¨Liberal democracy is in the grip of a corrupt elite and under friendly fire from a new elite on the rise. ¨

WHAT TYPE OF RESULTS DOES THE DEPLOYMENT OF THESE STRATEGIES PROVIDE?

Being faithful to a Marxist dialectic, there has been no clarity in the objectives of the new strategy deployed, and we assume there will not be, until the end: we are on a path that we do not know exists at the end...

Given that **Gramscian postmodernism** is the ideological support of three clear processes that are currently taking place, it is necessary to explain them: all democratic election. The first within the democratic framework. The second quick step to 21st Century socialism; the latter with a slow but progressive transition of the destruction of the bases and incentives that the liberal economy requires to function and a systematic deconstruction of its values. Apparently, the choice of one strategy or another depends on the belief of the strategic directors of each country in democratic as well as liberal values; that changes can be made institutionally, the strategic leadership capabilities of the leader, the solidity of the institutions of each country and the "political maturity" of the people.

Let's look at the facts of the three strategies being deployed:

Postmodernism strategy Gramscian (social democracy) that resists attacking the system based on private ownership of the means of production or violently attacking the culture, order, the rule of law, the bases, pillars, and incentives of the system): receives all the Gramscian and postmodernist contributions. Democratic seizure of power and application of progressive proposals within the respect of democracy and the framework of the law, that is, they are not launched in a tax manner or directed at the bases of the economy. This has been happening in some countries, especially European ones (it is what we call social democracy) in which the alternation to one side and the other occurs for the benefit of society and gradual changes. The changes are widely discussed in democracy seeing their possibilities and respective maturity. A fundamental aspect is that there is no attack on democratic alternation.

Hard Strategy Gramscian postmodernism - 21st Century Socialism: receives all the Gramscian and postmodernist contributions. Democratic takeover and rapid implementation of socialism by penetrating and reconverting military forces, eliminating private property and deconstruction of our social, economic, legal, religious, cultural values, etc.

It occurs in a society corroded by unrest, penetrated by indoctrination, with weak institutions for the protection of Democracy, with weak legislation for the defense of private property, - perhaps due to the fragility in obtaining property at its origin. by mechanisms not adhered to the law - with a breakdown of values and the rule of law. Total dismantling of the democratic alternation of power.

The use and formation of the violent civil forces that should defend the new system is observed with concern.

Soft Strategy Gramscian postmodernism: receives all the Gramscian and postmodernist contributions. Democratic seizure of power, slow but systematic deconstruction of our values and rule of law, imposition of progressive laws that attack the bases (incentives) of our free enterprise system, which allow the creation of value and wealth, which inexorably lead to the slow but progressive impoverishment of the economy, which finally leads to a collectivist subsistence economy:

"The entire remaining structure of the free market, including private property and the military, will fall on its own."

Almost all Latin American countries (including Spain) have been, to a greater or lesser extent, exposed to this type of strategy.

There is a long experiment in this type of society in Latin America (Argentina), where progressive taxes have been implemented, the tax burden has been greatly increased, it is an inflexible labor market, only a third of the population works (generates value and wealth) maintaining the rest of the population with subsidies, the decrease in well-being is progressive and unsustainable. Despite indoctrination, this situation is not sustainable, and a structural failure of the nationalized model will occur. As democracy - alternation of power - persists, these impracticable measures that have never worked anywhere will be reversed; people, society demands well-being and if it is allowed to choose its own path, it will do so in the name of its own and individual good.

Another way to approach the results that these strategies can generate is if we assume that there is no hidden evil or abuse of trust; and that only his proposals are full of naivety, dialectic and good nature. These last three variables recorded in their proposals and added to the agitation of slogans and charming proposals, come together in a cocktail of irresponsibility and arbitrariness without roots in an economic reality; It is a recipe that only leads to the abyss.

In any of the last forms above, they represent the most serious danger that liberal democracy and Freedom in Latin America have faced due to the degree of exposure in which society is left and the manifest vulnerability of civilization.

ANALOGY OF THE HOUSE TO EXPLAIN THE SYSTEM, DIFFERENTIATE A DIRECT ATTACK FROM AN INDIRECT ONE AND SHOW THE PILLARS OR BASES THAT SUPPORT THEM

What is the strategy for taking power? It is an indirect attack.

It is indirect because it does not target the military forces or private property; **Gramscian postmodernism** is pointing brick by brick at all the pillars (culture, religion, rule of law, order, trust, family, etc.) and the bases (incentives) that support the house and reproduce the system. It points to the ISA.

The strategy for taking power is indirect and "non-violent" (it develops new models of violence as it perfects armed civil groups that attack, corner and blackmail civil society and confront the public force with impunity).

The analogy of the house and indirect attack of Gramscian postmodernism against liberal democracy

Using the analogy of the house - where the house is the private property of the means of production - as a first step the bases and pillars of the house are attacked and deconstructed. The second and third steps are no longer necessary to execute; They can fall alone, since the guards that protect it (military forces), and the house (the private property of the means of production), will fall in the middle of Khaos (23).

How the system is reproduced

The system cannot be reproduced; What's more, it falls. This strategy demonstrates the depth of knowledge that its executors have about our economy - they live on a fixed state salary, they are incapable of setting up a company, however they see the gears of it and put in the stick - and the system itself since it prevents them from reproduce: order is important for investment, in Khaos (23) prosperity does not exist, without individual private savings there is no reinvestment, without inheritances the possibility of bequeathing your work to your children is removed, people need to be clear about the conditions previously prevailing before investing, you must have the security that I will receive my payment, the security of being able to withdraw my investment, if you do not obtain the product of your work for yourself you are not going to invest. Using the analogy of the house, houses under construction will stop while those already built fall.
Destroying the bases and pillars the system is paralyzed and there is no creation of new wealth. Public force and private force will fall alone.

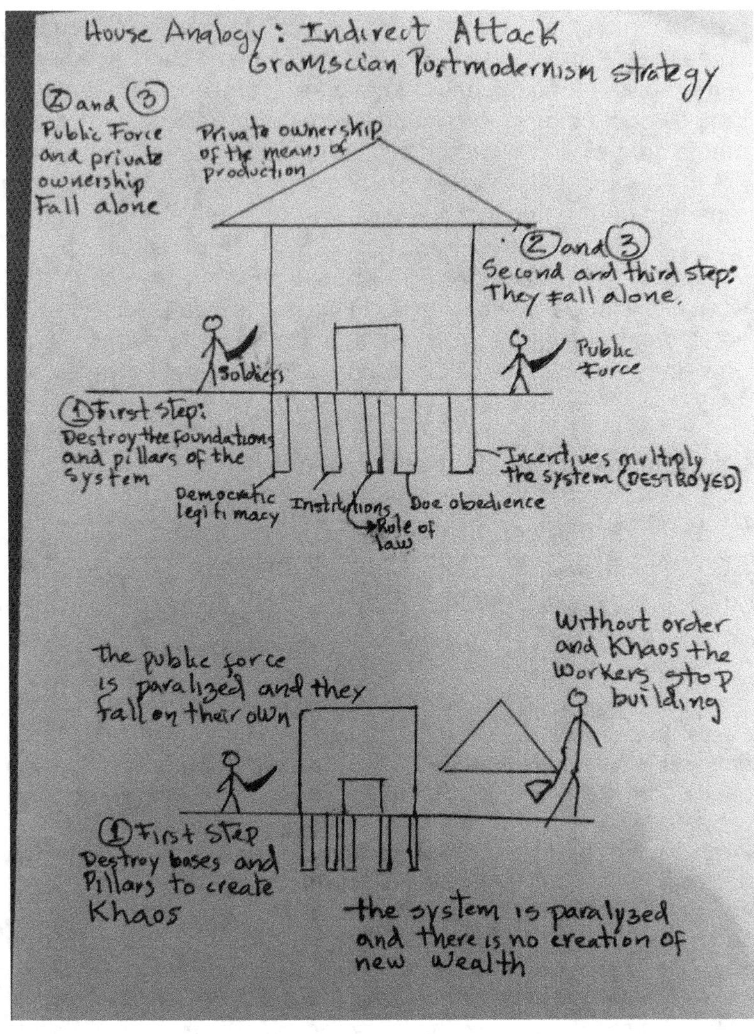

Things will never be the same. The implementation of this indirect strategy attacks firm concepts, deconstructs truths, creates multiple scenarios in which it subverts reason, unleashes previously contained forces, and exposes vulnerabilities. Additionally, networks grant acceleration plus the power of ubiquity that multiplies the effect. Traditional press media are being challenged by the networks; Now the networks are the tyrants, and the problem of media concentration is being repeated on the networks.

Dimension the danger of 500 people deciding the content of what 6 billion people in the world consume, via the press and networks. Imagine the above in the hands of any economically powerful group whose agenda is to seize political power at any cost!

Let's remember this title captured previously:

HOW TO IDENTIFY NEW PROPOSALS IN THE FUTURE THAT RETURN THE PATH OF SOCIALISM, AND WHICH INDEFECTIBLY LEAD US TO TYRANNY?

Necessarily these strategies are deliberate and systematic; This is the first element to identify to establish that there is a clear intention behind something. Trying to identify the pattern in an indirect strategy is where you most often make mistakes. The bases, order and incentives (such as the confidence that the investor must have; that the individual clearly feels that he can develop his own life project and generate the necessary methods for it) of our economy are not so visible. Furthermore, unexpected changes in policy, those that do not seem to make sense, are classic for undermining trust by inflicting more collateral damage than is visible (the collateral damage is visible in the decrease or destruction of individual savings, profits, People become discouraged because they do not receive the product of their work, etc.).

Continuing with the methodology, in this table we are going to summarize the concepts that animate both classical socialism and **Gramscian postmodernism** in their hard strategy. We are going to determine if it meets the concept, with what intensity or direction; to leave to the reader the definition of whether or not it has a tyrannical vocation:

Concept	Classic Socialism	hard Gramscian postmodernism	observations
Aimed at eliminating private property	✓		Its initial proposal is to eliminate the Inequality produced by neoliberalism. However, it may be a possibility.
Eliminate all formal and informal institutions that allow free enterprise to germinate, develop and endure.	✓	✓	**Gramscian postmodernism** Deconstructs them.
Eliminate culture	✓	✓	**Gramscian postmodernism** Deconstructs **them** .
Eliminate social order	✓	✓	**Gramscian postmodernis**

Concept	Classic Socialism	Gramscian postmodernism soft	observations
			m Deconstructs them.
Eliminate laws	✓	✓	**Gramscian postmodernism** Deconstructs them.
Eliminate religion	✓	✓	**Gramscian postmodernism** Deconstructs them.
Eliminate the rule of law	✓	✓	**Gramscian postmodernism** Deconstructs them.
Violent strategy that attacks the armed forces	✓		
Violent blackmail strategy towards civil society and civilian police forces		✓	**Gramscian postmodernism** **openly** **encourages** and supports them.

POSTULATES OF THE COMMUNIST MANIFESTO			
Concept	**Classic Socialism**	**Gramscian postmodernism soft**	observations
Expropriation of land	✓	✓	**Gramscian postmodernism** proposes

ownership and use of land rent for State expenses.			giving them to the landless. There is a promise to do so legally through the purchase of land.
Strong progressive taxes.	✓	✓	
Suppression of the right of inheritance.	✓	✓	
Confiscation of the property of all emigrants and seditionists.	✓	✓	The opposition is forced to emigrate to exile. The rest of the population is incited to attack them.
Centralization of credit in the hands of the State through a national Bank with state capital and	✓	✓	They intend to centralize unimaginable economic powers in the State.

exclusive monopoly.			
Centralization of transportation in the hands of the State.	✓		
Multiplication of national factories, means of production, plowing and improvement of land according to a collective plan.	✓	✓	In Latin America there have already been failed processes to protect the national industry (ECLAC).
Proclamation of the general duty to work, creation of industrial armies, mainly in the countryside.	✓	✓	"Universal work and a decent and fair salary" are proclaimed. ¨

Articulation of agricultural and industrial farms; tendency to gradually erase the differences between the countryside and the city.	✓	✓	
Free public education for all children.	✓	✓	And at the university level.
Abolition of factory child labor in its current form.	✓		This existed at the beginning of industrialization
Unification of education with material production.	✓		

What the previous comparison does is show us the ideological closeness between these two currents; It is evident that both doctrines share several concepts, differing in the time and way of achieving them.

METER OF TYRANNY IN GRAMSCIAN POSTMODERNISM

The following Test evaluates how **Gramscian postmodernism conceives** the different notions and ideas of the management of power, which any political group must consider. We bring them up because their type of strategy opens the possibilities of total power, leaving liberal democracy vulnerable. The success of the strategy is that it stimulates human desires for total power; Resisting this temptation will only depend on the strength of the institutions to repel the attack or the existence of laws that protect the institutions.

We are going to apply this Test to **Gramscian postmodernism hard,** which is what we identify as he is quickly going to install the dictatorship.

METER OF TYRANNY IN HARD GRAMSCIAN POSTMODERNISM

Power Factors or Actions	Tyrannical Rating from lowest to highest (1-2 Green. 3 Yellow. 4-5 Red, where 5 is maximum tyranny)	Observations: The concepts expressed here are extreme; They are shown so that they do not actually occur again.
Use of force against the population	5	It uses the violent force of related civil groups to blackmail society. Then, he corners the opposition into exile; Finally, when it is

		already installed, it uses public force with new laws to persecute the opposition. The concept of disposable citizens reappears.
Executive power concentration	5	They concentrate all powers, faithful to their dialectic, their dogma, and their method; And what is more serious, they reestablish the worship that existed in feudalism of the king, but this time to an all-powerful leader.
Concentration of judicial power	5	They concentrate all powers, faithful to their dialectic, their dogma, and their method; And what is more serious, they reestablish the worship that existed in feudalism of the king, but this time to an all-powerful leader.
Legislative power concentration	5	They concentrate all powers, faithful to their dialectic, their dogma, and their method; And what is more serious, they reestablish the worship that existed in feudalism of the king, but

		this time to an all-powerful leader.
Possibility of getting out of the tyrant through tyrannicide	5	After the process of concentration of powers in the state is finished, it is almost zero. Just a system implosion.
Use of indoctrination in society	5	There is a tyrant in every mind. All types of indoctrination and threats to free thought are instituted by the state.
Dissidents may be expelled	5	It has been established since Karl Marx's Communist Manifesto. It is the beginning of the exile.
Possibility of individual and collective organization	5	Association that does not originate in the state is declared enemy.
Possibility of turning the population against each other	5	It has been established since Karl Marx's Communist Manifesto.
Possibility of developing some type of property that allows one to defend oneself from the State.	5	They do not identify property as their primary objective; in fact, it is allowed for government supporters.

Possibility of losing life	5	Persecution is instituted both by related civilians who receive benefits from the regime, and by the repressive apparatus of the state.
Freedom Meter	5	Only the bureaucrat is free. Freedom for citizens is defined in terms of belonging to the party and what the leadership decides.
Equality Meter	5	All are equal; however, there is very little to distribute due to the wealth destruction that occurs in implementation.
Possibilities of receiving compensation for your work	5	**They begin a process of destruction of the concept of work; first taking from people the product of their work to give to another what is not the product of their work.** The concept of salary is destroyed: you must work as much as you can and receive as you need. They are societies that lose the incentive to work. The historical progress achieved in Liberal Democracies

		with respect to the remuneration of work is lost. They forget that the Human Being works for himself and his family; never for a stranger. That concept that existed in tribal societies, where everyone was related, is impossible to replicate in larger societies.
Possibility to choose your job	5	In the initial stages of the advancement of **Gramscian postmodernism,** and due to the destruction of the business fabric, it is difficult to find employment and have a well-paid job.
Religious freedom	5	The state religion.

Total 80 out of a maximum of 80.

This last measure is astonishingly worrying. We must and must be able to see the light or the darkness at the end of the tunnel and warn if the possibility of the advance of tyranny over freedom opens again in history... and it could be happening again.

For now, the reader has been able to gauge the potential of this new indirect strategy and the capacities of Gramscian postmodernism within the progressive strategy. The reader must be clear about the

Marxist basis, the additional postmodernist contribution to the Gramscian, as well as how its deployment (we will look at it in the next unit) gives it an advance on liberal democracy : it opens the way to the hard strategy of total power (Socialism of the XXI century); However, the soft one causes undetermined damage (never tested) in the bases and pillars of society, from which it is very possible that civilization will not be able to rise again.

A successful strategy for seizing power, whatever its hard or soft meaning, would make no sense if there was no proposal to exercise power. Is it going to be exercised to manage what has been received or change it? That change could mean the replacement of liberal democracy. For this reason, let us determine from the facts, if another way of expropriating and progressively moving towards Socialism has been modeled: although it has "renounced" going directly against the basis of the free market, that is, against private property, it has opted to go against the bases, pillars, and incentives that the system must maintain and reproduce. It is not enough to have ownership if there is no trust, if there is no trust in legislation, if market criteria are deliberately broken; that is, there is no basis for private property without the rule of law. If phenomena such as profit (progressive income taxes), private individual savings (accumulation in the form of savings is what makes reinvestment possible and which is reproduce the system), take away the product of your work, etc. are phenomena that are assimilated to expropriation (these topics will continue to be developed in subsequent chapters).

5

A PUZZLING STRATEGY

¨And this is how Freedom dies, with a loud applause¨

Padme Amidala

The tree of Liberty must be invigorated from time to time with the blood of patriots and tyrants: it is its natural fertilizer.

Thomas Jefferson

¨If you know the enemy and you know yourself, you should not fear the outcome of hundreds of battles. If you know yourself, but not the enemy, for every victory you win you will also suffer a defeat. If you know neither the enemy nor yourself, you will succumb in every battle. ¨

Sun Tzu on the Art of War

The key to victory is not in defeating the enemy, but in defeating the enemy's strategy; There lies your vulnerability.

Sun Tzu on the Art of War

SUN TZU: IF YOU DO NOT KNOW NEITHER THE ENEMY OR YOURSELF, YOU WILL SUCCUMBLE IN EVERY BATTLE

Hard Gramscian postmodernism seeks total power. In this unit we will return to the previous unit to deal with how the siege is carried out, the deployment of tactics, its effects on significant aspects of the structure of society, its characteristics, and tools.
The three deployments of Gramscian postmodernism seen in the previous unit, they must be understood in this unit from the point of view of their implications on the Freedom of choosing, looking for their indirect effects on property; That is to say, the reader must think what happens if he only has the property title but without the effects of using it in the free market because there is no trust due to the multiple confrontations that are generated, because there are apparently absurd laws that confuse, because they appear restrictive laws with countless new regulations, or because they destroy private savings, or attempt to control prices, or attempt to control production; All of the above is finally summarized in the elimination of the effects of property due to the attacks suffered on the rule of law. Is the reader facing another type of expropriation? We will develop these topics in the second part, first unit.

We emphasize that we believe that the advances of today's society occur through agreements, not through impositions.

I paraphrase the words of a wise former president of a small southern country: **We must agree on a minimum among society and respect it; then there must be the free exercise of Democracy.**

Not having denounced the greatest tyrannies on the continent demonstrates their nostalgia for tyranny. We do not rule out in advance that there are convinced democrats within their movements, who do not look favorably on the failed path to the abyss taken, however, their voices are not heard. What is heard are the calls to accelerate the processes generated from these strategies that are successful in their execution but failed in the creation of value and wealth. If we were to fall into the hands of unscrupulous people, who may be believing that they are bearers of good, of truth, who feel that oppression is only a lesser evil: we would once again be witnessing the rebirth of the death of Freedom in the hands of tyranny and dictatorship.

We identify two great successes of the Gramscian postmodernist strategy:

The first greatest success is to achieve, through dialectic and indoctrination, the nesting in each mind of a tyrant, in a way that made obsolete the simple way to get out of tyranny: killing the tyrant. For now, one tyrant lives in every mind of every indoctrinated individual.

The second great success is its ability to hide "an elephant in plain sight"; It has been very difficult for pure pragmatists to discover the true objectives of an irrational strategy from their own conception of "Not Wanting to Die", to use resentment, passion, fears, in short, the discomfort of society to sell their objectives with another name and thus cleverly plant a farce in the credulity of the population, in their desire to believe again and not lose hope. The fallacy is what explains why a strategy so painful for humanity can be successfully staged again.

FREEDOM THREATENED

Freedom is not given; Threats arise from the depths of the human being, it seems that it is encoded in our genes to try to dominate, to control, to make one's own ideas prevail over those who have others or those who have none, to see oneself like this. same as leaders.

The search for equality is the passion that accompanies man throughout the history of humanity; On that path of struggle, freedom has been found, by accident. This denotes the clear rational sense of equality as opposed to the freedom that must be felt: you have it, or you don't have it. People notice that they have it when they prosper, however, when they notice that they do not have it, it may already be too late.

What sounds paradoxical is that the human being in his essence is unequal so much so that everything he generates will be his reflection. Idealism feels morally superior, with the ability to redesign parts or elements, wanting to encompass even the entire system to make it unnaturally egalitarian. Idealism has repeatedly attempted to equalize in some sense (for example, monetary) people who are equal before the law, this can only be done by breaking that law, destroying all the institutions that guarantee that situation in order to be able to give perks to the groups that they consider will be beneficiaries of "their goodness." The search for blind equality is necessarily revolutionary and retrograde as far as the advancement of civilization is concerned. An additional element is added: idealistic approaches go against the incentives of a normal human being to live in society to produce, to have property, since the reason for property is to return the entire product of their work. which has originated from this; Ditto your job if this is your only currency you have. In this stalemate the new system can only be imposed under coercion and can only be maintained under oppression in tyranny.

A STRATEGY THAT UNINSTALLS CIVILIZATION

Understand that there is a war in which society is losing battles, understand the tactics that move with their own inertia and those that combine with unrest to attack the rule of law.

A previous battle that was not seen coming, fought in the World of ideas.

The first great lost battle has been taking place in the cultural field for more than twenty years in the indoctrination of young people; Today they are fertile ground for any strategy - no matter how bizarre - that is intended to be deployed by curbing their natural desire to get ahead by undertaking.

An invisible battlefield, outside of reality

The battles will be fought in the field of irrationality and towards the bases of the system. The opponent will not know that he is in a war until it is too late: his network of coherences, his training and his paradigms will not allow him to realize the seriousness of the matter: laughter will arise at the loss of absurd battles.

Exact definition of pawns, bishops

They identified the vulnerable groups that will execute the strategy, some of them will implement targeted and systematic violence to return the strays to the fold; and prepare the final assault. At the right moment they establish belligerence between civil groups, which groups must weaken, how to take advantage of the unrest for their objectives.

An intermediate battle that will be fought after democratically accessing power.

It will not be understood that the destination of a whole barrage of legislation that seems to have no roots in the common good is to undermine the foundations of the liberal democratic system.

Any loophole in the legislation and any weakness in the institutions and the very pillars of the system will be taken advantage of.

Young people are ready not to question laws, attacks on population groups, or legislation; in fact, they will bow down and applaud attacks on culture, on their way of life, on the foundations of society.

The incentives to produce value and wealth in the economy will be under constant assault until they are finally destroyed.

The final attack on the queen. How is the king?

Concentration of all powers, absolute suppression of the rule of law, society confronted on multiple fronts, the economy in ruins and large sectors receiving subsidies that will applaud the situation until those who produce leave the country...shortage, general rise in prices.

How are we going to face Humanity's passion for equality?

Equality seeking to share wealth will necessarily drag the entire society to a low average income. We must think of a different way to redistribute the wealth created. We must try raising the incomes of all classes to push society's median income up.

Put a limit on the search for equality? It might sound dare or hasty, but due to the serious events that have been unleashed coupled with the high risk of tyranny that passing an apparent turning point has brought, we believe it is appropriate to point out the limits that could be safe; one of them is:
Equality before the law, establishing that milestone that has been safe, and then generating all the conditions so that in full freedom individuals can achieve their goals of economic well-

being and try to become economically equal; knowing that phenomena of inequality will arise and that some will not achieve it. We will establish measures for exceptions and will not go backwards to the entire society.

Why don't they have proposals to create value and wealth and increase the average income of society?

The worrying answer might be: because they don't care.

Nothing changes, everything is transformed so that everything remains the same.

Thought is also recycled and reused, they come back with the strategies that have been successful and the same elements that have been successful in the past: nothing changes. The responsibility of a relaunch implies having the capacity for self-criticism and recognizing what did not work (this strategy did not make value judgments, nor did it define what was good or bad from the point of view of the damage generated) they only recontextualized in a way and time what didn't work. They showed that eventually, every twenty years a strategy could be relaunched, of course it is a new generation, and it is also an opportunity to rewrite history with different words, looking for a different accent. **Gramscian postmodernism** in all its meanings depends on the conditions of each country, the strength of its institutions, the capacity of legislation to protect the rule of law, the bases, incentives, and private property.

The time wasted trying to reinstall the truth: post-truth.

The nature of postmodernity that we have analyzed allows us to recreate a different narrative of history, situations, and truth; and this will be as strong and installed in individuals as the indoctrination, the use of networks and the issuer (if the one who deconstructs history is in political power, he could change it).

Yes, we must understand that it is another time, that the categories of truth no longer exist; What's more, the truth itself no longer exists. It brings us the duality of whether we play with the same tactics - since this is an already hegemonic strategy, which was not seen coming, which was not predicted - or whether post-truth is counteracted by evidencing the intrinsic dialectic in it - to do so we must possess the media and opinion leaders such as teachers, journalists, networks, etc. - if you do not have them, the work is only exhausting. And most importantly: start from passion.

Even history has been deconstructed, this proves that human beings have no memory and history is not written. The story is from what you can remember; and even so it is possible to deconstruct it to give another version that is rigged or attached to the reality that you want to show.

His role in democratic positions

It is a suicidal error to pretend or believe that in elected positions, they will manage the goods and wealth delivered into their hands, when they despise the method in which it was created and everything it represents. What has happened is going to continue happening, they are going to dynamite the pillars and bases of the system and all the values that allow it to grow and create well-being.

Youth and their connection with ideas of change

Historically, youth have always identified with advanced ideas; In Latin America they are connected with change, anti-corruption. This spirit of opposition is being taken advantage of by these new forces that hide their true and real plans against the established order.

The groups that are functional to tyranny and those that are not.

We are not talking here about those who participate directly, we are talking here about those who do not act and those in whom not acting makes them functional to the cause of destroying society, they remain undaunted, they vote out of emotions, but there is something, even if it is little, that lose: we must call on those.

Here it is possible that the bishops that are needed are located, in which they must be based to generate the counteroffensives.

We must remember that the world of ideas is in dispute. At this moment the balance is very unbalanced. We are interested in generating balance again and giving democracy a chance.

A successful counter strategy

Any strategy must involve removing the title of people from the communist oligarchy.

It must decisively incorporate inclusion and change must mean banishing discomfort. Create equal opportunities at the beginning and once. In the last part of this book we will give our opinion on what equal opportunities mean to us on the path to eradicating discomfort.

Identify the group that has to lose with the revolutions and propose strategies to increase their income.

Alleviate the difficulties of those who do not achieve it and have society in check.

To think carefully

How does a modern coup d'état take shape when the target is not whoever holds power, but rather the formal and informal institutions that allow the rule of law?

Answer: slowly fragment the order, destroy the pillars, the bases of the economy and the incentives to produce goods and services. We must take away power, legitimacy and due obedience (See Antonio Gramsci). **This response undoes the order based on the rule of law; and order is civilization.**

THE ALTERNATIVE TO CIVILIZATION IS HUNGER AND SHORTAGE: TOOLS OF THE NEW STRATEGY

Discomfort

We include it as a tool because despite being an instrument of exclusion of the right to reduce the possibilities of development of the rest of the population, as well as to remain in power, the new and renewed **Gramscian postmodernism** they have used this discomfort to denounce inequality as the result of something they hope to defeat (Neoliberalism). Now, the use of unrest is deliberate and systematic throughout Latin America, obeying clear patterns of using pressure on citizens, then they are chosen in democratic processes, not to reinstall the rule of law and the inclusion that would allow 70 % of the population in the middle class improve their well-being -depending on their training, they despise these values because at bottom they are free enterprise, and their purpose is to eliminate them- but to change one oligarchy for another and implement again an oppressive tyrannical system around the state: again the search for total power

Indoctrination

The Gramscian strategy has been deployed for more than 20 years with the intention of taking over schools, universities, journalism, opinion leaders, etc. It is repeated and repeated until it becomes true that neoliberalism is responsible for inequality, exclusion and poverty, rooting hatred in all youth.

The charming leader

Full of quick proposals that solve problems that have plagued us for centuries; This combative, problem-solving, charismatic leader emerges, who summarizes everything that tyranny needs.

The dialectical method

It guides the type of proposals based on the problems and the destruction of the adversary, with very easy solutions, that never say how and that promise change and anti-corruption. Deep down, all of them have a specific objective pointing, veiledly, to some of the bases or pillars of liberal democracy and the value system that sustains it.

Postmodernism

That unleashes new micro contradictions throughout society that replace the great classic Marxist contradiction of class struggle. This new strategy shoots in all directions and establishes many small fronts to end up eliminating all the categories that supported the values of society, civilization, attacking all codes of conduct (from schoolchildren to penitentiaries to by the laws), deconstructs all concepts, even the truth itself, rewrites history in a story that is beneficial... to Khaos (23) ...

Postmodernist leaders can be blamed for not caring about what the rest of the population cares about; and it is so because they do not care; They despise what matters to us all, in this case well-being. Their intention is to undermine the pillars of the previous system and promote change to their new imposed system; The path is doctrine; they are guided by the search for power for power's sake.

Both classical Marxism and **Gramscian postmodernism** coincide, in the sense of seeking revolutionary power. The first was found in the class struggle. The second, postmodernism has found revolutionary power in the small contradictions of society. The society: rather, civilization has managed to mediate a whole series of confrontations, contradictions or behaviors that do not benefit the social entity, through disciplinary codes, through the school, or patriarchy, or laws, or through the penal code; in other words, through a series of formal and informal institutions that serve the same purpose. If these contradictions could not have been mediated at the right time, it is very possible that civilization, as we know it, would not have occurred. Classical Marxism and Marxist postmodernism also agree that by unleashing them they release many emotions, anger and hatred and it is in that fertile ground where they once again agree to install an entire doctrine based on resentment, which comes from the dialectical method, for example. Therefore, it does not say how, and in which, in an underlying, progressive, not obvious way, the change involves another type of expropriation.

The violence

Violence no longer caused the armed forces of the state. It seeks to corner and intimidate civil society through strikes, demonstrations, street blockades, assaults on commerce and banks, reduction of basic services, reduction of mobility, etc. The blackmail is obvious.

They are replacing direct armed guerrilla violence; and being faithful to their new doctrine: they unleash, recycle, and sponsor new micro sources of violence. The khaos generated, the problems, the confrontations, are considered functional to their cause.

The target population

It recycles the worst: confronting and pitting the population against each other; In this case, the vulnerable – those who try to progress but cannot, those who do not try, those who do not want to do so, but want to live off of handouts, the criminals – receive financial support, receiving what is not from their work, and taking away from others what corresponds to their work.

Within this group there is a special one, which are the young people of Latin America who show a high degree of indoctrination, they go after the search for change and anti-corruption (they are against unrest).

Socialism communism perfected the cruel form of exile of its own citizens, those who do not consider confrontation and decide not to resist oppression. This practice was resumed and became common again.

Elimination of any possibility of counterpower

It will eliminate, lazily and without considering the damage to be caused, all private savings that are in sectors that are not protected by legislation or by formal institutions: pensions, severance pay, health, etc. The institutions and current legislation are the only ones that stop this tyrannical power in formation.

If current legislation allows you to destroy private property, you will destroy the business fabric, permanently ruining the production of basic and survival elements.

Concentration of economic and political power in the State

It prepares and concentrates power in the state for this or future hostile sieges on democratic power and the liberal order.

He will demand more powers for himself, for his supporters and supporters of tyranny; the destruction of the separation of powers is its objective; This is the first stage of tyranny.

Its doctrinal structure requires a tyrant, then it reorganizes the structure of the state around the tyrant; That is why it is important for them to transgress the law and not respect the rule of law (a structure that is about to be dismantled). The structure of the socialist state suits them well. At this point it will be impregnable; it will only fall under an implosion directed by its own leaders.

The population that executes the strategy

It is a seduced and indoctrinated group in which the tyrannical way of life lives within them; They have the capacity (given by the state, if it already has democratic positions) to force it on the rest of the population. They repress any deviation from doctrine through informal means.

The leaders of this new strategy are the same as the previous Marxist strategy that cornered Latin America and that made no other offer than to install themselves and impose themselves by force as a solution to an inequality caused by the neoliberal economic model.

The moral elimination of the ideological opponent

This is the method of dialectical response to a logical question: Marx and Engels instituted this type of response - always showing the opponent's flaws and disqualifying the opponent, accusing him of selling out to the bourgeoisie - and this is not going to change (everything that distances and avoids defending its own proposal under rational means). They have no way to defend their alleged moral superiority and the fact that socialism communism where they implement it, fails. They only have fallacy as a defense, the moral destruction of their opponent, and in this they are going to be relentless, attacking anyone who, for example, questions the need for a social plan: of course, they oppose it because they are a very bad person!

inequality

Raising this slogan replaces that of classical socialism to eliminate exploitation through the expropriation of private property; This made the social classes equal and now they could be free.

Now the **Gramscian postmodernist** promises to eliminate the inequality that neoliberalism produces; Is neoliberalism the free market, or is it the system of economic exclusion that the right implemented in Latin America? Do you plan to install the free market that occurs during the exchange of private property and with a system of free prices? The answer is no. In the end, the unspoken proposal is to eliminate the free market and install again the failed 21st century Socialism that inevitably can only be forced and installed through oppression and that can only be maintained through tyranny.

Laws, legislation, public morality, societal values, and the Rule of Law

They are the objectives to demolish in the end in the old classical strategy, now the first to deconstruct in the new **Gramscian postmodernist strategy.**

The morals and values of society are going to be attacked progressively and systematically - giving certain sectors of the population rewards and handouts to place them in favor of sedition - seeking to make society increasingly permissive in the face of the final assault on legislation. and to the bending of the rule of law.

The small attacks on the law (established order), which could be considered minor, and in their execution a certain reward is given to the individuals who allow the transgressions, are not minor, nor small; It is an unacceptable advance to the morals of society, to its values, so that by allowing the little, they consent to the much that is going to happen when they make the final blow.

Liberal Democracy

Liberal Democracy prepared for frontal attacks against the public force of the state, which classical Marxism proposed, but never anticipated violent blackmail towards the primary constituent (the voter locked in his house and blackmailed by small groups of violent protesters), nor an internal attack coming from the very exercise of power as proposed by **Gramscian postmodernism.** By definition, institutions are, from within, weak; precisely so that they do not oppress individuals.

Climate change

This is one more tool that covers their inability - or that they do not care - to create value and wealth, trying to insert into the unconscious a rejection of the development and well-being that progress generates. Their initiatives around the issue will mean a setback in development, bringing it closer to what socialism-communism can provide: equality in poverty.

Now this does not hide the need to create a higher level to the current free enterprise scheme that is in line with the preservation of the environment.

Rooting in Youth

This is what youth sees: ¨A political class entrenched in the State and has it for its own selfish benefit. A system that denies social advancement. This is how disappointment and hopelessness with our democracy set in among large segments of the population, convinced that the system is flawed.

All the vigor of society resides in the youth to carry on their shoulders the changes that are needed; by nature, they are anti-establishment.

The new generations have received a whole doctrinal topic in the last twenty to thirty years. The teachers have been functional by installing in the collective ideology of young people all the necessary dogmas to relax their value system so that they are fertile and functional for a new cause of change. For the moment, the hegemony of left-wing ideas resides within them, stimulated by their desire for change (as opposed to unrest) and anti-corruption. This is why they only follow the ones who are representing change and anti-corruption.

However, the single social class does not exist; and in this case youth does not belong to anyone; is in dispute.

When you see youth starting small businesses, trying again and again, not giving up, despite the discomfort; hope returns to me; They obey their deepest and most spontaneous desire for freedom, to get ahead and the path is, without them knowing it, free enterprise. What young people are really looking for is to eliminate exclusion and equal opportunities to unleash their full creative potential. It will not be possible to silence that innate desire of youth to be free, seeking the self-realization of their dreams.

What it is not said

The most important thing in any strategy is what is not said; what is not said and is avoided at all costs. These questions that remain in the air must be resolved because they compromise the future of civilization. The questions are: what does all this confusion and Khaos lead to? What does it lead to unleashing new confrontations between society every day? What does this permanent deconstruction and presentation of a new truth lead to? What does this relaxation of the values and morals of society lead to? What is happening that day by day is allowing the power installed and exercised from the executive a progressive advance on Freedom?

Inadvertently and during Khaos, tyranny advances...

All the actions that we are going to state below are **Gramscian postmodernist,** however, the principles that animate them have not changed in their essence since they seek total power: The deliberate marches of small violent factions, the favoring of minorities, the degradation of language, the actions accompanied by legislation against the empire of the law, the deconstruction of sexuality, unleashing conflicts that are contained by laws or informal institutions, apparent instability, deliberate attacks on the concepts of savings, trust and incentives, contradictory legislation. They are attacks on the liberal foundations of society. Cultural development and the advancement of civilization are tied to the liberal foundations of the history of society; **Gramscian** postmodernism in its systematic and deliberate attack it will not do anything else, but make large sectors of the economy disappear, civilization will go backwards and lower the average well-being of the entire society to subsistence levels. The free market cannot dispense with the institutions or moral norms that generate the order necessary for its permanence.

Finally, we have gone through the history of the political economy of humanity guided by the search for equality to verify that every extreme is vicious; Taken to the extreme, this search unleashes the lowest instincts, leading us to tyranny and loss of Freedom recently. found.
The change so that nothing changes. We see that human beings recycle concepts, present them in another way, innovate in the way they are presented; however, their objectives remain the same: total power and in their wake they will destroy civilization.

6

THE FAMILY, INSTITUTIONS AND RULES ARE RESPONSIBLE FOR ORDER WITHIN THE FREE MARKET

Individual freedom presupposes the autonomy of the subject in his personal environment and is only possible to the extent that the collective respects the principle of private property, an institution on which both the extensive order and the possibility of considering in our productive effort, realities beyond the directly perceptible horizon.

Frederic Hayek in his book Fatal Arrogance.

Moral institutions - especially private property, freedom, and justice - are not the fruit of reason but rather a second faculty to which man accesses through cultural evolution.

Frederic Hayek in his book Fatal Arrogance.

The church is replaced today by the school in its role as the dominant ideological state apparatus. It is combined with the family, as the church was before. It can be affirmed then that the crisis, of unprecedented depth, that shakes the school system in so many States in the world, often parallel to the crisis that shakes the family

system (already announced in the Communist Manifesto), has a political meaning. if it is considered that the school (and the school-family couple) constitutes the dominant ISA Ideological State Apparatus. Device that plays a determining role in the reproduction of the relations of production of a mode of production threatened in its existence by the world class struggle.

Louis Althusser in his book: Ideology and ideological apparatuses of the state.

There is no class struggle without antagonistic classes.

Louis Althusser

The ideology does not become dominant by simply taking power, it becomes dominant, hegemonic with the implementation of the ISA.

Louis Althusser

The family, institutions and norms are responsible for order within the free market.

WOULD THIS EXPLAIN WHY THEY ARE UNDER ATTACK?

We are going to use a reasoning used by Hayek in his book Fatal Arrogance where he finally defines the concept of moral norms as the set of non-instinctive norms (24) that allow human behavior to be ordered in society. The family - for postmodernist constructivists like Althusser - is, together with the school, the main bastion of reproduction of the capitalist system: yes readers; We are going to

confront the liberal vision of the family with that of Marxist historical materialism (25) taken up by Althusser. We'll see where it takes us.

This approach to the origins of non-instinctive moral norms, which allow a certain order, which in turn generates private property and its connection with commerce, therefore, with extensive order, is the midwife of civilization (of progress) as we know it. This cultural component will be used in the third part of this book, to try to understand the reasons why progress in Latin America was born without private property and full of corruption.

Human behavior in society is explained by non-instinctive norms; However, the concept of order and the very constitution of the family (in its most closed nucleus) is explained in accordance with the instinctive union.

Instinctive cohesion in the family

It is necessary to remember that human beings do not reach concepts as elaborate as "respect for private property as the basis of the economy" without going through initial stages where the first thing that is established is family cohesion - the basic cell with the most narrow - where the strongest glue at that level is instinctive filial love. Yes, instincts. The instincts under the genetic imperative to protect offspring, have a place for children and space for women allowed the first strong connection of the family (order was born). At this point we find no difference with the animal world. Human traits and characteristics such as learning, trial and error, differentiating what should or should not be done, attachment to tradition, allowed the development of moral codes (rule of law) of what we call civilization today.

In short, instincts and feelings united the first family organizations of society; however, it is the non-instinctive moral codes, accumulated over thousands of years, that allowed civilization (order spread).

It is also the time to point out that we should not make the mistake of underestimating the power of instincts - feelings such as anger, resentment, hatred or love - because these, if unleashed, have the power to return us to the time of the caves. This is so true that it is the key tool used by **Gramscian postmodernism**, which, taking advantage of the unrest, subverts order and defeats the rule of law to place society between the sword and the abyss.

In small, related tribal societies, solidarity and cooperativism prevail. However, it is no less a sociological error to try to extend this tribal order to larger or more extensive societies.

Relationships in larger societies - what Hayek calls the extended order - are necessarily maintained (civilization is achieved) with the set of moral norms in the rule of law. In this extensive order, societies can no longer apply the spirit of solidarity: they are societies in which no one knows each other; Nobody is going to give their job to a stranger (that only happens in the family environment); the stranger must have something to exchange. The mechanisms by which this exchange can occur is the rule of law that has previously been established through free pacts that guarantee that social, political, and economic relations occur with order and transparency. What is exchanged is always private property (this more elaborate concept already appears as a necessity of exchange and that it is only possible in order).

We will only access the extensive market (trade between large societies) of goods and services - which is called well-being and progress - only if we adapt our behavior to that framework of institutions, traditions of an economic, legal and moral nature that we have received. We can only incorporate ourselves by submitting to rules that have not been established by us and whose function we are incapable of understanding, in the sense that we understand how the things that we have built ourselves work; Hayek notes.

Now it is necessary to understand how elements that civilization gives us are inserted into simple aspects of life in society to deduce why it is an object of attack within a strategy. Elements such as language, custom, morality, laws and law are firmly interrelated with the free market, generating an order in which the individual is simply an element of a whole that he has not created.

All this knowledge, which is dispersed, is learned by imitation (of uses and customs). This is how the cultural system of values, of moral norms that shape behavior in society and in the market, multiplies.

This explains why in remote or excluded societies with less cultural development (civilization) the entrepreneurial spirit does not exist or is very weak; Then, entrepreneurship as an attitude is a learned initiative, it happens when being with someone who takes the first step or in contact with another more developed (civilized) culture; that's the benefit. Entrepreneurial behaviors are copied, imitated and adopted.

The extensive social order

In short, the strongest cohesion that exists in society is the family and is established by instincts such as filial love and reproduction. After the family is strongly formed, new rules or norms appear as a result of social interactions - with other groups - that improve social performance by inferring order to the new members. Imitation of these uses and customs is the most common way of learning them, feeling obligated to follow them. This is how the institutions that allow civilization are born.

In this order, based on these norms, a series of fictions and formal institutions are generated such as property, equality, laws, law and other informal ones such as family, brotherhood, parent-child respect, payment after a transaction, etc. Trade achieves the extension of this social order by allowing more developed populations to grow more than those that do not have access to it.

This is the extended social order in which other populations agree to accept the norms that allow commerce and therefore progress; They accept well-being in this way.

Laws or moral institutions are spontaneously created in society - call it civilization - which is committed to their observance for the good of itself.

Civilized society comes from an order generated from multitudinous human interactions that are reflected in formal and informal moral (cultural) institutions that are created spontaneously.

These habits, customs, beliefs or tacit or formal laws represent agreed restrictions on individual freedom that result in prosperity and well-being. These interactions have created a quantity of dispersed, non-transferable or copyable information and knowledge that is summarized in social norms (culture). As in all other areas of the human sphere, commercial relations and therefore economic well-being rest on order under the rule of law. Humanity is differentiated from animal organizations by civilization; The basis of civilization is these moral norms.

Trading in extensive order

Each human being intervenes in the social process when he seeks his own ends - this is the field of human action (Von Mises), social or economic and interaction with others - leading him to design ways to achieve them. This process, which occurs individually, generates the greatest contribution of information, personal, subjective, practical knowledge dispersed in special characteristics of time and place to a system. On the path to fulfilling their own goals, human beings dedicate all their effort, ingenuity and imagination, constituting a very powerful force of social, economic, political, legal innovation, etc. (human action) that makes the creation and maintenance of civilization possible. It constantly adjusts itself by creating formal and informal institutions that control every excess, coordinating or self-coordinating the necessary discipline of behaviors according to the development of society.

It is the practices and norms of conduct that have allowed the success of societies or groups of men. Its action in freedom is what allows progress.

Frederic Hayek pointed out the importance of moral norms and tacit pacts of behavior in society: We understand each other, we live together and we are capable of acting successfully because conscious and unconscious patterns of behavior are respected, which are not the results of coercion but the product of habits and firmly established traditions. The general observance of these conventions is a necessary condition for the order of the world in which we live and for the success of individual plans. All this results in freedom; Freedom, then, does not occur without a deep imperative of moral norms to which individuals voluntarily adjust.

What happens if these tacit agreements are broken, for example, in the family? Order is broken, khaos ensues!

The human being in freedom is constantly discovering new goals and means of achieving them; This is the incentive for that constant discovery that allows the advancement of society. Movements that in their essence are coercion or violence will impede and stop this engine of society and therefore progress. It is arrogant to pretend to know the laws of society by coming to redesign - correcting in its arrogance and fatal arrogance - what is considered incorrect. The above is impossible because there is no human reason that can house all the knowledge that society has spent thousands of years and that is dispersed in each person.

The present knowledge, thus given, in the form described above, is dispersed horizontally, it dwells in each citizen; It is not copyable (it is copyable only in the way in which imitation is understood; that is, it is not transferable to a book and then taught). If a policy were applied where the direction was central and vertical from top to bottom, it would once again imprison knowledge, annulling the spontaneous order, the evolution of social and cultural norms and with it, civilization.

It is tremendously irresponsible and would mean pushing society into an abyss by attempting to deliberately build (or deconstruct) moral institutions, language, freedom, the economy, private property, justice, the rule of law, religion or writing.

Communist socialists do not learn from every lesson that history gives and they try again and again, ruining progress and even taking many lives in each attempt.

We consider order because of observance and respect for moral standards and the rule of law. Order is a sine qua non condition for progress and economic well-being. "Order is civilization. "

THE POST-MARXIST VISION OF THE SCHOOL AND THE FAMILY

We are going to return to the Marxist terms and conception, since this will confirm our direction and give us the sense of urgency of the indirect strategy.

We had already mentioned in unit four of this same part, the special emphasis that Louis Althusser gave to the legacy received by the school-family binomial of the IEA (Ideological State Apparatuses) that identified them as the recipients of the church-family in the feudal era. In the same way, in unit three of the first part we talked about the "crisis in school and in the family (stated in the communist manifesto) that declares it with political meaning. For Althusser, the school is decisive in the role of reproduction of capitalist production relations.

These are excerpts from his writings in the book ideology and ideological apparatuses of the state:

The writing addresses the school as the element, the ISA capable of reproducing competent labor in accordance with the technical division of labor (workers, technicians, engineers). Not only are knowledge and skills acquired for work, but also the moral codes that maintain the system: receiving orders, ordering and ensuring predominance of the ruling class. It is not only about being qualified, but it must also be subject to the dominant ideology.

Why is its origin in the fall of feudalism important?

The French Revolution not only went from the aristocratic state to the bourgeois state, from the aristocratic repressive apparatus to the army, but also represented the attack and fall of the ISA church, subtracting its power by dividing its functions (remember the confiscation of church property and the civil constitution of the state).

The school received all that legacy from the church where the Church-family duo was replaced by the school-family duo in liberal democracy.

Why is school the dominant ISA and how does it work?

All ISA contribute to the reproduction of capitalist relations of production, that is, exploitation (Althusser notes). 2) each one attends in their own way: the ISA information, cramming information from the press, TV, daily doses of nationalism, chauvinism, liberalism, moralism, sports, religious sermons, etc. 3) the school uses all currents and great humanist themes, nationalism, moralism, etc. Althusser ends the idea with a statement that returns to the school and directly to the children as a battlefield. 4) **the school quietly performs very well: they take children trapped between the family state apparatus and the school ISA, taking advantage of their vulnerability; They are all skills covered by dominant ideology (language, calculus, natural history, science, literature) or more directly the dominant ideology in its purest form (morality, civic instruction, philosophy).** Althusser describes an abuse by the family and the school in instilling capitalist ideology.

Althusser goes on to describe the alleged abuse; He predisposes his readers to turn against the school-family: He prepares them from the age of six to be workers, others continue to be mid-level workers, small civil servants, intellectuals of exploitation (capitalists and businessmen), agents of repression (military, police, politicians) and ideological professionals (priests).

All culture is an ISA, but none as good as school... He concludes.

This unit focuses us on the importance of instinctive and non-instinctive norms accumulated for more than ten thousand years in the family and in all the institutions around society that have allowed development, commerce, well-being, and civilization.

On the other hand, it also identifies - through the methodology of historical materialism - the school and the family (ISA) as the objective to focus on in an eventual attack that blocks, reduces, and does not allow capitalist society to reproduce itself.

We believe that it is clear what the priorities and first executions will be in an indirect strategy: the school-family ISA. The effects could be catastrophic due to all the non-copyable (imitable) information that civilization has stored in the ISA and that is dispersed.

SECOND PART

FREEDOM AND PROSPERITY GO TOGETHER!

It's freedom's turn. However, in this second part we will change the methodology used in the first part of searching for the human passion for Equality, to do a case study by country. The reason is very simple: Freedom is not a passion, it has not been sought, it has been found, it has been built. It was barely discovered in the nearer part of recent history; Then, we begin to feel it, to touch it, to value it.

We will consolidate the fiction of freedom based on the right to private property; the power it confers.

We are encouraged to explain the concepts in each country about what happened according to the themes explained above: Rome to explain the strong concepts of slavery (its development in history with different names), the United States in contrast with its particularity of freedom with private property more weapons to defend it.

We will need to include a new concept: interventionism; We will compare it with the direct attack (expropriation) and the indirect attack (analogy of the house); Cuba and Argentina, in their order, will serve us for these purposes.

In short, we will look at how private property catalyzes freedom; This pair in the presence of order produced the greatest progress that civilization has ever had. From here we will return to Milton Friedman endorsing the concepts created around freedom.

1

PRIVATE PROPERTY AND FREEDOM

Freedom is a feeling; you have to feel it to understand that you have it or that you don't have it. When you start to feel like you don't have it, it may be too late to get it back.

All the forces of initiative and creativity of the human being were hidden in slavery and servitude; Only when Freedom was installed was talent unleashed and all those productive forces were unleashed, generating value and wealth like never before in the history of humanity, lifting large sectors out of poverty that for more than 20 centuries had known nothing but poverty. survival and extreme poverty

When you are born without Freedom, a question arises: can you miss what you don't know? Why are the bars so kind to these types of slaves?

In this unit we will locate freedom in the beginnings of private property, from day to day to the conception of this fiction as a right, however, the most important thing - still in formation over time - is that these elements make it possible for the human being achieves his dreams, his goals, giving shape to his plans. The discussion around the direct attack on property (expropriation, socialization, or nationalization with or without payment by the state) will be enriched with additional elements: taxes as advances on freedom and interventionism. We will arrive - hoping in the end that there is no discrepancy in the concept - to the true notion that the first (expropriation) is the elimination of the right to property and to dispose of it, while the second - interventionism - is the elimination of the effects of the property (such as disposing of it in the free market, having utility with it, producing, etc.) leaving only the title of property without any other function than being on a piece of paper: the indirect attack has these interventionist characteristics added to additional ones (elimination of the "order" and trust, necessary for the reproduction of the system). We are facing an innovation in strategy. The importance of this discussion is not minor, it is not semantic, it is of vital importance because it corresponds to the life model that we will give to our existence: in freedom and fulfilling our dreams or fulfilling the wishes and instructions of a bureaucrat, possibly in tyranny.

We begin this second part with three seemingly contradictory paragraphs (refer to the beginning) since the first places freedom as a feeling and the ability to do what you want; On the other hand, the second paragraph classifies it as the cause of humanity's escape from poverty. Finally, the third repositions it as a learned feeling, which must inevitably be lived.

Previously, in the main introduction of the book we identified freedom as a feeling, in the sense that it is not rational; However, several paragraphs later we gave it a less ethereal character: we held it responsible for the explosion of wealth and value that would reduce the poverty that had accompanied humanity since its beginnings. Two situations that seem very different; However, the sensations it produces when using it we fulfill our dreams or the unease that is felt when it has been lost are so different.

The three paragraphs plus the introduction contribute new arguments to the unfinished definition of freedom (we choose the word unfinished in its meaning that it is still under construction), trying to explain a little of the complexity that we are going to address in this part of the book.

We are not going to delve into the feeling; but rather we will return to the tangible aspects of freedom and we will do so from the sixth unit of the previous chapter where fictions, norms and institutions such as private property, freedom, laws, or rights were created in society, opening the space that we need in this second part.

PRIVATE PROPERTY AS A RIGHT

Human beings have the inclination to accept certain norms and institutions based on trade, development, well-being - where there is no coercion - as a precondition for civilization.

The acceptance of the concept of the right to private property (as a tacit agreement of behavior in society; later formal) and its effects lead to new challenges in terms of personal success. This is a necessary condition for the order of the world in which we live and for the success of individual plans.

Then, individual plans and above all the search for the means - their free action - to carry them out, enriches the generation of knowledge based on personal progress. Said progress occurs by virtue of the acquisition of property . The prevalence of the right to private property and the functions derived from it in satisfactory conditions of freedom and order is the means by which civilization is consolidated. This, concludes Hayek. Additionally, it is the incentive to generate a constant discovery of ends and means of achieving them that allows the advancement of society.

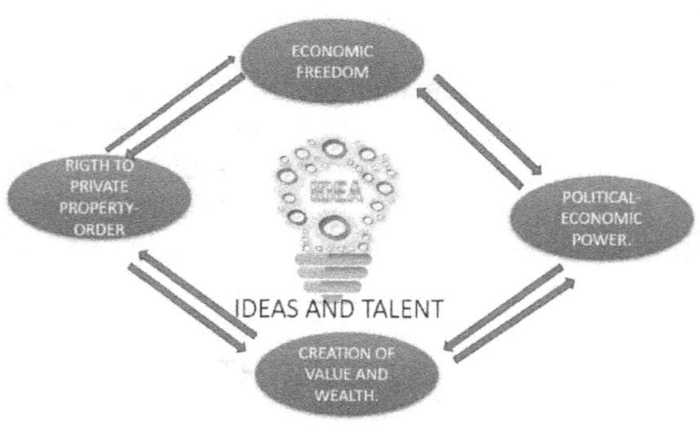

THE POWER OF THE FREE SOCIETY: PRIVATE PROPERTY AND HAPPINESS

In freedom you seek to fulfill your dreams; which is nothing other than the search for property (enterprises, your house, businesses, etc.) as well as the definition of the means to obtain it. In this process, a lot of dispersed, transversal knowledge is generated, fundamentally imitable by other people, this being the way in which it is disseminated in society. It was like forging steel. In each stroke, with each successful creative process that became part of the knowledge, that was copyable, the system was reproduced and added; it was forging freedom. It represented a power barely acquired by the masses by virtue of property – acquired property represented liberation – hardly of incipient creation. The only thing missing was the fiction of making that thing so valuable, so difficult to acquire, making it a right for the protection of it and its effects.

Reaching the concept of property and then moving towards commerce is only possible in the extensive order and under the cultural precepts that allow both to occur; Additionally, they are reproduced. This is why not only private property is under attack!

Freedom was developing in all those spontaneous and individual processes of exchange that took place day after day. It was amassed with each achievement of creating value and wealth, with each advance, with each invention it was consolidated, while society moved further and further away from poverty. They both won; one depending on the other.

Every glimpse of value or wealth that human beings were hardly able to create in the beginning, every new grain of property created and converted into value (freedom) was like a snowball that was preparing to roll downhill, destroying in its path, in the form no longer of a snowball but of an avalanche of anti-feudal revolutions, the prison of creativity and talent in which feudalism had imprisoned them.

Feudalism ended because freedom was no longer tied to the land, it was not necessary to possess it to be free; The intrinsic power that property brings to become free was possible through a new way that created much more value and wealth, that is, new property: it had arrived with the free market, industrialization.

The freedom that comes with having property. That tangible reality that you have manufactured, produced and treasured generates by extension other types of needs around freedom such as freedom of belief, speech, movement, etc. It is the midwife of other freedoms.

The point is that we are locating freedom-private property-happiness by virtue of the creation of value and wealth plus the definition of the means to realize dreams. Additionally, we are placing them at the center of the entire generation of knowledge in the civilized world. It is a materialist conception of the economic history of humanity, the truth is that it revolves inextricably around private property, order (culture and rule of law).

TAXES: HERE SOCIALIZATION BEGINS

Given the property, given its siege; The siege took the name of taxes.

The appearance of the state monopolizing violence is unavoidable; In all the multiple forms that it takes in history, they revolve towards its preservation, financing, growth, and extension to most areas that the individual allows. The imposition of payment of part of the individual's wealth to the state allowed its preservation.

In the third unit of this second part of the book we will see how the Americans at the beginning of their independence visualized two possible dangers: the first was the return of the English crown; the second the advance of the state itself over rights, property, and individual freedom; His specific response to this was reflected in the first and second amendments.

The early start of socialization: taxes

Americans foreshadowed the advance of the state over freedom by identifying the greatest risk that democracies with weak institutions can have; such is the case of Latin America. This advancement is manifested in many ways, being present in laws, regulations, rights, taxes, etc. The latter, taxes, precede any other, being the first thing that puts pressure on whoever exercises or monopolizes violence. The issue is simple: force is used to force and impose on people to subsidize, "through taxes," the state apparatus.

The way to approach this concept is elementary and arises from seeing the cases of taxes that must be paid.

The case of corporations and companies

We all see it as normal that all companies have to give a percentage of their net profits, however, it means the first advance of the state over freedom. For Colombia the tax pressure for companies is 35%. In the United States, the country of freedom, the percentage that must be paid is 21% (data after Trump).

Effective Tax Rate ETR. How it affects SMEs (businesses owned by ordinary people) in Latin America

For Colombia the visible tax rate is 35%, however, the effective tax rate says otherwise, standing at 84% for (ordinary people's businesses) SMEs and family businesses (see the development of this aspect in the first book of this series the fourth part, third unit: the rise of the left in Latin America in the midst of the era of unrest).

The ETR are fiscal and parafiscal taxes of an anti-technical nature (before the profit and income tax) that make it unviable for a company of ordinary people to be legal. This is the reason that 65% to 70% of ordinary people's businesses are immersed in informality. It is impossible to generate profit in this situation.

We will return to this topic later, in the fifth part, where we are going to propose creating an umbrella that eliminates all these obstacles to growth,

The case of individuals

In the United States it is between 24% and 46% depending on the state (2022 data). The income tax of Colombians is subject to certain limits.

These are the figures that determine whether a person must pay rent in 2023 in Colombia:
- His gross assets on the last day of the year exceed 4,500 UVT, that is, $171,018,000 Colombian pesos.
- Your gross income is greater than 1,400 UVT, or $53,205,600 Colombian pesos.

There are many other taxes, for example, the consumption tax that can reach 8.2% in the United States and 20% of all the elements that we Colombians consume or buy. For the United States it is easier to get closer to the total value of taxation (in companies and in individuals); while, in underdeveloped countries, the issue becomes complex due to the two economies (formal and informal or underground) that are managed.

The sum of prosecutors and para prosecutors for individuals in Colombia who belong to the formal sector is 50% of the salary, that is, when you receive your payment, 50% of it has already been taken. If you add the 20% VAT, it is already around 70%; Please compare with a 100% salary tax level that is assimilated to slavery (27) (the product of your work does not belong to you).

In order not to go wrong

In this book we propose a broader range of state participation, beyond providing order, justice, and basic services. We believe that state participation in the private economy is beneficial in certain sectors that are clear for development, however, due to high investments, risk or lack of security, the private sector will not execute them. We talk about the development of innovation sectors, the construction of infrastructure - with private money - that works very well in developed countries, but the collusive permissiveness of state and private corruption has discredited it. It includes the monitored participation of private individuals in services that constitute rights such as health, sanitation, education, pensions, etc.

However, it is not the topic of discussion of this writing.

Therefore, the discussion here is not about whether state intervention is good or bad: it is inevitable.

The state, an instrument of tyranny

What we need to differentiate is when certain individuals in the name of the state, seeking equality at the expense of freedom, attempt to torpedo or replace the creation of value and wealth that is based on private ownership of the means of production, given that in this case it is Collective, that is, state property, demonstrated less social impact, since it was not capable of producing new wealth, which reduced the wealth already created, which sent new people who were not before into poverty. Additionally, its essence is coercion - given the characteristics of going against human nature - which inevitably ends in tyranny, increasingly challenging the stability of civilization. Transferring the creation of value and wealth from private property to state property confers as much power on the bureaucrat as the transfer has been made.

The above only demonstrates an inertia of the state, which is taken advantage of by the intrinsic desire of some people to advance individual freedom that begins through traditional means, reaching states close - through taxes - to the nullification of the effects of work (taxes at 100%, for example). This is one of the indicators that show how close slavery is; Another indicator is how much of the national income, that is, GDP, the state consumes; In Colombia it is 34% in 2021, in the USA it is 43% in 2020. Where is the people's money better: being spent by the same people who produce it or being spent by the state? These two indicators are not enough to generate reliable alarms of its progress on the bases, pillars, or incentives of the system of producing value and wealth.

Then, the big question is: can alarms be generated? What type of alarms should be set and when should they be activated?

In short: the advance of the state over freedom, and in this case economic freedom, has always been present, making it impossible to resist it in many cases. **What we must establish are the desirable limits of its advance and at what moment it interferes, stops, transgresses, supplants the bases, pillars, and incentives of the system of creating new value and wealth, equality before the law, the rule of law, In short, individual freedom. Let us remember that the possibilities of getting out of poverty are encrypted in the exercise of individual freedom.**

WHEN THE STATE BECOMES A DANGER TO FREEDOM

Every space that is ceded to the state is an advance on freedom; This is how each right that is requested is a small part of the freedom that is irremediably lost. Each right that is given to a certain part of the population (minorities, vulnerable sectors, etc.) represents a loss of equality before the law, which is the fundamental principle on which our system is based. Every beginning of tyranny is based on the bankruptcy of this principle that almost always begins by showing goodness towards a suffering minority, making arbitrariness imperative to help them. This is why the tools developed in the first part, fourth unit are necessary:

METER OF TYRANNY IN **HARD GRAMSCIAN POSTMODERNISM**

The factors or variables analyzed in that unit help establish the first signs of the appearance of tyranny. Let us remember what they are: the use of force by militias against the population, the concentration of all powers in the new leader, the impossibility of leaving the tyrant after the concentration, the permanent and irruptive indoctrination about the freedom of certain groups and even of children, the impossibility of organizing as dissidents to be an option for power, difficulty in obtaining income that is not possible around the state, etc.

The previous signs regarding this type of advance on freedom are clear, showing us that we are facing an indirect attack; However, we are not used to being attacked without first declaring war, so the success of the strategy is that it places the siege on society in a gray area. The next step to get out of the gray area is to recognize the strongest indications to establish that the apparent spontaneous Khaos is due to deliberate actions because of apparently meaningless measures (they respond to human action). A third step is to identify their systematicity (repeated in several countries). Deliberate and systematic are these from which an unexpected disorder arises (lack of confidence, discontent, feeling that the horizon is lost, family and social instability, multiple threats and contradictions arise, progressive taxes that destroy more wealth than they collect. , predation of savings dedicated to increasing per capita investment, equality before the law is dismantled, tearing down the rule of law, profit and profit are eliminated, destroying the incentives to produce

- the system is not reproduced -, they are favored groups to the detriment of others) and Khaos, a lot of Khaos appears everywhere. These are the children of the Gramscian postmodernist dialectic.

The middle and upper class is under attack, the rest of the population instrumentalized. Despite all this, what is worrying about this whole issue is that the population that has been manipulated and subjected to extremes is the one who is responsible for defending the system (through a cultural battle) to re-establish institutionality if the democratic order has not yet been altered.

Finally, the moment and the most appropriate measures to stop the advance on freedom must be given by the institutions. If not, it will be a setback in terms of order, civilization, and the rule of law...

The concept of shared well-being deserves special analysis; At this moment, what we must be clear about is that progressive taxes and laws or regulations that determine predistribution or redistribution attack the bases and incentives of the system. This is a substantial topic that has its own space in part four.

THE FENCE IS ACCENTATED: EXPROPIATION AND SOCIALIZATION

We need to become familiar with some other administrative concepts against property and attacks on economic freedom; that is, the application of administrative or legal measures that replace the direct action of defeating an army in the way of advancing private property and its effects. Expropriation, socialization, or intervention may or may not include defeating an army, however, its effectiveness is undeniable.

Expropriation and socialization mean the abolition of the right to private ownership of the means of production (factories and land) and their management by private parties. Both terms, eventually used in direct action, after violence, could be confused. On these two topics there are extensive studies given by the experts we cited at the beginning; We are rather interested in the consequences of interventionism in its indirect form.

The traditional way of attacking private property is direct - with its stages of violently defeating the defenders of the system, expropriating property, removing the foundations, culture, laws, the rule of law and incentives that allow its reproduction. which has always been associated with the term expropriation, nationalization, or socialization. The possibilities are wide from here: expropriate and distribute the shares equally among the workers. -Various coercive ways of imposing equality have been tried that always end up generating new inequalities. How is the above explained? All this development would initially eliminate inequality, however, it would be destabilized almost immediately by the free action of human nature that would ruin the advances achieved in terms of equality: some would sell their shares to use it in other things of interest, others They would waste it, in others there is no concept of saving and investing, new workers could enter, or some of them leave the company, a more productive company would make its employees earn more than a less competitive one, etc. Socialization (nationalization or expropriation by the state seeking state or collective property) would solve these difficulties where the state itself would be the employer and each worker would receive the "just vital universal wage." Syndicalist concepts are a destabilizing element for the ideas of socialization because workers can seek a share of the property or increase their income above what the state intends to give or the company can give (they are interest groups in their normal actuation); these unionist concepts only work in free enterprise when property is private; That is, the worker would reach his maximum income as part of the interest group opposed to businessmen (investors and entrepreneurs), otherwise he must adapt to the socialist universal living wage, whose value is negligible in all countries.

INTERVENTIONISM: ANOTHER FORM OF ATTACK ON ECONOMIC FREEDOM

To give further illustration to the reader who is more familiar with the interventionism that plays in the field of attack on freedom, the indirect attack **(Gramscian postmodernism)** is an interventionism that has previously undergone a massive process of indoctrination, in which additionally , a deliberate and systematic attack is made on culture, order, religion, family, the rule of law, incentives (they prevent the reproduction of the system, being difficult to detect because individuals do not receive them directly). Traditional interventionism is directed towards people in the form of laws or regulations that aim to protect sectors or interest groups. In several forms - of traditional interventionism - the damage generated is reversible - to the extent that the economic sectors can support it before bankruptcy - such as "fair price laws", minimum wage, restricting certain imports, etc. However, in most cases, - and let's take the freezing of prices as an example - interventionism forgets that the industrial fabric is connected and that the final products of one sector are the inputs of another, so that when it affects Some of the chain must affect the next because no one is going to produce at a loss. It is clear then that every intervention requires a greater and deeper one.

Example: if the prices of forage for cows rose and that causes the price of meat to rise, which is the input for sausage companies, the entire chain raises prices at different times. It is not enough for a bureaucrat to freeze the price of a sausage (he tries to protect consumers of sausages who are from lower strata), without freezing those of the entire chain; condemning them to produce at a loss or close due to bankruptcy. In short, it ends up extinguishing the social purpose not of a company but of an entire sector; The worst scenario unfolds that can only end in the worst way: hunger and scarcity. Interventionism in all its forms is incompatible with the free market, always leading to more socialization. Double challenge: Planning and competition are exclusive in the face of a free enterprise model that is deeply discredited.

This union of bureaucrats and state workers who are guided by socialist norms (norms that they apply in the most visible and fail to see what is under the iceberg) do not understand that what must be done is that those vulnerable groups that are trying to protect (target group of the price freeze) have - increase their income - how to buy those foods at market prices (subsidies, work or entrepreneurship). Later in this book, we will propose solutions in this sense; We will touch on the most difficult ones: work and entrepreneurship.

There are laws that, due to their effect of restricting private action on certain aspects, have a socializing objective on human action; A very clear example is the excessive regulations and costs imposed on NGOs, removing private action from that area under the pretext of avoiding the loss of taxes and mismanagement of capital. The state must prosecute the crime already committed, not restrict freedom, it is professed.

EXPLANATION OF THE INDIRECT ATTACK IN TERMS OF INTERVENTIONISM

Interventionism allows us to detect the origin of the attack, this is indisputable, however, for the majority it is not possible to quantify the immediate or long-term damage caused to the system of creation and reproduction of wealth: it leaves you the ownership of the property, although it eliminates the effects of this, not allowing it to be determined what or how much to produce, or at what prices, nor to determine the quantities or when. In short: it remains in a gray area since it maintains ownership; It is easy to determine the origin - unlike what we have studied in indirect attack - but it eliminates the effects of ownership, being closer to the classification of indirect attack. Private property only remains nominally.

Another attack - which does not look at the consequences -
on the social function of private property.

Any of the measures against property that we are analyzing have pernicious effects on the well-being, health and life of the population - which the executors do not seem to care about - or on their doctrinal lust, their dialectical discourse, their imperative morality (they feel obliged to coerce regardless of the consequences because they are bearers of a greater good), intoxicated with dialectics or in their magical thinking they irresponsibly assume them as collateral damage that prevents them from measuring the damage caused to the population. Or they simply don't care.

The clearest way to measure the depth of the attack is by measuring the effectiveness of blocking the social function of the affected private property; that is, in the manifest shortage of the intervened product or service (significant groups of the population are affected in key sectors for life itself such as health, education, food, distribution, pensions, food, etc.); said with examples:

If the attack is against the health sector

How much can the remnant of companies in the health sector that survive serve the population? How many people are expected to die from this attack?

If the attack is against a food producing sector

How bad is the impact that it could generate scarcity or hunger? How many companies went bankrupt, what population sectors do they serve? How many children, elderly and helpless people affected?
The impact of the population in terms of scarcity, death or general impoverishment of the population is inevitable after a direct or indirect attack. In this same second part, at the end we will be explaining the technical reasons why the impoverishment of sectors or industries occurs, after the irresponsible attack.

THE IMPORTANCE OF THE MOMENT: WHAT IS ALL THIS DISCUSSION ABOUT?

It is about the definition of the life model!

The evidence found in the previous chapter shows a deliberate and systematic strategy with the same tactics in different intensities - as different as the country in which it is being applied - but all with the objective of changing society (immediately or progressively) from the bases (and replace them with others) demonstrating that the proposed model is incompatible with the current one.

This reality forces us to strip ourselves of good things and get rid of the romantic halo that an unequal idealistic struggle has, to expose the harsh reality in terms of way of life: all this is about the model in which we are going to live or die in society, it is about to choose the pattern that will organize the society. Choosing between what we are living in brings with it a reduction in poverty, but at the same time intolerable inequalities. A model where we have divided power (so that it does not oppress us as individuals); but due to cultural issues, as well as due to its designed weakness (and voter inaction) it allows corruption and unrest to become embedded. On the other hand, the other model has proven to be indolent in its installation process, causing large sectors of the population that oppose it to emigrate, subjecting large sectors to poverty and a generalized decline in the standard of living; Simultaneously, it can, in the search for a greater good (equality), lead us to totalitarianism, tyranny and oppression (since its essence is coercion). In one, evidence shows that dreams can be fulfilled by following consumers' desires; On the other hand, in the other we will fulfill the wishes of a bureaucrat. Which model best meets individual aspirations and the objectives of society? What model can be articulated in democracy so that if we don't like it, we can repent?

In places where freedom has been lost, many try to resist, circumvent the new laws, others simply give up or emigrate from the country. The countries are left for a few... the mediocre (today they are specialists in living off state contracts; they have sold their soul to the future tyrant; they never go to work). In those who nest tyranny will become censors of the truth, they will tend to force due obedience, they will be rulers of non-collectivist action, shouters of improper conduct, beaters of transgressors. Just as it happens with a few in the networks who become aggressive champions of the candidate for tyrant.

OUR CONCERN

The People, the common people, are not interested in the effectiveness of private property, nor in political parties, nor in alternation, nor in democracy, and even less in freedom; Additionally, they do not have the time to stop and think about this; They are overwhelmed trying to be middle class. They are interested in more banal things such as salary, savings, food, entertainment, whether they will have rent, etc. This is its advantage and its weakest point depending on who takes it.

2

WE ONLY KNOW FREEDOM IN THE LAST 200 YEARS OF HISTORY: ROME

¨Libertas est naturalis facultas eius quod cuique facere libet, nisi quod vi aut iure prohibetur¨

"Freedom is the natural faculty of doing what one wants, unless prevented by force or law."
The concept of Liberty in Rome defined by Florentino.

Slavery (27) is a natural issue.
Aristotle

We refer to Rome because it was the slave empire par excellence of the ancient world and the Middle Ages. Its feudal economy with its characteristics - which interest us - studied in previous chapters (METER OF TYRANNY IN FEUDALISM). However, it additionally concerns us to identify the basic features of slavery.

Our thesis is that the economic and political phenomena in history have very little new, but a lot of recycling and more of refining old methods by correcting flaws (we will verify this in unit four of this same part when talking about Cuba). We will see in detail what is distinctive about a slave state, and we will confront those characteristics with new economic-political systems that evoke its practices. The reader will be able to compare them with other economic-political projects (Liberalism, Socialism and Progressivism) that are occurring in the modern and contemporary age.

Slavery was one of the most enduring institutions in history; that is, the most successful in the sense that it met its objectives no matter how cruel and inhumane its methods were (this is not an axiological evaluation, it is an evaluation of the ability to be effective).

We will verify that the great currents and doctrines that are shown as new and innovative are nothing more than refinements of successful schemes in the past. We will also discover in the imprint on each system, the imperfections of human beings and their deepest tyrannical desires.

A serious analysis of Freedom goes through the analysis of slavery in Humanity. -This is the topic of unit two-. We are going to do it by looking at the beginnings of Slavery and its peak in Ancient Rome, we are interested in its characteristics, the conditions that make it persist. The phenomenon of Freedom in history is a relatively recent event; Its counterpart, slavery, has been with us since the beginning of time and is renewed from time to time. It is necessary to understand, in their context, the deep compelling reasons for **Slavery and Servitude to endure "naturally" over time** and only change their name under other clothes.

The Western Roman Empire existed from 27 BC to 476 AC when the Middle Ages began in Europe.

In Rome you could be a slave by force or by right: by force you became a slave of the empire or of a Roman citizen if you were a prisoner in war and by right since the son of a slave is born a slave or the son of a naive (free) man is born ¨naïve¨. You could, however, go from citizen to slave and vice versa. Many of the institutions of Roman law, such as paterfamilias, slavery, guardianships, etc., were aimed at safeguarding the assets and patrimony of the empire in the hands of the most capable Roman citizens to guarantee taxes and thus maintain the preeminence of the Romans by guaranteeing their wars. Wars were what allowed the wealth creation system to reproduce; That was the basis of the Roman economy, that is, each war added more land, more subjects, more taxes. Rome did not destroy the economic bases of the people it invaded or changed customs or religions; He devastated their armies to clearly subject them to vassalage with the consequent payment of taxes.

WHAT ARE THE REASONS FOR SLAVERY PERSISTING IN ROME?

First, it was legal and the slavery of ancient times, which later became known as serfdom, was the basis of the feudal agrarian economy; Nothing was conceived without slaves or serfs in the Middle Ages.

Second, the Roman slave was subject to his condition by force of arms, because he was subjected to defenselessness (no access to weapons), he did not have access to economic power (he could not have assets and therefore had no assets to exchange and /or buy weapons), he had no power even over his own children, submission was absolute, since his food depended on the boss, as did his defenselessness and inability to organize for confrontation.

There was no moral imperative for that condition to change in those times.

Now that we are clear about Roman slavery, we are going to define its basic features; that will serve as elements of comparison to see if in the future any other form of government wants to be similar:

BASIC CHARACTERISTICS OF A SLAVE STATE (MEET YES, NO)

Characteristics of the concept of Freedom	How it happened in Rome for the slave	Compliant
Policy	They have no rights.	✓
Free opinion	They have no rights.	✓
Mobility	He is prohibited, he lives where they tell him. If he escapes his punishment could be death.	✓
Properties	The slave had no right to own property. He himself was property.	✓
Access to weapons (defense or organization)	They did not have access to weapons. The Roman legions carried weapons and were made up of citizens and later mercenaries.	✓
Life	His life did not belong to him; The Roman citizen, his patron, could dispose of it at any time. They were speaking work instruments (livestock; like a cow).	✓
Home	The slave had to live where his master (patronus) determined.	✓
Job	The slave must work in what his master determines.	✓

	100% of the product of your work is taken away from you.	
Control over your family or offspring.	The slave (son of a slave, born a slave) had no control or power over his family or offspring; They were subject to the parental authority of the patron - paterfamilias.	✓
Feeding	It is given to him by the boss.	✓
Salary	They have no rights. They have no salary.	✓

After the time of Rome and feudalism has passed, we will not find in the rest of history a written document that says that one is a slave, nor the social recognition of this as a virtue of that society. Modern slavery has been perfected, forcing us to look for characteristics in Rome (slavery) and in Europe before the French Revolution (serfdom) that lead us to identify that some other system has recycled this mechanism that has been successful for more than 10,000 years. in the history of mankind.

Each of the basic characteristics of a slave state must be reviewed by the reader in each political-economic system that has existed since the 18th century; It will not be difficult for the reader to identify which of the characteristics of the concept of freedom it takes up, such as politics, free opinion, mobility, property, access to weapons, life, residence, work, etc., and what type of imprints are recorded in that system according to with the "great leader" who interprets or formulates them.

3

BIRTH OF FREEDOM IN THE UNITED STATES: FREEDOM WITH PRIVATE PROPERTY AND WEAPONS TO DEFEND IT

America is the land of opportunity which has produced, in the last 200 years, the greatest freedom and prosperity for the widest range of people the world has ever seen. It is still the land in which people of many races, different beliefs and origins are free to cooperate, to achieve their individual goals while at the same time retaining a diversity of values and opinions.

Milton Friedman

"We hold these truths to be self-evident: that all men are created equal; that they are endowed by their Creator with certain inherent and inalienable rights; that among these are life, liberty and the pursuit of happiness."

Thomas Jefferson

In unit three, we will touch on the second aspect that we are interested in looking at, which is the uniqueness of the appearance of Freedom in America (United States); how the beginning of the "American Dream" is legally and politically consolidated, which recognizes for the first time that Freedom without property and without weapons to defend it is only a "nice" feeling. Its great contradiction: Freedom for

the white male man with property and weapons; against black slavery.
In the first part of this book, we had looked at this issue, but from the
point of view of Equality.
In this unit we are going to explain with the example of how fictions
and institutions that are beneficial are consolidated into laws,
analyzing that the defense of freedom is a particular issue of the
individual and that ultimately the power to defend it must be enabled
in the laws.

The United States is the land of economic inclusion and the
"American dream." These two events occurred due to the early
demarcation of their ties with England and the advance of
Freedom in those lands, where the bases of colonial feudalism
could never be established, so that they never had to carry out
a direct attack against the bases. of something that did not
happen (as was done in the French revolution); They did not
experience the exclusion generated by immovable social
classes. This would explain its strong uninterrupted growth due
to the explosion of talent and creativity - in Liberty, in the full
development of the extensive order, with permanence of the
rule of law, protection of business culture, in preservation of the
bases, pillars and incentives that It allows the system to
reproduce itself - for more than 250 years, bringing the
banishment of poverty as we know it.

To talk about the birth of Freedom in the United States is to
understand it in two contradictory senses: the one that
concerns us and the one that gives it a new singularity and
meaning is Freedom with economic inclusion, private property
and weapons to defend the Freedom achieved. Its counterpart
is that it is only for white men and in a country that at that time
black slavery persisted and women could not vote.

This contradiction could not be clearer in the writing of Thomas
Jefferson in which he only referred to white men at a time when
black slaves were considered property; However, this

controversial issue could separate us from the development of two of our objectives: the first, equality before the law (only for whites at that time; this would explain the great economic differences between whites with property and freedom, compared to blacks without freedom or property). And the second, the freedom to pursue your goals, your happiness.

In this unit we will see how freedom is expressed in laws (as evidence of many concepts seen in the first part), having private property as a background; Both generate confidence to reproduce the system, in an environment respectful of extensive order and the rule of law. As a result, we have an explosion of value and wealth that will be generated over the next 250 years.

We will explain the United States' first and second amendments in their historical context and invite two experts on the topic; will deduce how the "American Dream" is shaped and its meaning in terms of the well-being achieved by its population. For this we invite you to reread the first unit of this same part: PRIVATE PROPERTY AS A RIGHT.

1776 independence of the United States.
1789 constitution of the United States.
1865 abolition of Black Slavery in the United States.
1920 women vote: nineteenth amendment.

FIRST AMENDMENT OF THE CONSTITUTION OF THE UNITED STATES OF AMERICA

Congress shall make no law respecting an establishment of religion or prohibiting the free practice thereof; nor limiting freedom of expression or of the press; nor the right to peaceful assembly of the people, nor to petition the government for a redress of grievances.

The primary objective of a constitution of a country is to prevent the State, as a "constituted superior power"; becomes a tyrannical, oppressive, and abusive entity over individual freedoms. That desire was clearly expressed in the first amendment. The strength of the first amendment is that individuals with economic freedom can claim other freedoms such as freedom from coercion of expression and whoever wants to listen, let them listen. In the same way with the press, the right of assembly and creed. Avoiding coercion in these respects can then be extended to preventing individuals from becoming someone else's instruments; That is, they serve another person other than their own interests (remember that we have associated serving our interests and seeking the means to realize them with the well-being of society through the collaboration of other individuals in the creation of value and wealth). This simple last idea arises in all individuals spontaneously.

SECOND AMENDMENT OF THE CONSTITUTION OF THE UNITED STATES OF AMERICA

(Taken from the National Archives, is: "A well-ordered militia being necessary to the security of a Free State, the right of the people to keep and bear arms shall not be violated.")

In the second amendment, and after freeing themselves from the British Crown (the overseas superpower), the Americans understood that the next second power that could become an oppressor was a closer one and predicted that it could be the state itself.

FREEDOM THE AMERICAN STYLE

Now the concept of Freedom for the American encompasses other aspects such as the ability to defend it when required. Given the scenario of the possibility of an oppressive state, the people must have economic power (property and assets) with effective means (weapons and organization) to defend them. A very different scenario was being configured from those of the revolutions in Great Britain and France, in which political power was taken away from despotism, class equality and equality before the law were achieved when the socioeconomic rise was being achieved by incipient mercantilism. In America, the despot, who resided in England, had already been defeated; There had been unprecedented incidents of land transfers to non-noble settlers, and they were preparing to form a state that could eventually become the new despot, if they let it. Given this, they consolidated the freedoms that would allow them to fulfill their individual dreams in addition to generating all possible means to achieve it (knowledge) with weapons to protect it.

Around these ideas, Americans have created inclusive public and private institutions, with an entire institutional framework in the rule of law that allows the majority access to goods and property (the American dream), the creation of the order necessary for development of a large market in which these goods are exchanged; finally, lethal weapons and the ability to organize into militias. "If the state becomes an oppressor, it will face a militia of equal proportions to its power."

HOW THIS CULTURE OF ECONOMIC FREEDOM IS FORMED

The model of conquest and colonization that Spain implemented in Latin America, from Mexico to Patagonia, failed again and again in North America (North Carolina 1585-1587 and 1607 Virginia), because the Indigenous people resisted being enslaved and there was no gold (9) - see book: why countries fail, Daron Acemoglu and James A. Robinson. Pages 33 to 43-.

The Virginia Company, the company that owned the land before the British crown, was in charge of conquest and colonization, trying again and again to transfer the feudal model of administration. They suffered failure after failure, because they could not enslave the Indigenous people and the colonists did not allow themselves to be subjected to servitude.

The colonists were fleeing from the Virginia Company's coercion and death threats. In 1618 even, outside the prevailing ideas of the time (in the feudal economy property was only owned by the nobles), the Virginia Company decided to change the incentives for the colonists to work hard by distributing land per head - fifty acres to each. settler and fifty more acres for each member of his family and servant he could take to Virginia - the settlers received houses being released from their contracts; Over time, a cultural aspect about property and the power it represented was going to take shape. The culture of property tied to power would mark Americans and their Institutions from now on. In 1619 a general assembly was introduced that gave effective voice to each adult male and property owner in the laws and institutions that governed the colony. "Democracy" began in the United States.

In Maryland and Carolina, The Virginia Company again sought to establish a rigid, hierarchical, and elitist society based on land ownership and attempted to subdue the colonists as tenants to pay tribute to the Lords; failed again. The colonists had many options in the new world, and they escaped.

In 1691 they managed to eliminate the political privileges of the Lords (Lord Baltimore).

A DEMOCRACY BASED ON PRIVATE PROPERTY AND THE RULE OF LAW

In 1720 the thirteen colonies had similar governments; a Governor and an Assembly based on the voting rights of male owners. Women, black slaves, and propertyless white people could not vote.

In 1774 the colonies formed the first continental congress to define its members and the collection of taxes: prelude to the war of independence. An economy was built on strong foundations and institutions that would preserve the incentives of the free market plus a legal culture that allowed commercial, economic, and social relations to occur with order and transparency; the economic system was reproduced.

The following is a "deconstruction" of the second amendment, in which we analyze each of its parts and place it in a legal and historical context.

Our guides will be constitutional experts Jeffrey Rosen and Jack Rakove.

ONLY 27 WORDS (second amendment) THAT MOBILIZE A COUNTRY

"A well-ordered militia being necessary to the security of a Free State, the right of the people to keep and bear arms shall not be violated."

Militia

What is a militia?

At the time of the American Revolutionary War, militias were groups of able-bodied men who protected their towns, colonies, and ultimately states. "(When the Constitution was drafted), the militia was a state institution," Rakove explained. "The states were responsible for organizing this," he added.

well organized

What did "well ordered" mean?

One of the biggest challenges in interpreting a centuries-old document is that the meaning of words changes or drifts.

"Well ordered in the 18th century tended to be something like well organized, well-armed, well disciplined," Rakove noted . "It did not mean 'regulation' (as a synonym for bringing order) in the sense in which we use it now, it is not about the regulatory state. There have been nuances there. It means that the militia was in an effective way to fight," he concluded.

In other words, it does not mean that the state was controlling the militia in a certain way, but rather that the militia was prepared to do its job.

In the debate over the second amendment, the words "a well-ordered militia" continue to be one of the most cited and discussed parts.

for security

What type of security does this fragment refer to?

To understand this, you must consider the climate of the United States at the time. The country had just fought a war, gained its independence, and was expanding westward. There were enough reasons to feel insecure, so "safety" had an obvious meaning:

"You have an expanding country, and the primary defense use of the militia would be to protect local residents from attacks and invasions," Rakove said.

It also meant physical protection from government overreach.

"The idea of a state militia could also be attractive because it serves as a deterrent against national tyranny," Rakove said. "At that point, if government forces tried to take over the land or overstep its boundaries, then you would have a ready institution – the militia – that would outnumber any army," he continued.

Obviously, with the size and scope of the modern American military—plus the fact that militias as we know them no longer exist—that notion is difficult to imagine today.

of a free state

What did a free state mean?

It may seem obvious, but Rosen and Rakove agree that the Constitution includes a lot of contemporary moralism and not all the terms are well defined.

In this case, the meaning of "state" is what it seems to be.
"This immediately refers to 'state' as one of the states of the original colonies," Rosen explained. "When he wrote the

Constitution, James Madison had the Virginia Declaration of Rights of 1777 at his side and essentially copied and pasted the language from there," the expert said.

But it could also refer to a broader understanding of freedom. "So here," Rosen continues, "George Mason (the author of the Virginia Declaration of Rights) is not just talking about the free state of Virginia. He is also referring to a broader state of freedom.

the right of the people will not be violated.

What kind of right?

This is another of the most controversial fragments, which helps to better understand how the creators of the Constitution thought about complex ideas such as "right."

"When we think about 'rights,' we think of them as regulations and exemptions," Rakove said. "Back at the birth of America, they had a different quality. "They were more moralistic," he explained.

Rosen noted that this perspective is reflected in the Declaration of Independence.

"The framers definitely believed in natural rights: that they are granted by a creator," he maintained. "They believed that we are born into a state of nature before forming governments and that we are endowed with certain fundamental natural rights," And these natural rights include the right to religious expression, freedom of expression, property, among others. But, Rosen clarifies, they did not specifically include Second Amendment principles in that set.

The village

Who are the people?

Even the term "the people" – the most basic of all – has limits. "When you say the people, you mean individual people," Rakove maintains. "But, if you go to Article I, Section 2 of the Constitution, it says that the House of Representatives will be elected by the people. So, who are the people? Who has the right to exercise that vote? As you see, you can use the term "people" to refer to a collective mass, but there are also categories of people that can be excluded," he explained.
Ultimately, when the Constitution was written, slaves were considered property and women could not vote.

Additionally, there is a more basic issue of semantics: By "the people," does the Second Amendment refer to individuals as private entities or as militia participants?
The legal consensus is that the Second Amendment applies to individual rights, within reasonable regulations. More on that below.

own and carry weapons.

What are weapons in this context and what is the scope of carrying them?

In the case of "District of Columbia v. Heller," the Supreme Court decided that Second Amendment rights did apply specifically to the possession of firearms for self-defense.

The decision struck down the Firearms Control Regulations Act of 1975, which harshly regulated gun ownership in the District of Columbia.

In an excerpt from the decision, the Court considered the strange approach of the amendment. The judges divided the text into an operating clause – "the right of the people to keep and bear arms" – and an introductory clause – "a well-ordered militia being necessary to the security of a free state." The court determined that the relationship between the two fragments, as well as the historical context of the creation of the Constitution, clearly provided an individual right.

The term "guns" is also constantly changing, and there are ongoing debates about assault weapons and new firearms technologies.

"One thing people differ on is whether assault weapons bans are constitutional," Rosen said. "They also disagree about how we should interpret the Constitution: whether in light of historical terms or new technologies," he indicated.

The term « arms » is also an ever-changing one, and there are ongoing debates about assault weapons and emerging firearm technologies .

Finally,
"The authors did not mention the right to bear arms as one of the natural rights," he added. "Although, it is fair to say that in the face of the right to alter and abolish government – to the extent that modern people claim to have that right – the framers did believe in it."
"In that sense, it is historically correct to say that the perpetrators felt a natural right to self-defense."

What does the whole amendment mean?

For its modern application and current purposes, Rosen agrees that it is necessary to change the way the Second Amendment is presented to courts and tribunals. For the most part, the decisions have remained consistent since the Heller ruling in 2008 and a very similar ruling, McDonald v. City of Chicago, which was decided in 2010.

"It is truly surprising that since these Supreme Court decisions… the lower courts have upheld almost all of the gun regulations they have asked to review," the expert said.

Words like "militia" and "law" are loaded with historical context and nuance that can act like a Rorschach test, leading even the most well-intentioned interpreters to different conclusions. If there were clear answers, these 27 words would not be so incendiary.

Jeffrey Rosen is a professor of law at George Washington University, as well as president and CEO of the National Constitution Center (NCC). This organization's website has a fully interactive version of the Constitution with commentary and primary documentary sources.

Jack Rakove is Professor of History at Stanford University. His book «Original Meanings: Politics and Ideas in the Making of the Constitution » won a Pulitzer Prize in History.
https://constitutioncenter.org/interactive-constitution

BASIC CHARACTERISTICS OF A SLAVE STATE (MEET YES, NO)

If we ran this test in the United States around the time of racial slavery, to be fair, we would have to run two (2) at the same time; one, that of racial slavery towards blacks, which would obviously lead to a slave state and the other, that of white men, which would lead to the birth of freedom with some borders of private property, economic inclusion and weapons to defend the freedom of the possibility of an oppressive State, never seen in history: the future of the defense of freedom, overshadowed at its birth by racial slavery (in 1950 blacks were 10% of the population and whites 84%; in the In 2020, blacks rose to 12%, Hispanics to 18% and whites 68%).

GROWTH AND WELL-BEING

The data that we are going to generate below will help us measure the impact of the arrival of economic freedom with access to private property in the United States and compare, denoting the marked difference in income (and in all the factors that point to the well-being of the population) with Latin America where the events of liberation, of departure from feudalism did not come with access to property; In fact, they were plagued by exclusion, corruption and socialism until today .

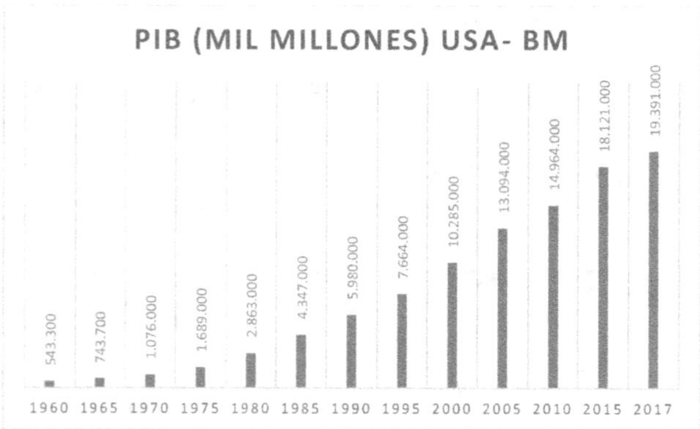

GDP per Capita: USD 59,531

This freedom in the United States has meant that each individual, seeking their own ends and integrating their own means to achieve them, has been able to generate value for society 10 to 15 times greater than if they did so by following orders in a collectivist society. A few of them will be successful as entrepreneurs, but the vast majority have participated in the realization of those dreams, contributing their efforts according to their capabilities to receive important benefits in terms of well-being generated by the new wealth created in an amount that has allowed the phenomenon. of the wealthy middle class that has dismantled any theory based on the exploitation of labor. This is the great achievement, the greatest scope within the social sense of private ownership of productive goods in which the greatest example is the United States of America.

Most of the population lifted out of poverty.

In the United States, a family of four (4) people to be considered poor must earn US$30,000 per year, US$2,500 per month.

The reality is that the income of one (1) immigrant in Florida is US$12 per hour, which working eight (8) hours a day gives an average of US$2,880 per month (these values are if you work only one (1) person in the family; that is, it moves away from the poverty level twice as one more person adds to the income). This is due to the high number of companies present in that market, which in turn generate high demand for labor; The freedom of enterprise makes them compete with good salaries, making them grow sustainably and permanently.

The Gini index is not a good indicator in this environment of abundance and well-being and could only be used to stoke hatred, resentment, and envy in society.
Gini coefficient (35) USA 0.418.

4

THE CUBAN REVOLUTION: FREEDOM MORE THAN HALF A CENTURY LATER

Let the springs of collective wealth flow in full flow.
Karl Marx in the Communist Manifesto

The life of a human being is worth millions of times more than all the property of the richest man on earth.
Che Guevara. On a banner in Havana.

We are going to talk about the Cuban reality - from this narrow corner of Liberty - seen on several trips by one of the authors. The main task of this unit is that the reader knows, but at the same time can get rid of the aggressive image of the traditional direct attack that leads to socialism communism (this image discontinued, the current indirect strategy does not allow him to see) and manage to reconcile concepts with a new form - strategy - that manages to impose the same failed, tyrannical, and impoverishing system.

We must, for reasons of pedagogy, state it, however, only seeking to move the reader away from these clear signals offered by a direct attack - knowing in what sense it comes, how and who generates it - and its consequences that the island experiences today. The reader must refer to what we saw in the first part to document the direct and indirect attack and its effects on the ownership of private property of productive goods and its effects on the elements that allow it to reproduce (culture, laws, currency, etc.).

We will see how the Cuban system is maintained and erected even more by denying the basic aspects of the individual. From where socialism communism learned (history is learned by human beings) - it revamped and refined past regimes - to make itself an impregnable regime, which only an implosion coming from above, from power itself, can overthrow.

In previous units we showed the spontaneous way in which only in a free environment can the search for the specific ends of each human being that lead to economic happiness (obtaining private property) be better achieved in a cooperative environment that allows each one receives according to his or her ability to contribute. This is the first step that in turn paves the way for the search for more political freedom. We reference the unpublished case in the United States whose process was endorsed with the signing of the first and second amendment.

Cuba is going in the opposite direction. There is a violent revolution (direct attack) with the dismantling of private property, the violent dismantling of culture, of all the bases, foundations and incentives that allow the reproduction of the capitalist system. It is replaced by a new socialist culture that changes idols, paradigms and establishes a new way of interaction in the daily lives of ordinary people with the almighty state; It's a new way of life.

CUBA THE EXAMPLE OF A DIRECT ATTACK

House analogy- direct attack on liberal democracy

Regardless of the degree of corruption, poverty, or economic exclusion that Cuba had before 1959, the forces that overthrew the dictator Fulgencio Batista were not coming to reestablish liberal democracy (which they despise).

Since Lenin, Marxism-Leninism had been installed in popular ideology as the great revolution that defeats the regular army (those who take care of the house); Next, they install themselves in power to doctrinally (this word -doctrinally- is used in the sense that what guides their actions is a belief that does not measure consequences; it is only guided by an all-embracing power that in itself does not need anything else, only in itself is it necessary, it is blessed...) to expropriate the lands dedicated to the production of sugar and its entire industrial process, that is, the private ownership of the means of production (bringing down the house in the terms of our analogy). In Karl Marx's terms, end the infrastructure that is the exploitation of one class by the other through private property and immediately cease its effects - since its owners, upon losing ownership, lose their ability to order what, how much, how to produce and access to the profits of its exercise - (these are the foundations and pillars of the house and incentives to produce).

How the system is reproduced

The free-market system can no longer be reproduced, the entire system has been left in the hands of bureaucrats: property, the effects of ordering production, administration are centered on the state, the state is the entrepreneur, the only one that can be an investor according to a collective plan to which all individuals are subject.

Socialism communism begins a dismantling of all the concepts that have been created around the free market. The family, culture, laws, religion become a virtue of preserving the new system and a process of rapid dismantling through indoctrination begins. The capitalist system not only requires private ownership of the means of production but is made up of what Karl Marx calls superstructure (culture, language, religion, salary, work, laws, etc.), which mitigate the clash of a class. against the other and allows their reproduction.

THE DAY TO DAY OF ORDINARY PEOPLE

Communist socialist societies are not that different from liberal democratic societies when it comes to the daily lives of ordinary people: they have eliminated inequality by removing all wealth in the hands of the upper and middle classes by lowering the entire population to be a new class of ordinary poor people or in the process of impoverishment). The ordinary poor people (no longer the group that has not made it in capitalist society), are now the bulk of the entire population except for the state bureaucracy (the population is only allowed economic survival actions). They are societies that have eliminated the upper class and the middle class.

The mythical story of facing a superpower.

Cuba has always been looked at, seen with admiration, and shown as an example of stoicism and gallantry. I must clarify that I have never admired stoicism that hits a stone, but rather intelligent stoicism, measured gallantry. I have always been skeptical, and I have preferred to go see, to realize things personally - that no one tells me -. I felt a certain pride, but at the same time I had a certain concern, but, as I always wanted; before showing my admiration, my respect... See if it was true!

The first contacts

On my first trip, what I observed was that they hid everything from me, the ordinary Cuban was afraid. Cubans could not enter foreign places and/or talk to foreigners. The second time I went, I spoke with Cuban friends exiled in the United States and they got me to go live in Cubans' homes: to live their reality.

A different reality than what they sell.

I found myself in a sad country.
Yes, the people had high standards of education, in fact, ALFberto (all name has been changed), a man who carried my suitcases, had studied some fermentation topics in the former Soviet Union; It had titles that I didn't understand well. He spoke very well about the revolution; of their values; However, he preferred the US$5 that I was going to give him for the two days; instead of receiving the "Just and Revolutionaries" US 15 dollars a month if you work for the state.

- What was happening?

- Was he facing a revolutionary evil, or did he not believe in the revolution?

No, he is simply a human being who is moved by needs and incentives. The revolution did not calculate this: the frustration, the employment of so many enlightened people, the incentives, and the desire to earn more, to be better, for you and your children to do well. The revolution forgot that it was going to deal with ordinary human beings who behave like ordinary human beings.

I learned that ALFberto later emigrated to Ecuador (because while in Ecuador he contacted me), and later to the United States; His closest friends tell me that he suffers from Stockholm syndrome because strangely, for all Cubans in exile,

ALFberto still speaks well of the Cuban revolution (Stockholm syndrome? Or is the land calling, not intending to definitively lose his connection to the land? In any case, the regime's political use of this human need is reprehensible).

The indoctrination received from state institutions clashed with his deepest instincts to use a freedom, which he did not have, in the search for a better future for himself and his loved ones. Once this last aspect was denied, he only had to face the coercion of the state or not resist anymore and emigrate; He chose to emigrate. This is the reality that all the totalitarian systems that have been tested live: the massive emigration of their most precious human resources - the entrepreneurs, the restless people, the intelligent ones, the innovative ones, those who do not expect things for free, those who take on challenges, those who mark progress-.

ISA COMMUNIST SOCIALISTS OR, SAID ANOTHER WAY: FORMAL AND INFORMAL INSTITUTIONS THAT REPRODUCE CUBAN SOCIALISM

The reader can realize and identify that what we are going to look at next represents the socialist ISA or, in other words, the formal and informal institutions of the new Cuban socialist system. You will notice that they are all designed to compel a state that is based on oppression; That's why I would try to keep it. It requires oppressive and coercive ISA. They are the apparatus of violence of the ISA state of the superstructure.

Currency

In those times there were two currencies: one for the people, Cuban pesos, and another CUC, convertible to dollars minus the 10% that the regime kept. The exchange rate is 20 CUC for $480 Cuban pesos.

The state interferes with the conditions that the currency must reflect:

-It does not work as a unit of account to determine the prices of products since they are set by the state, however, that only works in state warehouses that are always out of stock. The products move in a secondary market (black market) and in a small and incipient economy free of basic subsistence products. In these last two markets there is inflation reflecting scarcity.

-A means of savings in a subsistence economy does not make sense since it does not represent future investment. The only saving function is to convert it into currency; to preserve the value of foreign currency for later consumption that can be obtained or received in CUC.

-As a means of exchange for the exchange of products and services in an economy that only works in one direction, with subsistence levels being intermittent.

Salary

Monthly salary US 15 ($480 pesos), bus fare $10 pesos, a small pizza $10 pesos.
Let us remember that pure socialism, communism, does not agree with the division of labor or that different jobs have different salaries. Its doctrinal vision is equality without considering each person's individual effort, skills, knowledge, or special talents.

Send me to the warehouse!

It was a notebook to claim food at the warehouse (Mandao a la Tienda), at first no one wanted to show it to me. It was 5 pounds of rice, 2 pounds of beans, 5 pounds of sugar, 1 pound of butter, 1 tube of pasta (every 3 months), 1 chicken for five people. The saddest thing they told me was: that lasts 2 or 3 days. Then you must go to the farm (market) to solve and the prices are as follows: 5 pounds of rice $25 pesos, 1 pound of beans $16 pesos, chicken thigh $30 pesos, pork meat $40 pesos, an egg $1.10 pesos.

Solve

It is going to the street where the two markets exist (the black market for products that are not found in government warehouses and what is produced illegally by people); These products move through the laws of the free market. An incipient barter capitalism was created, where everything was obtained, which has allowed Cubans not to die of hunger.

Even though the doctrinaire communist socialists do not recognize the market, the same laws are fulfilled in them that, like gravity, even though you do not believe in it, it must affect you if you jump from the tenth floor. Price inflation – reflecting scarcity and consumer choices – affects them too.
The Resolve in Cuba demonstrates the failures of the doctrine in the rapid replacement of knowledge learned over centuries in the extensive order. Spontaneously, simple people resolve in their own way, still maintaining consensus regarding the culture of payment and other important aspects of the rule of law so that barter and incipient trade can take place; despite the restrictions, aversion, and condemnation that the system generates towards basic survival models like this, which of course, are based on the free market.

El paraíso del revés

Clothes

The donated clothes are sold by the Government. Good clothes go to the black market: pants US$30, t-shirts US$15. In Cuba there is a black market for everything.

Job

There is no work, they told me. You only get in construction and agriculture; The professional does not want to earn $480 pesos. If you want a good job, you must buy it and it costs between $20,000 and $30,000 pesos. The most sought-after jobs are as drivers and those in contact with foreigners.

Until a while ago, simple, artisanal, and individual jobs that were assigned by the state were released and self-employment was regulated in a country in which there is no guarantee of receiving the fruit of one's work and has even institutionally disregarded the incentives to produce it privately. The damage is catastrophic in the ability of that people to move forward.

A flawed system that produces no new private value or wealth

Cuba has tried to return some economic freedom through self-employment to have private growth that helps reduce poverty. They are aware that this is the path, however, this means the recognition of the historical error of the very bases of socialism communism that Karl Marx established. These steps are fruitless because the system is tainted by the distrust generated by an economic system without foundations, pillars, and incentives - the communist socialists They are very good at destroying it, but very bad at creating it - at producing and creating value and wealth. We will talk about this aspect in a general way later.

Family

The concept of family, as we know it, has become secondary after having left the education (indoctrination) of children to the state for more than six decades. Society now revolves around the survival of the state. The damage to institutions like the family is unforgivable: you can't even trust your children; They may be listening.

Socialism communism (36) fragments the family, which cannot be trusted; indoctrination for the defense of the state begins in schools; your children no longer belong to you.

Culture of the foot

The neighborhood Cuban is going to deceive you, scam you and take any advantage from you if you give him the chance; Yes, it is not violent. He is resolving.

That "liveliness" is sculpted in the culture of the Caribbean; vividness that is difficult to tame by any doctrine, no matter how strong its influence. It shows that there are things firmly rooted in the human spirit that cannot be forced under coercion or laws.

When I returned, there were many people waiting for the remains of rice, sugar or whatever I was going to leave. I bought and left them food; I left them every pair of pants I had.

Given the above, we are going to analyze the concepts associated with Freedom:

Cuba is one of the last two living exponents of socialism communism; in such a way that we will not run the Test of Tyranny since we already ran this one for Socialism at the time. The Tyranny Test approves it.

BASIC CHARACTERISTICS OF THE CUBAN STATE

We are going to run the Test that we apply to slavery in Rome; should show the degree of proximity that the communist socialist regime can achieve to slavery.

We will see if it complies with them or not and we will mention how these new uses, customs and socialist laws occur. (YES, NO)

Characteristic of the Freedom Concept	How it happens in Cuba	Compliant
Policy	Only if you belong to the Single Communist Party, do you have access to participate in its closed elections.	✓
Free opinion	There is only the official opinion; Those who disagree commit a crime.	✓
Mobility	If the Cuban "deserts" he loses all his citizenship rights, he cannot return to the country for several years (formally, up to five) and his family is not allowed to leave the island. Due to the planning of all services and products, you cannot move around the Island, you must remain in the place of registration or risk being deported to your place of origin.	✓

Property	Socialism communism by essence considers property as the cause of inequality. In some cases, you are allowed to have your home, but it can be expropriated if you do not behave in accordance with the canons of the party. If the individual has economic power, he could eventually compete for political power with the party.	✓
Access to weapons (defense or some organization)	Weapons are exclusive to the regular forces of the state.	✓
Life	The Cuban can maintain life, if he does not rebel against the communist party (state).	✓
Home	Cubans are not free to move to other places on the Island; they must remain where they are registered, or risk being extradited and committing a crime.	✓
Job	The Cuban cannot choose work, in fact, until recently (02/06/2021) " more than 2,000 activities" were authorized in which "the exercise of self-employment is allowed", which would imply the major reform in the communist country, where	✓

	the government and its companies dominate the economy; before they could only legally carry out 127 work activities; jobs such as manicurists or shoemakers were from the state.	
Control over your family or offspring.	Communism breaks the family unit, and the most important thing is the party; children are indoctrinated at school. Socialism-communism forces the family to despise a member who does not agree with the ideas of the party.	✓
Feeding	The Cuban has a card given by the state where the ration to which he is entitled (when available) is located monthly - sent to the store. If he does not do what the state says, his ration is poor, he and his family suffer.	✓
Salary	He does not have a significant salary, historically it has been US$15 a month. The product of all your work is supposed to be received by the state.	✓

In conclusion: Cuban socialism communism perfected slavery, making it an impregnable regime.

CUBA: AN UNPUGNABLE REGIME

The Cuban regime achieved it: the defenselessness of the individual.

One of the clearest characteristics of slavery is to dispossess the individual (so that he cannot defend himself) and generate a state of helplessness around the person so that he believes that nothing can be done. Cuba achieves it: the job does not belong to you, you work for the state, you cannot have enough income to defend yourself from state aggression, you cannot choose your work, the salary is ridiculous, you survive only with the ration card (the mandate to the store); If something is missing in the house, you have to go out and solve it.

Cuban Constitution: the system defends itself.

Constitución
de la República de Cuba

PREÁMBULO

NOSOTROS, EL PUEBLO DE CUBA,

inspirados en el heroísmo y patriotismo de los que lucharon por una Patria libre, independiente, soberana, democrática, de justicia social y solidaridad humana, forjada en el sacrificio de nuestros antecesores;

por los aborígenes que se resistieron a la sumisión;

por los esclavos que se rebelaron contra sus amos;

por los que despertaron la conciencia nacional y el ansia cubana de patria y libertad;

por los patriotas que a partir de 1868 iniciaron y participaron en nuestras luchas independentistas contra el colonialismo español, y a los que en el último impulso de 1895 les

ción impuesta por capitalistas, terratenientes y otros males sociales;

por los que promovieron, integraron y desarrollaron las primeras organizaciones de obreros, campesinos y estudiantes; difundieron las ideas socialistas y fundaron los primeros movimientos revolucionarios, marxistas y leninistas;

por los integrantes de la vanguardia de la Generación del Centenario del natalicio de Martí, que nutridos por su magisterio nos condujeron a la victoria revolucionaria popular de enero de 1959;

por los que, con el sacrificio de sus vidas, defendieron la Revolución y contribuyeron a su definitiva consolidación;

por los que masivamente cumplieron heroicas misiones internacionalistas;

por la resistencia épica y unidad de nuestro pueblo;

ideas de emancipación social de Marx, Engels y Lenin;

APOYADOS

en el internacionalismo proletario, en la amistad fraternal, la ayuda, la cooperación y la solidaridad de los pueblos del mundo, especialmente los de América Latina y el Caribe;

DECIDIDOS

a llevar adelante la Revolución del Moncada, del *Granma*, de la Sierra, de la lucha clandestina y de Girón, que sustentada en el aporte y la unidad de las principales fuerzas revolucionarias y del pueblo conquistó la plena independencia nacional, estableció el poder revolucionario, realizó las transformacio-

Article 1: Cuba as a "socialist State of law and social justice, democratic, independent and sovereign, organized with everyone and for the good of all as a unitary and indivisible Republic, founded on work, dignity, humanism and the ethics of its citizens for the enjoyment of **Freedom,** equity, equality, solidarity, well-being and individual and collective prosperity.

Article 3: in the Republic of Cuba, Sovereignty resides non-transferable in the People, from which all the power of the State emanates. The people exercise it directly or...

Article 4: "The defense of the socialist homeland is the greatest honor and supreme duty of every Cuban.
"Treason is the most serious of crimes, and whoever commits it is subject to the most severe penalties."
"The socialist system that this Constitution endorses is irrevocable."
"Citizens have the right to fight by all means, including armed struggle, when no other recourse is possible, against anyone who attempts to overthrow the political, social and economic order established in this Constitution."

In article 1 it mentions freedom within a confusing context where the state and a series of values prevail that really distract from humanity's historical claim (freedom).

In article 4 it institutionalizes terror; authorizing and legalizing the violent actions of "civilian" paramilitary groups of oppression in favor of the Government, against the dissidents of the regime: the system defends itself.

Contrasted with the constitution of the United States (calls for liberty), the Cuban Regime calls on the population on defend the state; that is, they legalize paramilitarism. Normally the groups of armed civilians or collectives or whatever name they receive, will eventually carry out the dirty work by executing and carrying out tasks against civilians, which in the hands of the regular forces would be actions against humanity. The division that it manages to create in society and the formation of terror groups to persecute dissidents is an unprecedented creation.

Where the Cuban people went wrong

The Cuban people ignored several aspects that serve as alarms when forming a state and a constitution:

The first.
Throughout history, slavery and servility have dominated; From the moment human beings have tried to organize, one interest group has given itself the right to dominate and oppress the other.

The second.
The most successful political economic system in history has been absolute monarchy (rigid class stratification of society into nobles, clergy, and serfs); that is, tyranny. This system was sold by the nobles as an extension of "God on Earth."

Third.
We had mentioned that the objective of constitutions was to limit the powers of the state over individuals.

Ping pong out, down with the worm, down with the scum (chorus)

After the case of the Peruvian embassy in the 1980s, the regime instituted days of contempt for migrants (dissidents); of which there were many ways to do it.

One of them was to sing this chorus, while stoning the naked migrant. In particular, i heard two stories in which my interviewee participated - and in which he showed pain and regret, but which helped him understand that something was wrong - in which they sang it to him, while they were being stoned: first to a classmate, later to a teacher (because of the respect they had for her, they did not stone her). His crime was to seek a better future, to understand that it was impossible in the revolution and to follow his instincts in the search for personal fulfillment. The above is nothing different from what has been repeatedly done by all individuals who face the same situation in different parts of the world where socialism communism has been implemented in any of its presentations.

If we look at the definitions provided in this writing about political regimes, in general, socialism-communism is exceptionally impregnable because it reverses history by reviving the absolute monarchy at the head of the communist party, concentrating unimaginable powers, reducing and keeping people in poverty. almost all sectors of the population, recreating in the constitution the most refined fictions to remain in power indefinitely despite and above the people.

Only the regime can be changed; The only way, and I hope I am wrong, is for an implosion to occur, from within: the Cubans, if this premise is confirmed, are condemned to their existence without freedom!

Why don't the Fathers of the Revolution make a ¨mea culpa¨ (my fault) and recognize that they took the wrong path, freeing all those people to try again to rebuild that nation? The answer is simple: doctrine, pride, does not let them; believing that with only good intention everything is possible. The cemeteries are full of good intentions.

THE ELIMINATION OF ECONOMIC EXPLOITATION AS A CONCEPT TO ELIMINATE INEQUALITY

This was the Marxist-Leninist promise, which in the Cuban case was a continuation of the direct strategy whose purpose would be the establishment of a regime in which, by eliminating the cause, private property, exploitation would consequently be eliminated. The final step, being consistent with the philosophy of historical materialism, would be the change of the superstructure and installing new ISA -paradigms that we know as formal and informal institutions that allow and reproduce the system- (culture, family, laws, policies, new institutions that guarantee the permanence of the regime, etc.) of life around collective property in which the socialist just man would be happy.

I leave it to the reader to determine whether structuralist rationalism (philosophy below socialism) does not suffer from fatal arrogance when attempting to understand how sociology, economics, and politics work around human beings. Likewise, to evaluate the cost of leading the lives of many people who have not asked for the revolution, much less to be dragged into such utopian ideas.

GROWTH AND WELL-BEING

The data provided by the Cuban government is unreliable: the GDP per capita provided by them is US$8,821 for 2019; However, these values are debatable (they are false; it is impossible for socialism to produce innovation, value, or wealth) when contrasted with its exports of US$1.7 billion and imports of US$3.7 billion. There is another value that seems more real to us in which we would approach a true value of US$2,018 per capita that includes the basket of services that the state provides poorly. We have no doubt that the communist elite must have high standards of living in a country that cannot feed its population.

We are going to use the salary of US$15 a month, although we recognize that the value of groceries, transportation (which we found free at that time), education and health are left out.

The income comparable to the salary gives us US$180 per year. Compare it with that of the United States or other developed countries where poverty has an income 15 times greater than 98% of the population in this repressed country.

5

LATIN AMERICA: FREEDOM UNDER SIEGE IN DEMOCRACY

What does Freedom mean that makes millions of people flee from where it does not exist? Is it the scarcity that socialism generates, the deprivation of freedom, coercion? Many Cubans lose their lives trying to cross 90 miles that separate them from Florida... many do not make it. Seven million Venezuelans have fled socialism. We saw their starving bodies; many lost their lives in the attempt. Despite the risk, nothing stops them from trying again and again.

Taking from the rich and giving to the poor in any way possible: it has not worked. This only allows the practitioners of tyrants to look kind and benevolent.

We are interested in real examples of the indirect attack in which the ownership of private property of the means of production is preserved, however, the intervention on prices, reduction of incentives such as profit and profit (through high income taxes or progressive), high regulation of labor hiring, imbalance of the union interest group, high taxation rate, actions to prevent the order that generates investor confidence, blockage of laws, minimum wages that are too high (coercive predistribution) , that business does not occur due to the dismantling of the rule of law, the appearance of enormous amounts of small conflicts in all aspects of society, etc., etc., means that in the end the businessman cannot choose what and how much to produce because well either there is no use left for it, it cannot do so at those prices or there is legislation that forces it in some way. Property has lost its effects, and the owner is a simple administrator in the best style of a planned economy in transition to a "higher" collective stage; Collectivization occurs when scarcity overwhelms and the next step is required to guarantee production and the new order.

Some will be laws, other policies, many just strategies, others simple redefinition of doctrines or names, however, all create unease, raise spirits, disinhibit small revolutions, generate feelings; The sum of them configures the khaos. We will analyze the policies, whether they are won in the cultural battle or those generated from points of power; Their common denominator is that they go against some "normal performance" of social, moral, economic, or political relations; Furthermore, they are necessarily imposed, obligatory. They go against everything established. We will look at them trying to determine their final objective within the established order. We will see in real cases where this innovation that we call Gramscian postmodernism takes us, those cases being the ones we are going to analyze.

DOCUMENTED ACTIONS OF INDIRECT ATTACKS AGAINST ECONOMIC FREEDOM

Pension and health funds

In 2008, the progressive government of Cristina Fernández de Kirchner nationalized US$30 billion dollars belonging to 9.5 million contributors saved in pension funds.
Today that money is lost within the spending of a giant state; a possible hostile adversary was reduced to nothing, private individual savings were eliminated, in turn eliminating

investment, that is, forward growth, the future reproduction of the system that would reduce the potential poverty of the new generations that jump into the labor market ; All the bases and incentives to believe in an individual savings system again are broken. They did it... this unusual success with so much impact is going to make them want to repeat it throughout Latin America.

Pension funds do not originate spontaneously in free enterprise, they are born from a law that seeks to protect workers in the final stage of their life, in which they can no longer work. They are products of human design just as socialism is; However, its objective is to take obligatory individual savings (parafiscal) to finance the private pension system administered by private parties. -They are generated by parafiscal taxes, they create businesses with other people's money for their friends; This is what gives it that moral questionability at its origin. The administrators are large private companies - part of the precept that private companies are better administrators - that profit from money that they do not put out of their own pockets. This creation has turned the funds into large private sector investors (stimulators) and at the same time buyers of state debt.
There are two interest groups, within the free market system, that are not seen well by Marxism; They are the investors and businessmen; The latter have the idea of business, they take money from investors seeking to fulfill their dreams or objectives. In the socialist model, the investor would be absorbed by the state and the businessman by a public official or administrative bureaucrat. This last approach, apart from reflecting ignorance and apathy to find out more about how the subject works, what it brings us is the danger of acting under doctrine and not the pragmatism of understanding something that works. Additionally, these private funds have given

additional power to traditional economic groups, potential rival enemies of any socializing plan.

The nationalization of pension funds does not seek to improve the system, it seeks two objectives, both doctrinal: the first is political, to give more power to the state to the detriment of private parties that could dispute that power. The second economic, eliminate individual savings (which takes away power from individuals and large companies) private. It seeks to prevent the reinvestment of capital and the reproduction of the capitalist system that they so despise.

Other funds (for example severance pay) that manage parafiscal taxes - they are taxes, the product of a law, but they are not destined directly to the state, but rather to funds, companies or private provisions for a specific issue or service - also have the same structure and will be the target of these same nationalizing proposals.

fair prices

Through Decree No. 2,092 dated November 8, 2015, with Rank, Value and Force of Organic Law of Fair Prices, published in the Official Gazette of the Bolivarian Republic of Venezuela No. 6,202.

Resolution 823 of November 11, 2022, in Argentina.

This policy is sufficiently explained in the second part, first unit under the title: INTERVENTIONISM: ANOTHER FORM OF ATTACK ON FREEDOM.

If you have a political setback you change to a democratic attitude

On September 4, 2022, Chile widely rejected the new constitution drafted by left-wing extremist sectors.

Every time there is a large or significant setback in which society clearly rejects the imposition of a norm or law, there is a change of attitude, an apparent and temporary diametric change, in which the questioned leader becomes a democrat who respects everything. what was agreed. The strategy has a disconcerting effect in society accustomed to having a culprit with overwhelming evidence; - plays with established paradigms, changing attitude requires showing what people expect to see - the repentant is given another chance. This strategy works; It generates time, a new opportunity, which is what is ultimately sought. However, that opportunity may be the final one. It reminds me of the parable of the snake that suddenly changes and allows the rabbit to cross the river on its back; In the middle of the river, it changes again, eating the rabbit. She says: - well, this is my nature.

If you have a political setback, another strategy is used and that is to separate yourself from the leaders who have taken the path of hard Gramscian postmodernism (21st century socialism).

September 13, 2023. The Colombian president compared his Nicaraguan counterpart to Augusto Pinochet, due to the persecution of the Nicaraguan poet Gioconda Belli. On the other hand, the Chilean president sent him a note of protest for referring to his country's police officers as "criminals."

Daniel Ortega called Gustavo Petro a "traitor" and called Gabriel Boric a "pinochetito": what happened?

After they receive the "pardon, based on oblivion", they relaunch from the same point where they were, their once good relations with the tyrants.

The criminal is a victim of society, reducing the number of crimes reduces crime.

"If we achieve that a series of activities in Colombian society that are considered crimes today are not considered crimes in the future, then by definition there will be less crime in Colombia," said Petro on August 19, 2022, in the speech he gave at the inauguration ceremony of the new director of the Police.
It is not a naive proposal; it seeks to affect the legal system, the rule of law and all the paradigms that society has in this regard. It is based on a new precept of **Gramscian postmodernism:** power brings truth, so despite being absurd it must be discussed because it comes from power. It unleashes the small contradictions that exist around crime, delinquency; generates small revolutionary foci. It involves attacking institutions and destroying them.

Dismantling of the entire constitutional framework that corresponds to the visible framework of the entire free market system and protects all its relationships.

Change or modification of the doctrines of police entities regarding demonstrations.

Taken from Infobae on July 28, 2022.
Salamanca said that "Esmad is going to be reviewed: one, its doctrine; two, training. Here there is a position of guarantor with the human rights of Colombians and that is clear for the institution."

Likewise, he mentioned that said review will be carried out considering the ruling issued by the Council of State in 2021 in which it orders patrolmen, non-commissioned officers and officers of this squad to undergo training and understanding of Decree 003 of 2021, which establishes a strict protocol for the use of force during a citizen protest.

It is a preparatory act to confront different and small civil interest groups in society. It generates a positive effect in that it recreates the great revolutionary confrontation between proletarians and bourgeois that should have occurred before the seizure of power. This is also achieved by changing the doctrines of the entities that administer and execute the violence of state weapons; They cannot enforce the law, their belligerence is taken away; that is, changing the police doctrine in this case that prevents it from confronting any civil movement, even if it is armed, or inhibiting the rights of other groups or manifest violence against sectors not inclined to the goals.
At the same time, groups related to the final ideology are allowed to demonstrate, not to be subdued by the police forces and generate Khaos.

Piqueteros in Argentina

On October 13, 2021 (text taken from infobae).
The picketers announced that they are going to cut this Thursday, starting at 9 in the morning, the main accesses to the City of Buenos Aires and isolate it, as well as at least 17 provinces.

November 10, 2022. Taken from the Los Angeles Times.
The protesters - many of them from the leftist Polo Obrero - reject the official decision to put a ceiling of 1.35 million beneficiaries on the state program "Potenciar Trabajo", the main one in the country, which grants tasks to unemployed people or people with

little income and He pays a monthly sum that represents half of the minimum wage of 57,900 pesos (about $347).

It transforms social mobilization into a militia against democracy. Its function is to pressure the growth of social plans related to its policies, hinder the normal development of the free market economy, increase tax pressure on those who produce; Khaos, suffocate the system. Confidence to invest is lost. Mobility is essential for the capitalist system to reproduce.

Chavista collectives Venezuela

Hugo Chaves creates the Chavista collectives on April 10, 2006, to protect the revolution
Replacement of the constitutional armed forces with paramilitary forces that are loyal to them. These paramilitary forces can be and were effectively directed against the dissident population.

First line in Colombia

May 27, 2021, Gustavo Bolívar exceeds the goal of 100 million pesos in his vaki to support the first line.

Argentine profit law

The Income Tax Law (No. 20,628) was implemented in 1974.
In fact, the General Confederation of Labor (CGT), the most important union center in the country, has tirelessly reiterated that it is a "work tax" and that "salary is not profit."
However, although under other names, many countries around the world implement it as a redistributive measure, mainly in developed nations such as Spain, France, the United Kingdom, Japan, or the United States.

Highly questioned in poor countries, even though it is used by developed economies where salaries are high, it is a clearly redistributive measure and attacks incentives for paid work.

Laws that dismantle the right to free enterprise in real estate

Case of second and third house laws in Spain.
Law 5/2018 of June 11, which modifies the law of civil procedure regarding illegal occupation of homes, came into force on July 2, 2018.
They are faithful to the socialist maxims of ownership only of the first house. When there are people who, due to their vocation for savings, ability to do business around the real estate issue, block it by allowing the occupation of the private property of the second and third home; In the process, they violate the rule of law and institute the arbitrariness of their regimes built around tyrants.

Criminals as spokespersons for peace

It seeks to create Khaos and hopelessness before the rule of law.
Give preeminence to certain interest groups against the armed forces to generate small security problems that bring the revolution closer, that break the institutional order.
They uncover the character of small revolutions that they consider to be the small contradictions solved by civilization.

Decarbonization or energy transition in the face of climate change

Madness either hopes to awaken small contradictions or sees a quick way to economically adjust society downwards, to decrease, to reach the just society that they imagine of low consumption; That society is therefore less demanding of them in generating value and new wealth in what have proven to be the worst students.

They adjust their manifest inability to produce new value and wealth to all policies that imply the destruction of the wealth created, to drag the well-being of society to its levels of pre-wellbeing and generalized poverty.

Pact with prisons

Overwhelming and generator of Khaos, it goes against the formal institutions of prison and the informal ones constituted in the collective imagination that the criminal must pay for his crime in prison. Break the rule of law. Unleash small revolutions and discontent.

Labor reforms, including subsidies.

Destabilize the balance that must exist between interest groups in society. Ingratiate yourself with certain minorities to instrumentalize them towards violence.
The previous paragraph should not be taken to mean that minorities should not be helped or that they "per se" are a problem for society. What he is trying to point out is that it does not help them at all when they become instruments of violence to install some other doctrine foreign to their interests.

Economic degrowth laws or regulations that destroy sectors.

September 1, 2022
Irene Vélez, the minister of mines, said the following at the National Mining Congress: aware that Colombia sells what other countries buy from it, she said in front of businessmen in the mining sector that it is necessary to ask other countries to

"decrease in their economic models" to refer to the need for a change of model in which countries buy fewer mining products so that producing countries sell them less and thus reduce climate change.

Outside of a firm and irresponsible desire to reduce the impact of fossil fuels on climate change, the minister reflects her contempt for the capitalist model and adheres to irresponsible reasons (for coming from a poor country where the biggest problem is hunger and poverty).

What he is really doing is hunting down his model full of economic impossibilities (the options offered by his socialist model to reduce poverty are very modest and decreasing in relation to the problem posed) within a series of ideas with ideological doctrinal roots in the climate issue. Their approaches are crazy and suicidal for an underdeveloped economy.

6

ARTIFICIAL EQUALITY AT THE EXPENSE OF FREEDOM

The failure of coercive laws to impose equality is because they go against the most basic instincts of human beings.
Milton Friedman

Any society that places equality before freedom will have neither. The society that places freedom before equality will have something of both.
Milton Friedman

Any policy directly aimed at a substantive ideal of distributive justice must lead to the destruction of the rule of law.
Friedrich Von Hayek in his book The Road to Serfdom

We will try to respond, based on what we have seen until now, to the question of a member of the audience as to why the intention to establish equality fails again and again, this being such a sublime concept. The questions have been reiterated: why and how does equality fail? How difficult is it to get back on the path of growth? Why and how does it impoverish society?

Equality is a product of human design (modern constructivist rationalism) that aims to solve undesirable events of human interaction in freedom, which is inequality. The relationships that occur at that level are spontaneous, obeying the intrinsic order of human social and economic events; going against them already implies fatal arrogance. That said, we will address other topics regarding the effects of the imposition - by coercion, pardon the redundancy - of equality in contrast to the duty to be and be human (exposed by Milton Friedman) and we will show how it is manifested in the indirect attack trying to go about blocking (using the tools given by this book) the very creation of wealth that it causes.

Milton Friedman tells us that human relationships are not fair, life itself is not fair, there is no justice in sports, in beauty, in health and much less in the wealth that depends on certain skills and abilities for business. Nature, creation is not fair, but we will not dare to judge beyond that, nor will we try to answer why; We will not judge God, we will simply accept Him. We will refer tangentially to the issue of the false morality behind equality. What we cannot miss is that it is a political strategy that has proven to be successful time and time again; so successful that despite going against everything established, it finds convinced defenders who help lead a mass, who inadvertently cross an uncertain path carried by a promise to receive something that another has worked for, that another has built.

THE IMPOSITION OF EQUALITY FAILS AGAIN AND AGAIN

The failure of coercive laws to impose equality is because they go against the most basic instincts of human beings. Milton Friedman explains it by bringing up a phrase from Adam Smith: "it is a uniform, constant and uninterrupted effort of each human being to improve his conditions to improve his own life and make a better world for his children and his children's children." If a law interfered with that, he would try to avoid it, break it and, unable to resist it, he would emigrate from the country.

Friedman notes: The implementation of coercive laws in search of equality faces the opposition of the basic instincts of the human being to prevail humanity, generating all the effects of leaving the laws. These types of laws have been implemented in all types of countries, different cultures, in different economic models, with various alternatives and in all of them they have had the same effect: resisting them.

Their installation is preceded by either violence, or the exaltation of feelings such as envy, anger, frustration, or hatred, with great popular support, or by the recent process in Latin America of dismantling the free enterprise system that produces value and wealth. All these strategies that use the same variable (equality or inequality) and articulating feelings are only effective when they are articulated in some deep discomfort. The strategy is winning because the contenders underestimate the forces that hide feelings (hatred, frustration, envy).

Then, after the party, the hangover occurs and the measurement system based on well-being returns, however, due to the degree of tyranny installed, it may already be too late for some. In countries with different stages of progressivism (26) and in which democracy continues, they vote for change. In totalitarian regimes in which, due to oppression, they cannot change them, they resist them, try to overcome them to finally emigrate.

However, the deep damage to the system has been done and the terrain of doing business is flawed. The challenges are considerable; Among them, the most difficult are those that are inserted in the culture (those that have taken humanity centuries to develop), -the extensive order: we understand each other, we live together and we are capable of acting successfully because the conscious and unconscious patterns of behavior that are not the results of coercion but the product of firmly established habits and traditions - the clearest example is trust.

All of these patterns of behavior that enable progress are used more successfully by some who have learned or developed business skills or are more astute; or they simply see it clearly (that's humanity); These are the businessmen, for whom not consuming today represents savings to invest in the future, they are the ones who, seeking their own ends and generating their own means to achieve them, make the economy grow. It is the one that several accompany in their dream and together they build new wealth. Obviously, there is going to be inequality in that act in which a few generate enough wealth to drag the vast majority out of poverty. A few following their instincts, seeking their goals to fulfill their dreams generate value fifteen times greater than if they did so following orders in a collectivist society. Historical evidence proves it, eliminating them is condemning the entire society to poverty.

It is an issue of morality, claim the most doctrinaire, claiming a false morality for their coercive acts and demanding to accelerate the process.

The parallel markets that exist in Cuba demonstrate the false communist socialist morality; ordinary people impose their survival against any false morality. So there is no high morality in the laws of prices, or in not allowing each human being to seek their well-being or that of theirs or to have to buy more expensive goods, or to submit to a union; Ordinary people do not need to rationalize it, but will feel that everything is prohibited; Their tendency is to break the law, they will only obey it because of the consequences of prison and in these cases they will never be guided by a feeling of justice. The talented will migrate to where they can use it for their own benefit.

FAILED IDEAS THAT HAVE BEEN TESTED IN ALMOST EVERY LOCATION, POLITICAL AND ECONOMIC SYSTEMS, COUNTRIES AND CULTURES. IDEAS CLEARLY INCOMPATIBLE WITH FREEDOM.

The imposition of equality through direct clash and violent and devastating revolutions

Collectivist ideas have been put into operation throughout the world, mainly in countries of the communist socialist orbit such as Eastern Europe, the USSR or China; where the direct attack (Marxist-Leninist) violently destroyed the free market model, over its ruins and devastation of lives, to rebuild property in favor of the state, the superstructure that sustains it with the political tyranny that maintains it.

In a mixed model with extensive state ownership, five-year plans in democracy

In India, an economic planning system with five-year plans was established as soon as British colonization had ended, and in the best Soviet style - in democracy - plunging the economy into a downward spiral and society into more poverty. The preeminence in India was state ownership over private ownership. Already in the 1980s, stagnation was on the horizon; the economic failure that was consolidated in the 90s with the abandonment of the five-year collective plans.

England, the cradle of the free market, also experienced its socializing process - in democracy - that paralyzed its economy; Additionally, it created state and union bureaucracies, new millionaires who lived behind the regulations. Taking the fruit of someone's labor to give to another what is not the fruit of their labor was the rule until Prime Minister Margaret Thatcher abandoned that model. Europe to a greater or lesser extent has felt the effect of these policies. In these economies, the weakness is noted in the defense of the ideas of the free market or that inequality is unbeatable as an idea despite the fact that it inevitably drags the entire society downwards in well-being and restricts the economic future of future generations.

The case of several European countries with social democracies

Social democracies such as Sweden and the Scandinavian countries have opted for a welfare state that is financed by an industrial plant and a private business network that operates the most tenacious free market.

Argentina and Latin America with Gramscian postmodernism (it is happening again)

The Argentine case comes from being an economic power at the beginning of the last century; after decades of interventionism - which have severely limited the effectiveness of private property to generate growth and reduce poverty - which has stagnated its economy and begun to decline. This country - preserving democracy - has additionally suffered from the onslaught of **Gramscian postmodernism soft** focused especially on labor laws and regulations, redistributive laws, productive sectors that maintain ownership of private property, but suffocated by tangles of regulations and taxes that are around the level of slavery, the tax burden on natural persons is around 70%, equality ministries, laws for the defense of minorities, all the cultural aspects that allowed the reproduction of the system have been under attack with laws, policies or regulations. The results have not been long in coming: today its poverty has grown to 50% of its population, 8 million workers support 20 million people with checks from the state. Latin America has suffered the attacks of this same type of slow, deliberate, and systematic policies, but all of them open the possibility of the path towards total tyranny as the country's institutions allow it.

They fail and repeatedly fail over and over again.

No experiment has worked that involves destroying the social function of private property, neither seeking its replacement by state property, nor preserving property by attacking only its function, nor half-assed regulations , nor full tax burdens or seeking redistribution, nor the searches for the unionist state, nor the socialist just man; All of them have failed because they face the reality that human beings only work for themselves and their loved ones, they do not work willingly for society (someone unknown) or for a greater good. You can force him, however, as soon as he has the chance he will resist or ultimately emigrate.

They have understood it in part, they no longer compete with the free market on an equal basis trying to see who produces more value and new wealth. Socialism communism is proven not to produce wealth - they will no longer keep Marx's promise: the rivers of socialist wealth will flow - it is a model that in that sense represents involution. Their new presentation is more about trying to resemble and join any movement that must necessarily destroy wealth or go backwards in reducing poverty with the excuse of saving the planet.

Despite the above, they continue stubbornly trying to prove something that society has not requested, has not asked for. Strategies must be designed to confront them, so that they are not destroying the achievements achieved by society or that lead it to the abyss.

WHICH IS DAMAGED (BREAKED) AFTER THE IMPOSITION OF SUCH EQUALITARIAN MEASURES

Communist socialist countries (direct attack) and their return to economic freedom

The violent direct attack completely destroys the wealth created, nullifying the social function of private property; That is to say, all the wealth that each company generated represented in the products or services it manufactured, (if the sector produced syringes, there are no more syringes) the money that went to other companies in the form of payments or transfers will cease, threatening the sector and the business fabric with bankruptcy; all the people who worked in that sector are unemployed.

The decrease in income, that is, in the wealth represented in money of that sector or company is no longer there; society is immediately poorer in that absolute value.

The question is: why is it a bigger problem if the promise is the replacement of that private company with another from the state?

First, private property has proven to have a better social function; That is, it produces better products and services at a lower cost.

Second, because what guides them is doctrine, they do not stop to weigh the damage to the economy, they do not consider the deaths they could cause in vulnerable sectors. They do not understand that the entire business fabric is interconnected: society will lose all that effort and value.

Third, the state official is faced with the challenge of replacing years and years of accumulation of Know How deprived, of the replacement of a social function (in this example the production of syringes -shortage-) that does not happen overnight (the examples analyzed show the delivery of entire companies and sectors to people who know nothing about the issue). At that moment the officials are taking a whole list of socialized companies for which it will not be done immediately because it is not a priority (these companies are vandalized by the borrowers); Additionally, it is possible that its continuity is not in the plans of the leading official. Repeat this example for thousands and thousands of products, food, hygiene items, safety, health, etc., etc. The reader, to get an idea of the problem, must visualize many, many former indoctrinating bureaucrats waiting for orders on what to do, in a medium of capital circulation that they are unaware of.

Remember that the bases and pillars on which the free market economy was based have been extracted; there is no trust or order.

Finally, the person who takes care of other people's things has not been born ¡

No one today who was not a fanatic would defend socialism-communism as a means of producing well-being and wealth; It is only enough for basic public services in survival sectors. The writers who have accompanied us, including Hayek and Von Mises, have sufficiently explained the structural flaws of this system; now, doing it again is not our objective.

We have pointed out that the system once installed is impregnable, so that the countries that have left socialism-communism have done so because their elites have decided to implode (in the case of the Soviet Union and satellite countries) to try to survive the competition of the other. superpower opening spaces of economic freedom. In cases like China and Vietnam, their leadership has demonstrated the ironclad nature of their establishment, that they have not hesitated to give up economic freedom because they know that their regime will not fall. Due obedience in these systems has always been overwhelmingly compelled by the weapons held by the state. The countries that have returned to the free market have done so in a painful way (closing of companies with losses or poor quality products, products that have no outlet, etc.). Upon leaving socialism, the system is flawed because individuals do not feel secure that they will receive the fruit of their efforts, the rules have been lost (rule of law), the bases and pillars must be recomposed, as well as incentives.

Countries that apply egalitarian measures (Gramscian postmodernism-indirect attack) while preserving democracy

The indirect attack blocks the ways in which the system reproduces, that is, the economy does not grow and at a certain point begins to decrease. If the economy does not grow, there is no way to absorb the new individuals who enter the labor market; or they become poor or supported by the state with money (intermittent aid) taken from taxes of those who still work.

The cocktail is toxic, however, with a slow death: the reproduction of the system is stopped, capital is drained from it, it is impossible for it to function well so that it decreases. The businessman finds himself in a limbo in which he retains ownership of the production goods, but price regulations, impositions, taxes, the unease generated by the khaos of cultural attack, absurd labor laws, etc. prevent him from producing, functioning, sell and effectively carry out the social work of private property; Next to the difficulty for business survival there is always the omen of bankruptcy. Each company that is defeated by the strategy unleashed, that does not achieve it, is lost wealth (its constant value in money), unemployment and social work that society loses progressively.

Where democracy is preserved, the political freedom of people allows them to evaluate the systems, they do so by estimating the well-being perceived according to their work , according to the number of opportunities that the system provides to achieve their own objectives. of his family; That is, people resist, evaluate the well-being and the little progress in which they live and decide to change it. People do not evaluate welfare-deficient systems in accordance with the moral sophistry (justice and egalitarianism) that egalitarians propose. Human beings are not yet prepared for such high moral designs; He simply wants to live better every day. The return to liberalism will be a necessity. This is why extremists call to accelerate the process to a harsh Gramscian postmodernism that ends in loss of freedom and tyranny.

Recomposing the economy is easier after Gramscian postmodernism than in the previous case. The business community that survives this onslaught will be disoriented, but ready to quickly return to the path of progress, after the suffocating measures and laws are repealed; It's in your genes, it's there.

The two direct and indirect strategies fundamentally seek the same thing: attacking the productive system that creates value and wealth; one does it directly immediately (falling into the void of poverty immediately, to try to rise again with state property). On the other hand, the indirectness is unnoticed, progressive (falling into the void little by little, hitting and bouncing from stone to stone -progressive poverty-). The first had the full support of the Soviet Union with high morale. Once the discredit of the system occurred with the fall of the USSR and China, Latin America opted for the second, unnoticed, slow option. The substantial difference is that they decide which comes first: attacking private property or attacking the culture, bases, pillars, and incentives of the system.

By destroying incentives, both strategies leave the system undermined towards the future; such simple spontaneous themes - but ones that have taken centuries for human history to develop - such as having the product of our work, seeking one's own benefit and that of others, having utility, payment according to work, according to time, etc, they no longer exist . Confidence to invest is flawed. This is the largest "expropriation" carried out.

WHY DOES A DIRECT OR INDIRECT ATTACK IMPOOVER THE POPULATION IN A GENERALIZED WAY?

Before any act of war, the bearers of the drums, the first thing they do is dehumanize the possible recipients of their actions.

This has been the attack on free enterprise, where previously, on the one hand, its detractors have attacked basic concepts such as profit, wages, work, etc., completely ignoring the interconnected effect of the creation of wealth (of the repercussions of its bankruptcy on the business fabric, on people's lives, on the well-being of ordinary people) as well as ignoring the social value of private property (services or products); on the other hand, the process of indoctrination, of discrediting free enterprise in young people. This does not mean to ignore the fact that there are no freeloaders, exploiters, abusers of private property who use it to ignore the common good, revealing all the evil that human nature brings to both sides.

Placing the concepts on the fore, then intoxicating the executors with dialectics, clothing them with a greater good, with a superior morality, giving them the character of liberators makes them blind executors who cannot measure the damage caused , the damage is reflected in the millions of lives damaged or put at risk by the destabilizing adventure. For structuralist rationalist ideologues (socialism communism) they cannot continue to be "collateral damage" in times when we have reached the consensus that humanity is not ready to put aside its selfish personal well-being or that of its loved ones; much less put the common good first, no matter how good it may seem, that is. We share the idea that something must be done to benefit the population unknown by a successful, but exclusive minority (as exclusive is the human being when he reaches a pedestal on which he expects recognition) of the free market.

THE DAMAGE (IMPOOVERY) IN THE BUSINESS FABRIC OF A COMPANY OF ORDINARY PEOPLE

We are going to try to explain from the same business fabric of a small business (a real case of a business for ordinary - ordinary - people). For this we are going to use a graph used in the first book that shows where all the money is directed (read wealth created in a small business). This graph will allow us to feel the calamity that the bankruptcy of a company represents and identify all the connectors it has towards other supplier companies, buyers, state entities, parastatals, workers, individual savings of workers, future savings of workers, banking, services public, toilet, etc, etc.

We all lose with the closure of a wealth-creating unit - company -; Please check the column (WHERE THAT MONEY GOES):

INCOME	JANUARY	WHERE THAT MONEY GOES	% About the sales
Sales Product 1	174,269,051		
Sales Product 2	0		
Sales Product 3	0		
Sales Product 4	0		
Sales Product 5			
Sales Product 6	0		
Financial and Others	0		
TOTAL	**174,269,051**	19% goes as VAT to the Treasury	100%
EXPENSES			
Salaries	25,055,108	It goes to the Worker and he spends it at Home	14%
Severance	2,283,665	To severance companies and invest in large companies	1%
Interest Cease	274,040	It goes to the Worker and he spends it at Home	0%
Cousins	2,283,665	It goes to the Worker and he spends it at Home	1%
Vacation	1,113,663	It goes to the Worker and he spends it at Home	1%
Cheers, ARPy Pension	3,595,935	To ARP and Pension companies and invest in large companies	2%
Compen Box	1,148,667	Compensation Funds and invest in the worker	1%
Aids/Bonuses	720,000		0%
Cellular Assistance			0%
Area training technique	3,500,000	To training companies	2%

Prepaid Medina			0%
Professional services			0%
Subtotal Personnel Expenses	**39,974,743**		23%
Tax Audit Fees	987,218	Tax Auditor by Law	1%
Legal Advice Fees	1,083,225	Lawyer	1%
Cio Tax .	0	Tax	0%
Stamp duty			0%
Office Rental	2,256,151	Property Owner	1%
Public Services Water/Electricity	438,686	Public Service Companies	0%
Office Transfer Expenses			0%
Insurance	287,578	Insurance Companies	0%
phones	510,410	Telephone Company	0%
Cell phones	764,340	Cell Phone Company	0%
Legal	203,366	Notaries, Treasury, Banks	0%
and Office Maintenance	221,899	Maintenance Companies	0%
Depreciation	5,771,847		3%
Subscriptions, Magazines, Newspapers			0%
Messaging, transport and mail	779,044	Logistics Companies	0%
Cleaning, Surveillance and Cafet	692,871	Cleaning Companies	0%
Stationery	243,524	Various Companies	0%
External Consultants	2,567,106	Consulting and Knowledge Companies	1%
Representation Expenses	57,674		0%
Telemarketing			0%
Marketing and advertising	3,058,200	Marketing Companies	2%
end of year expenses			0%
INTERNAL TRAVEL.			0%
Tax leaving the country			0%
Maintenance and Accommodation			0%
Air Transport			0%
Ground transportation			0%
LOCAL TRAVEL			0%
Maintenance and Accommodation			0%
Air Transport	122,328	Transport Companies	0%
Ground transportation			0%
Unforeseen 0.3%			0%

Subtotal Administration Expenses	**20,045,465**		12%
Financial expenses	827,510	Banks	0%
Arrears Interest - DIAN			0%
Expenses not Ded.Impto.4 x1000	1,036,596	To the Treasury	1%
Other Non-Deductible	147,700		0%
Subtotal Other Expenses	**2,011,805**		1%
Total spends	**62,032,014**		36%
Commissions pending payment 2013	2,000,000	It goes to the Worker and he spends it at Home	1%
Current Commissions		It goes to the Worker and he spends it at Home	0%
Manager Variable x Operational Profit		It goes to the Worker and he spends it at Home	0%
Cost of Sales Product 1	113,449,152	Supplier Companies	65%
Cost of Sales Product 2	0	Supplier Companies	0%
Cost of Sales Product 3	0	Supplier Companies	0%
Cost of Sales Product 4	0	Supplier Companies	0%
Cost of Sales Product 5	0	Supplier Companies	0%
Cost of Sales Product 6	0	Supplier Companies	0%
Subtotal Cost of Sales	**113,449,152**		65%
TOTAL	**177,481,166**		102%
Monetary Correction - Adjustments x Inflation			0%
Profit Before Taxes	-3,212,115	IT HAS GENERATED WEALTH FOR EVERYONE AND EVEN NOT 1 PESO TO THE OWNER	-2%
Income and Complementary Tax			0%
Profit from Distributing to Partners			0%

The description of the previous example should in principle stop acts that harm or affect a wealth-creating entity (company), even if the origin of the property is flawed.

Paths must be opened so that this entity (company), which has not had the opportunity or the right to first defense, can do so by demonstrating its worth to society.

If this small company is closed, if it produces syringes, it means that there will no longer be anything to inject people with; Its twenty workers are going to go hungry because they have no income, all suppliers, individuals or connected companies will receive the negative impact. The reader must amplify this example to simulate a massive direct or indirect attack where, in the direct one, the entire private economy collapses, or in the indirect one, an entire sector goes bankrupt or the bankruptcies occur in stages.

If large companies are closed, all the wealth they produce, represented in money, goods and services, stops flowing; When it is closed, it leaves a dark void that generally impoverishes the entire society: the doctrinaire executors fulfill their objectives of taking power away from the upper classes, however the most serious damage is done to the lower classes from whom they take away food. , health services, education, housing, salaries, etc.

Additional impoverishment due to inflation

In this space we are going to explain the dark void left by the closure of a large sector in the economy; all in terms of inflation.

It is necessary to keep in mind the following premise, which has been proven not to be true: the demand subsidy, that is, the subsidies and grants given to the population create inflation. This premise was disproved precisely in the first government of Lula Da Silva where he claimed to have reduced poverty by 44 million people through subsidies. The previous agreement is not true, it did not reduce poverty; With subsidies he secured votes for the next election, postponing poverty; However, what it did demonstrate was that subsidies can be paid without inflation; This is true if and only if the quantity of products and services remains stable in the economy, that is, there is no closure or bankruptcy of companies, but, fundamentally, if currency is not issued without compensation in production or productivity.

In the cases that we are analyzing, the objective of undeclared war is their progressive bankruptcy. The sum of all these companies is the sum of the wealth of the attacked sector. When they go bankrupt, there is a vacuum of products and services that the state intends to fill with emission or with subsidies or subsidies that it has removed through taxes from those who still produce. The larger the bankrupt sector, the larger the placement of money that will not have an effect on the supply of products and services (now scarce) and will push prices inexorably upward.

Individuals perceive, but do not understand, the growing loss of wealth and well-being. They feel that money buys less and less, because basically some irresponsible people left the market with nothing to buy.

The economy with bankruptcies, that is, under attack, in the long term adjusts downwards in poverty; Does the question arise as to whether this is the fair and low-consumption society that they expect? If so, they have already arrived.

Or is it that they don't understand that everything is interconnected in a way that we are just beginning to understand...

The business phenomenon is very young; not everything is studied. There are chapters to be written about the business fabric, the minimization of bankruptcies, the relationship of the connecting vessels with the social function, the interconnection of spending between social classes.

All very new phenomena.

What would happen if the companies that the strategy attacks are all in the health sector? How long would it take for society to re-accumulate all that knowledge - snatched away - in the provision of the service?

The incompatibility with the creation of new wealth

All the socializing models that have been tested in one way or another throughout humanity, in which they have wanted to impose equality under coercion, fail in the creation of new wealth.

Why can't they create new wealth? The reason is very simple: the evidence shows us a relationship between freedom and the generation of talent and business ideas. Egalitarianism is incompatible with freedom. The moral bases of collectivism face the basic characteristics of an individual who is going to create new value and wealth: the individual only produces it for himself and his people; While egalitarianism seeks to benefit a collective, all egalitarianism is about truncating the individual. You are not going to become a more moral man in communist socialist terms simply because you force yourself to do something you are not prepared to do. Trying to reestablish human morality through coercion is something abject, absurd, and it has been sufficiently demonstrated that it does not work.

THE FATAL ARROGANCE OF SOME AND OTHERS

We do not fully understand the phenomenon of business interrelationship

There is a case that happened to us in the midst of the COVID 19 pandemic that explains a lot about the lack of knowledge of the communicating vessels between the business fabric. This applies even to large companies, although their relationship with the companies of ordinary people is very rare; or at least that's what we thought:

During the pandemic, it occurred in Latin America (or in almost the entire underdeveloped world) that the upper classes - who had savings since they had high incomes, also because they worked in the formal sector - retired to their homes, cut off all contact other than to receive food from the formalized system. We saw, astonished, how many people - who had no savings and who were dedicated to small, family businesses - took to the streets to sell anything to get something that would allow them to sustain themselves. Confusion surfaced side by side in the discussions we had with a colleague from London, they did not understand why we were doing it (going out in the middle of a pandemic to risk our lives) since they received their check at home -in its world of developed economy, everything is legal where the state knows exactly who its citizens are. While here in Latin America, people who work informally were either dying of hunger or dying of COVID 19; you had to choose.

Apart from this, the important fact is that we do not know the degree of interrelation that, despite the exclusion towards lower classes, exists between the upper and lower classes, even between formal companies and ordinary people.

What is clear is that the relationship exists, it is very strong and if large companies were to be absent, a dark void would open in our well-being. Therefore, the solution to inequality is not to destroy large private companies, it is to help the companies of ordinary people to consolidate alongside large companies to reduce exclusion.

Wrong right and left policies

Another aspect that both suffer is the policies made for developed economies.

It is very clear that the IMF missed something substantial in its policy of trickling down from the upper classes to the lower classes in the form of work and opportunities; forgot that 70% of our economy that generates work is informal with clear restrictions on accessing the growth given in the other formal sector. On the other hand, union policies are aimed at that same formal sector, where a higher salary with better conditions can be negotiated. The same does not happen in the companies of ordinary people in which the boss is the mother or father, where they pay what they can to a workforce with very poor skills offerings.

Equality is that everyone has the minimum opportunities to use their abilities and talents regardless of their beliefs, race, social class. Pretending that everyone should be equal in income, level of work, etc. conflicts with freedom.

Milton Friedman: There has been no society that, by denying economic freedom, has had civil or political freedom: the tyranny is manifest. You can't have a free society without free markets.

There is more freedom where there are more opportunities; consequently, there is more income, and the cycle leads to increasing opportunities (opportunities measured in terms of access to property).

Democratic freedom implies the alternation of power in the administration, the protection of principles, of values that the entire society agrees on. There are two parts: the first must recognize and accept not destroying these values or destroying wealth. The counterpart must commit to defusing the unrest, eliminating exclusion, bringing most of the population closer to progress.

Liberalism, progress is only possible with budding freedom, and this is best expressed in democracy.

The free-market works based on private property, its effects and the social work it generates.

7

ALL THE FORCES OF CREATIVITY OF THE HUMAN BEING WERE HIDDEN IN SLAVERY AND SERVITUDE

Most people throughout history and many people today have lived or live in tyranny and poverty. Freedom (understood as the sum of all freedoms) with political freedom has never existed together without economic freedom. Far more people in the world live in tyranny and poverty than in freedom and prosperity.

Milton Friedman

Economic freedom is stronger if a country has more entrepreneurs and more people who depend on itself.

Frederic Hayek

In this unit we will only establish the role of economic freedom in the history of humanity; Your defense will be your results.

The advance of civilization and the reduction of poverty makes sense - when it is explained in terms of Freedom - because it has allowed all creativity to be unleashed, it has freed the talent that slavery and then servitude had kept prisoner in previous centuries.

Both detractors and those in favor recognize that the free market has lifted most of the population out of poverty and hunger.

Economic freedom generates economic growth, innovation and science, new companies, in short, new value (in an inclusive environment that allows private property, that preserves the rule of law while maintaining incentives to produce) that absorbs the growing population and reduces poverty. There is no evidence that there is another more effective way to remove poverty from humanity.

If you look back in human history, there has only been poverty. Humanity has maintained the same levels of poverty almost unchanged in the last 10,000 years; It has only been decreasing since the year 1700 where only one phenomenon explains this reduction: the appearance of Freedom; economic freedom.

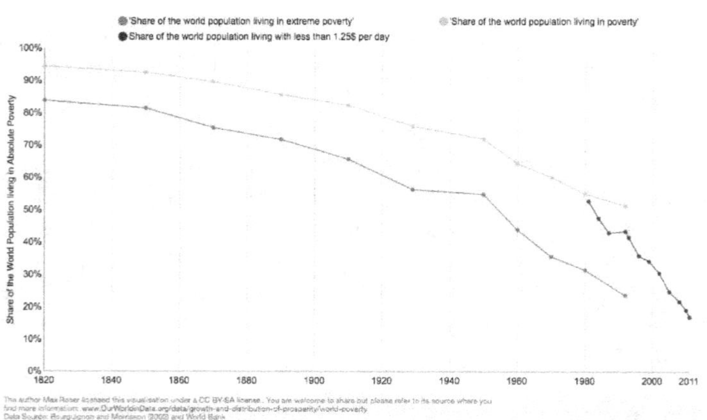</p>

A strong chapter begins in terms of results in terms of value and wealth creation, and poverty reduction:

All poverty indicators have fallen since freedom arrived in history.

Poverty has been reduced from 98% of the population in the year 1700 to less than 10% as of 2020 according to the World Bank.

Extreme poverty, defined as the situation of those living on less than USD 1.90 a day, has fallen from 88% in 1700 to today, probably affecting between 9.1% and 9.4% of the population. world in 2020, according to the Poverty and Shared work Prosperity Report.

What does the comparison of free societies versus more egalitarian societies show us?

The consequence of this analysis is supported by the fact that the countries with the greatest freedom are those that have given the greatest fight to poverty; In them, their poor have between 10 and 15 times more income than the 98% of the population restricted in freedom. The above also demonstrates that the social function of private property is more powerful than the social function of state or collective property.

And in general, where there is more economic freedom, there is more of any other freedom.

CONCLUSIONS: EFFECTS OF FREEDOM

The most notable conclusion is that liberalism must be allowed to produce value and wealth, which it has proven to do very well. It has no aspirations to decree equality or happiness unless it is material happiness.

Its results are very simple: reduce poverty; as well as the means it uses (without coercion): letting it happen, letting it happen. It does not promise happiness or the achievement of ideals by decree. It is demanding in that it tells you that everything depends on you, that you save, that you reinvest, that you be productive. Nothing comes without effort, our grandparents told us, tradition also says.

Progress in freedom generates inequalities as humanity is unequal; eventual damage to the environment, depending on the work and the pressure on the natural resources of a system that has no maximum arrival point. All human problems as human is human action. Inevitably, sooner or later we will arrive at a solution without messianic saviors.

We do not want to cover with prudery or with a false morality what we consider to be correct in human actions: the human being, when left free, seeks his own interest, seeks his benefit and that of his loved ones, trying to fulfill his dreams; Other people collaborate with that idea, with that dream and receive a fair payment to the extent of their contribution. This apparently selfish attitude in the eyes of some indirectly helps society through the wealth created, the utility generated, the social service that the private property of that company provides to consumers, the best use of resources by giving a good product to the best price, in the generation of work for people who can only offer their vital force, taxes to the state, etc. This book is not about exaggerated consumerism, placing an upper limit of arrival to the system, nor about the need to change the measures so that this is not the inaccurate indicator of economic growth.

THIRD PART

THE ORIGIN OF THE DISCOMFORT: CORRUPTION AND THE CULTURE OF EXCLUSION IN LATIN AMERICA

This third part is about Latin America and the reasons for its poverty: it started from a feudal scenario (very similar to that of North America and Europe, however, the results were different). Surely there is no single answer; In this writing we hope to shed light from a cultural point of view. We will base ourselves on the history that occurred in those places, trying to isolate events that differentiate the extensive order that occurred in each case. We will extract situations, stories that reflect the uses and customs of the time in question (first unit of this part), anticipating that they will be copied by future generations, which will give that color to today's culture (second unit) that On the one hand, it allows them to differentiate, discover, and achieve success; on the other hand, it allows or does not allow open trade between the population, which must be the result of the extensive order (third unit).

How do the exclusion and corruption that arise in unrest in Latin America take hold?

What sectors develop with the advent of freedom?

Does private property monopolized by the Spanish and white Creoles have anything to do with progress?

1

EUROPEAN FEUDALISM TRANSFERRED TO LATIN AMERICA IN ITS USES, CUSTOMS AND LEGAL ISSUES AROUND PROPERTY (28)

Unrest, as a synonym for exclusion, has always existed, it was just that it was instrumentalized (against right-wing government) in Latin American politics after the fall of the Berlin Wall.

In Latin America we are an amalgamation of various races and cultures.

Why does corruption in Latin America have the same connotations from Mexico to Patagonia? Why do we deny our color? Where does this amalgam of careerism, bribes and the good life come from? Why don't we value hard work (34)? Do the culture and way of life trap us in underdevelopment?

We are going to use story telling as a methodology to answer these questions; This requires that the reader has read in the first part, the sixth unit with the title: THE FAMILY, THE INSTITUTIONS AND THE RULES ARE RESPONSIBLE FOR ORDER WITHIN THE FREE MARKET. WOULD THIS EXPLAIN WHY THEY ARE UNDER ATTACK? and understand these issues related to non-instinctive moral codes that end in uses and customs; moving on to the creation of private property in the extensive order. This is what happened in North America and

Europe, then we must identify its difference with Latin America. The methodology is simple, we are going to stage situations taken from the feudal era and transferred from Europe to the new world and then explain and contextualize the concepts that concern us. This will be on the first unit.

This third part is about the cultural causes of poverty, exclusion, and corruption in Latin America. The reader will determine the reasons why the extensive order was not given as it was in other parts of the study, that is, identify what there was originally that prevented private property from remaining in the hands of a large part of the population, identify how Exclusion combined with corruption did not allow trade to be extended to the majority.

The reader will see the effects of the colonial administration system imposed by the Crown on the uses and customs that converge towards the extensive order. The aspects that the colonial administration system blocked and therefore will not occur are: order (in the sense of the absence of the rule of law), extensive order (which is trade, since the majority does not achieve private property), the freedom to negotiate; Corruption prevails (since business occurs between whites and around the State) and economic inclusion to this day (since this was a primary aspect of the feudal order in which only white nobles owned property).

The reader, using his or her knowledge of the uses and customs, should be able to relate the little entrepreneurship we have with the environments of exclusion; It is explained in that this is an imitated behavior (or attitude), which for obvious reasons occurs very rarely.

So far, we have achieved clarity of the unprecedented characteristics of how Freedom is installed in North America, that is, with land ownership, economic inclusion, and weapons to defend Freedom. Here lies the fundamental difference with Latin America: where colonialism (feudalism) is strengthened and ends with convulsive wars of independence that do not bring about the deconcentration of land ownership, they drag an economically exclusive culture - with a racial component - and a different conception of the progress of each racial group and the mixture that is formed.

The extensive order that occurred in North America, after property was acquired under the rule of law, has allowed it to grow uninterruptedly for more than 250 years.

THE ORIGIN OF CORRUPTION AND EXCLUSION IN LATIN AMERICA

DEFINITION OF CULTURE:

The first thing we must do is agree on the definition of culture. We understand it as the way of life of a social group, whose most important glue is "race" and is expressed in terms that make them distinctive of that social group, such as customs, music, knowledge, laws, morals, beliefs. , art, habits, skills, ways of loving, relating, codes of conduct, norms, religious beliefs, the sense in which success is seen, values, traditions, etc.

Culture will determine your behavior and the way you interact with the environment; that said, it is also a determinant of your economic success.

WHERE OUR CULTURE COMES FROM

Culture is learned (imitated) through tradition, uses and customs. We are going to move to the colonial past and extract situations to stage events that leave their mark on our current behaviors, marking a historical process where progress only occurred in certain sectors.

SCENE 1: IT WAS THE TIME OF THE COLONY.

The situation of the indigenous people

The memories of the conquest had already been erased from the memory of the aborigines (original community owners of the land), more than twenty (20) years had passed since that genocidal war and their memories only came in the form of those immense tanks (29) with a head and four legs that neighed and carried a human figure that shone like dull metal, killing in the distance with a deafening sound. Now was the time of oppression, of forced labor, of the denial of the human person. The times of facing them without any opportunity had passed. Now was the time of servitude and slavery in the manner exercised by civilized nations; It was the time of the mita and the encomienda (30); In exchange, forgiveness of life was received with the salvation of the soul.

The situation of the Kings of Spain

It was necessary for the Spanish nobility to transfer an entire infrastructure and form of government of land ownership to the newly discovered new territories; that was the feudal system (31).
The first act of copying the system of government was to give nobility to those rootless and adventurous people who came from the safety of Spain to conquer new territories in the name of the Catholic kings. The second act, after making them close to the nobility, was to give them possessions to manage in the new world. Now that it was legal, the immense wealth of the new territories could be exploited. The laws were clear, only

nobles and gentlemen would inherit, so the spoils of war were safe.

NOW LET'S GO WITH THE QUASI-HISTORICAL STORY OF THOSE WHO HOLD ECONOMIC AND POLITICAL POWER BY TRANSFER OF THE CROWN OF SPAIN.

Let's go back to colonial times. We are in the bosom of a noble family by royal cession and pure Spanish blood (descendants of Spaniards, who had come in search of land and power that they had not achieved in the peninsula due to their situation as servants of the crown).

SCENE 2: THE COLONY. HOW BUSINESS WAS DONE.

We delve into the conversation between a merchant and an encomendero.

"I don't know what we're going to do," said a gentleman encomendero to his brother in a meeting with a merchant. The encomendero had titles of nobility from the crown and that allowed him to do business and own property in the name of the crown. The merchant did not have the blessing, for his trade, of the Spanish crown.

- Many of these mestizos (32) say that they are not Indians (33) and demand their freedom, they say that they are mestizos, that for this reason they should not be in the mita or in the encomienda. Who is going to take those impure jobs in the fields and in the mines? - the encomendero asked.

-Don't worry, we will buy black slaves. -the brother clarified. Clarification of the previous text: The hard work, the field work, was carried out by servants; The nobility was only dedicated to war and social events.

If the merchant wanted to remain in the business, he had to offer participation, that is, a percentage to the encomendero, in order to allow him to continue his venture and grow his business.

-I come to offer you 40% of this trading business and we will be able to grow it if we take it and sell it on the plain to your great friend De Las Casas who has permission from the Crown to sell it in the central market. I will take care of this impure, but lucrative work, so that your majesties do not get dirty (30). –The merchant questioned to close the business by linking the encomendero.

We follow the Methodology of reviewing medieval behaviors and customs to define the cultural aspects that impact our degree of development today.

The owners of all the means of production (the land in feudalism; the colony in South America) were the white Spaniards who had received nobility and property. These property relations have been inherited in the last 300 years (with gaps, restitutions and return to concentration). They can only be broken when freedom in commerce and the market is opened, creating new sources of wealth in sectors other than those that come from the land and it is the moment when mestizos, Indians and blacks were able to access property; in the ¨free market¨.

COMPARATIVE SCHEME OF INDIGENOUS ADMINISTRATION AND GOVERNMENT (YEAR 1400), SPANISH CROWN (YEAR 1492), COLONY (YEAR 1830) AND CURRENT EVENTS

Next, we are going to analyze certain concepts (economic system, freedom, work and equality before the law, races, political power, and ownership of the means of production) in which we will see again how the concepts are combined in Latin America. of class equality, equality before the law, freedom, access to private property for comparative purposes in history going forward in this same writing and for comparison transversally with what has been studied in parts I and II of this book regarding the revolutions of Europe and North America. The melting pot of races: white (owner), mestizo, indigenous and black (majority and economically excluded) marks in Latin America the most important characteristic in the advent of "Freedom" that the liberating deeds should carry. Freedom had unleashed progress in the societies studied so far; This did not happen with any of the Latin American races; Or rather, progress was racially selective given that the determining factor that differentiated them was access to private property.

The reader must observe that the unprecedented advent of Freedom in Latin America does not unleash talents or creativity in the production of value and wealth as was seen in Europe and North America, -if there is generation of any value or wealth it is around those who already held economic power -; with some exceptions: they were all white Creoles because it was never accompanied by access to private property for different races; In the same way, they were restricted by exclusion and by the rigging of only being able to do business around white power.

CONCEPT TO BE ANALYZED: ECONOMIC SYSTEM

Explanation of the first example: The economic system for the indigenous population in 1400 (before the discovery) will be contrasted with that of the Spanish peninsula in full discovery (1492), in the South American countries subject to colonization between the discovery and independence (1492-1830) and that of the American countries today.

Indigenous population (1400s)
Primitive Socialism

The Spanish peninsula (1492)
Feudalism: Noble: he owned everything. Servant: had no possessions; This begins to change with capitalism.

South American Countries (Spanish and Portuguese colony, years 1492-1830)
They moved the feudal system to the New World. They created a parallel, giving political power, possessions and nobility to the white Spanish adventurers and prisoners who made the conquest. In exchange for submission to the Metropolis.

Current American countries (2000s onwards…)
Free market (Capitalist)

CONCEPT TO ANALYZE: CONCEPT OF FREEDOM

Indigenous Population (1400s)
Tribal, slavery ties existed.

The Spanish peninsula (1492)
Noble: he was free and could do anything. The Servant: was tied to the land, belonged to the region and of the same race. He was subject to the Mita and the Encomienda. Black slave: he had no right to his life .

South American Countries (Spanish and Portuguese colony, years 1492-1830)
Creole or white Spanish: Free. Indigenous: With a 1/4 soul at the beginning, he was subjected to a "Light Slavery System" Mita and Encomienda where he had to give his work and possessions to the mitayo or encomendero. Black Slave: ¨soulless¨. It belonged to his life to the white Spanish.

Current American countries (2000s onwards…)
Free. Freedom before the law of all races.

CONCEPT TO BE ANALYZED: WORK AND EQUALITY BEFORE THE LAW

Indigenous Population (1400s)
Tied to mother earth and in harmony with nature: hunting, fishing, gathering and incipient agriculture and livestock. Preeminence of the chief and his family.

The Spanish peninsula (1492)
Noble: leisure, parties, politics, arts, painting, dedicated to war and defense. They considered hard work impure. The Servant: Agriculture, livestock. Only serfs and slaves worked. There is no class equality.

South American Countries (Spanish and Portuguese colony, years 1492-1830)
Creole or white Spanish: leisure, parties, politics, administration of Crown property. Indigenous: semi-slave work in agriculture, livestock, mining, the difference is that your soul had to be saved with religion. Black Slave: Slave work in agriculture, livestock, mining. without soul. There is no class equality. With independence there is no access to the land, it continues to be centralized in the white Creoles.

Current American countries (2000s onwards…)

Exchange of work for money. The greater the contribution, the greater the pay. Instituted class equality and equality before the law.

CONCEPT TO ANALYZE: RACES

Indigenous Population (1400s)
Same race. Social divisions: Chief and common Indian.

The Spanish peninsula (1492)
Same race. Social divisions: Noble: superior race blessed by God, blue blood. The Servant: commoner.

South American Countries (Spanish and Portuguese colony, years 1492-1830)
Different races: Creole or white Spanish: superior race blessed by the Crown with titles of nobility to be able to access political positions and administration of possessions. Indigenous, mestizos and blacks: excluded from access to property.

Current American countries (2000s onwards…)
Equality before the law and equality of races. Promotion is supposed to be by Merits.

CONCEPT TO BE ANALYZED: POLITICAL POWER

Indigenous Population (1400s)
Main authority chief, succeeds matrilineally in the majority of cases

The Spanish peninsula (1492)
You can only access a political position if you belong to the nobility or buy a noble title or earn it for important feats or achievements towards royalty.

South American Countries (Spanish and Portuguese colony, years 1492-1830)
You can only hold political office if you are white Creole or Spanish. Otherwise, you must be in collusion with the "privileged circle" to have preeminence .

Current American countries (2000s onwards...)
Democracy: elections. The feudal scheme in terms of corruption was moved today; power does not come from a "privileged circle"

CONCEPT TO BE ANALYZED: OWNERSHIP OF THE MEANS OF PRODUCTION

Indigenous Population (1400s)
Community property. Community socialism.

The Spanish peninsula (1492)
The King, the Nobility: they were the owners of all possessions. Feudalism begins: wealth only came from the land. End of feudalism and beginning of capitalism (new owners): the property owner, merchant, potter, etc. was frowned upon. Those who achieved economic power gained access to titles of nobility and nobility and could only maintain their economic activity if they maintained close contact with the nobility.

South American Countries (Spanish and Portuguese colony, years 1492-1830)
The Spanish crown held the property on behalf of the Creoles or white Spaniards: they were the owners of all the possessions. Home colony: wealth only came from the land. End of colonialism and beginning of capitalism (new owners): mestizos with businesses could become as rich or richer than

the Spaniards, however, they could only integrate into the economic fabric if they maintained close contact with the whites or Creoles who maintained political power. .

Current American countries (2000s onwards...)
Free enterprise: If you have a business idea, you can be as rich as your work and persistence give you. The feudal scheme in terms of corruption was carried over to the present day; Businesses are around the "privileged circle" and protected by laws of political power.

COMPARATIVE SCHEME OF INDIGENOUS ADMINISTRATION AND GOVERNMENT (YEAR 1400), SPANISH CROWN (YEAR 1492), COLONY (YEAR 1830) AND CURRENT EVENTS

	Indigenous (1400)	The Spanish peninsula (1492)	South American countries (Colony 1492-1830)	Current American countries (2000s onwards...)
Economic system	Primitive Socialism	**FEUDALISM. Noble:** he owned everything. **Servant:** had no possessions; This begins to change with Capitalism.	**They moved the Feudal System to the New World.** They created a parallel **by giving political power, possessions and nobility to the Servants, adventurers, white Spanish prisoners** who made the conquest. In exchange for submission to the Metropolis.	Capitalist
Freedom	Tribal	**Noble:** he was free and could do anything. **The Servant:** was tied to the land, belonged to the region and of the same race. He was subject to the Mita and the Encomienda. **Slave:** he did not even have the right to his life.	**Creole or White Spanish:** Free. **Indigenous:** With a 1/4 soul at the beginning, he was subjected to a " Light Slavery System" Mita and Encomienda where he had to give his work and possessions to the Mitayo O encomendero. **Black Slave: without soul** . His life belonged to the Spanish.	Free

Work and Equality before the Law	**Tied to Mother Earth and in Harmony with Nature:** hunting, fishing, gathering and incipient agriculture and livestock.	**Noble:** leisure, parties, politics, arts, painting, **WAR AND DEFENSE.** They considered **HARD WORK IMPURE. The Servant:** Agriculture, livestock. **ONLY SERVANTS AND SLAVES WORKED. There is no Class Equality.**	**Creole or White Spanish:** leisure, parties, politics, administration of Crown assets. **Indigenous:** SEMI-SLAVE work in agriculture, livestock, mining, the difference is that you had to save your "Soul with Religion." **Black Slave:** SLAVE work in agriculture, livestock, mining. **WITHOUT SOUL There is no Class Equality.**	Exchange of work for money. The greater the contribution, the greater the pay. Class Equality and Equality before the Law established.
Breeds	Same race. Social divisions: Chief and common Indian	Same race. Social divisions: **Noble: Superior Race blessed by God, Blue Blood. The Servant: Plebe.**	**Different races: Creole or White Spanish: Superior Race blessed by the Crown with Titles of Nobility** to be able to access political positions and administration of possessions. Indigenous, mestizos and blacks: excluded from access to property.	Equality before the Law and equality of races. Promotion is supposed to be by Merits.
Political power	Main authority chief, succeeds matrilineally in the majority of cases	**You can only access a Political Position if you belong to the NOBILITY** or buy a Nobility Title or earn it for important feats or achievements towards Royalty.	**You can only hold political office if you are Creole or White Spanish** . Otherwise you must be in **collusion with the "Privileged Circle"** to have pre-eminence.	Democracy. Elections . The FEUDAL scheme in terms of CORRUPTION was moved to the present day; **Power DOES NOT come from a "Privileged Circle"**

Ownership of the Means of Production	Community Property. Community Socialism.	**The King the Nobility:** they were the owners of all the possessions. **Home Feudalism:** wealth only came from the land. **End of Feudalism and beginning of Capitalism:** The property owner, merchant, potter, etc. was frowned upon. Those who achieved economic power gained access to Titles of Nobility and Nobility and could only maintain their economic exercise if they maintained close contact with the Nobility.	**Creole or White Spanish**: he was the owner of all the possessions. **Home Colony:** wealth only came from the land. **End Colonialism and beginning Capitalism: The mestizos with COMPANY could become as rich or richer than the Spaniards** , however, they could only integrate into the economic fabric if **they maintained close contact with the Whites or Criollos who maintained political Power.**	FREE ENTERPRISE. If you have a **BUSINESS IDEA** , you can be as rich as your work and Persistence gives you. The FEUDAL scheme in terms of **CORRUPTION was moved** to the present day ; **Businesses are around and** protected by **Laws of political power. ¨Privileged Circle¨**

What can we extract and learn from this comparative administration scheme?

Property relations were limited by race. Mestizos with businesses could eventually become as rich or richer than white Spaniards, however, they could only integrate into the economic fabric if they maintained close contact with the whites or Creoles who monopolized political power.

The reader remembers that the origin of birth was very important, being a white Spanish peninsular was not the same as being a white Creole.

The unhealthy habit of doing business around political power was inherited, so that good businesses are: building infrastructure, building schools, providing services that the state should normally provide, that is: negotiating with the state. These businesses do not require innovation, competition, cost reduction, novel ways of negotiating; They only need fixing, paying bribes, careerism, and corruption.

Exchange relationships (trade) depend on the relationships you have with those already established and with those who manage political power, there is no free enterprise.

If you do not belong to the "closed circle", these will reduce your chances of doing business; You must have the endorsement of the "gentlemen".

Hard work is considered impure.

Entrepreneurial jobs were frowned upon by society.

Nothing was based on merit. Success depended on making friends with access to power and having the degrading cunning to create businesses that would allow him to take advantage of careerism.

Does this have any resemblance to the current reality in some Latin American countries?
Have we dragged the worst of colonial feudalism into our times? Are these customs part of our culture today?

After the colony ended with the advent of independence and republican life, the titles and a large part of the properties were swept into the hands of whites, no longer so noble and noble, however, in the collective unconscious they continue to be revered. both to the whiteness of their color and to the possessions and economic power they still hold. Many have migrated from land-based economic power to agro-industrial businesses that have allowed them to increase their money. Free enterprise was the key so that those who were not nobles could have money, the dynamics of doing business opened new sectors such as commerce, services, technology, internet, etc. However, we carry the worst feudal vices of doing business around us and only with the help of political power. Society views very well those who use tricks and cunning to grease the hands of politicians to take over businesses around the state. These are the only "entrepreneurs" who are well regarded; These are the same ones who make our roads, schools, infrastructure, etc. in a mediocre way.

The following are graphically the results of the transfer of this corrupt scheme of negotiating with the state (contractor-government) in the example of the construction of a school:

CONTRACTORS AND THEIR BUSINESSES IN THE COLONY'S DRAGGED FEUDAL SCHEME

CURRENT CORRUPTION SCHEME DROUGHT FROM THE COLONY							
CONTRACTOR-GOVERNMENT							
SCHOOL CONSTRUCTION							
BRICKS	COST OVERRUNS	BELLAQUERIA	WARNED	ILLICIT PROFIT	THEY STEAL RESOURCES	SELFISHNESS	COST OVERRUNS

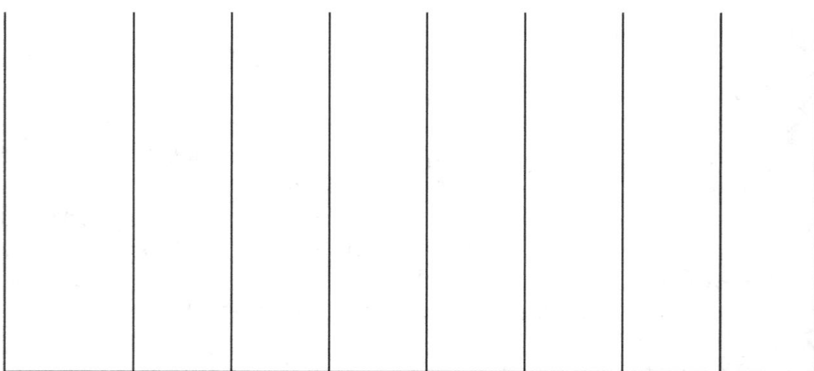

The types of businesses expected from this corrupt pseudo-feudal scheme are:

-Photo fines and the entire scheme of traps around it, which do not seek compliance with the law, but rather to fleece the taxpayer.
-Tax collection.
-Poor health services.
-Public hospitals.
-Poor- and poor-quality infrastructure construction.
-Pension and health schemes, where private savings that originate in parafiscal funds go to the companies that administer the system - in the case of pensions, health, they deny or delay services - where their owners are friends of the legislators.
-And all of us who have to suffer since they have a rigged law so that in a tax manner, we are obliged to give them our money.

CONCLUSIONS

We drag the worst of the political-economic system of the feudal era and transform it into socially acceptable corruption.

It has an even worse aggravating factor: it frowns upon hard work, entrepreneurship, and private initiative.

The issue of corruption, understood as the rigged way of doing business around power, drags on as one of the worst characteristics of the feudal era that today is part of the way of life, the way of doing politics; It is therefore cultural; It is also transversal to Latin America, affecting any type of government that is installed (regardless of its origin). The power for power's sake (without control) to which some new political currents aspire will only multiply this effect. We are reliving what we experienced in the seventies, but with a different political nuance.

In general, the advent of freedom brings with it the release of the innate creative forces in the human being; with them the creation of value and wealth, the reduction of poverty. However, we can infer from the regions analyzed that this creation of well-being occurs with different intensity depending on the racial ingredient, the type of freedom that society has in each part of the world that we are considering: it is clear that in North America the Black slaves did not develop that potential and its results are seen until today when they are just beginning to reach the income levels of whites. In white Europe (Anglo-Saxon, Frankish, German), with the end of feudalism, class equality and freedom, impressive levels of income and well-being (less inequality in prosperity) were achieved. Finally, in the case of Latin America where, due to its special connotations, European feudalism was transferred as a colonial administration system, a segregation was imposed, an exclusion to the dominated races that transcends their uses, customs, legal issues around the property (24) until today. The impact continues to this day where the concentration of private property is still racially and socially segregated, leaving large sectors of mestizos, indigenous people and blacks excluded from development. The ways, uses and custom of doing business around the Spanish and white Creole race (the only one allowed to do so) impacted the effect that free enterprise should generate on income, on the reduction of poverty of all races that were under its effect. There was no free market, nor the creation of private property, nor extensive order, nor the rule of law (order); It only happened for whites.

In fact, it has taken several generations for the mixed classes to own their homes today.

Exclusion is not only reflected in material conditions such as access to credit and financing but is also reflected in the business customs that are imitated. The baggage, knowledge, and attitude necessary to undertake are taken by society in the process of learning and imitation which is impossible when the general feeling is to exclude certain sectors. The excluded classes have no mirror from which to copy patterns, much less norms beneficial for their well-being and progress. We are going to try to explain the concept with a popular saying that has great meaning, although not literally, in our environment: son of a tiger comes out painted. To bring it closer to the context we want, it must be removed from the genetic issue, since culture, norms, as well as language are learned by imitation or common uses. The most accurate term would be in this context: the son of a tiger learns to paint himself if he sees his father or his peers doing it.

Aspects around culture and ways of life are necessary to establish the differences that have allowed some to be successful and others not. At the end of this book we are going to formulate our proposal on how to promote development - in the companies of ordinary people - for which we must take into account this aspect of how it should be woven into our cultural environment, however, I am sincere, we are still orphans of ideas on the matter.

2

TODAY THE CULTURE OF EXCLUSION IS A WAY OF LIFE

Culture, as a form and way of life, is a key determinant in the way you conceive progress and success.

We are going to review some of the effects on behaviors and customs that carry over to the current era as cultural traits that do not help entrepreneurship or the creation of value and wealth. For this purpose, we will extract current situations, of which we have taken note, because they reflect learned behavior (modes and customs). We will continue with the narrative methodology, but this time with real events that occurred today.

In the end we will try to understand how the discomfort influenced the desire of each person (which arises from individual freedom) to carry out their life project through the process of creating value and wealth.

FIRST CASE:

It was a poor neighborhood where a talk had been given on entrepreneurship (starting a business) and what could be obtained through risk; There were several people willing to undertake it, they wanted to do it. One of them started selling products. He had barely started when his neighbors made him the recipient of ridicule, jokes, and jokes. When I asked him how he felt, he told me that he didn't feel sorry... I understood that they had given him social punishment, however, he resisted because according to the information received by us, they; the others obeyed their ignorance.

Finally, he gave up his attempt to continue selling.

SECOND CASE:

This other case arose from a conversation in which, after a girl requested help to study, it was explained to her that I had financed my studies by selling clothes; The girl was convinced. I trained her on how to buy, how to sell on credit, who to sell to, and who not to sell to.

After a while, and seeing that I didn't see the girl doing this task, I asked her mother:

-And tell me how your daughter has been doing, she is selling clothes. TRUE?

The response was overwhelming. - Never. We will remain poor, and we may die of hunger, but with dignity.

THIRD CASE:

This is a question that I have asked many times, to try to see how many times I receive the same answer and this one has been repetitive:

-And your son is going to be a businessman or businessman? The answer. - No, he is studying to work in an important company.

FOURTH CASE:

On a visit to Colombia by two London friends, one white Anglo-Saxon and the other black African British, one of them asked me, while we were on a mass transportation bus (Transmilenio).

- Why were there almost no white people in Bogotá, had they only seen one or two? quite inappropriate question about the place and because several understood English; They realized that they were not seen as white. So, what race did they think they were? I received grim looks when I explained on the bus that we were a mix, that the people from the capital were a clearer mix because they were indigenous people who didn't sunbathe as much as they did on the coast (it was very interesting the expression on people's faces when they discovered that they weren't seen as white).

Summary of current cases

These four cases summarize the effect of ideas repeated over time (such as exclusion) -over and over again-; As they become part of the collective imagination, becoming determinants within the values of the culture, they outline your attitude towards how you consider paths or jobs as part of your development of your well-being.

HOW DISCOMFORT (EXCLUSION) AFFECTS PROGRESS

We have summarized in the first book: THE RISE OF THE LEFT IN LATIN AMERICA IN THE FULL ERA OF UNREST the six major themes that have transformed the unrest today, which, added to the exclusion, to the denial of access to private property, contributed to our poor performance in value and wealth creation; in the banishment of Latin American customary poverty.

In Latin America the majority has been racially excluded: The indigenous people seek to return to primitive socialism, the mestizo triethnicity seeks to develop in the extensive order where exclusion does not allow them; On the other hand, the upper sector has developed a sector that occupies 30% of the population while the other 65% seeks equal opportunities that allow them access to private property.

The steps in history followed by Latin America on its path to progress have been the following:

Before 1492 we lived in tribal conditions of primitive socialism.

From 1492 to 1830, where the feudal system of servitude towards whites in Europe was transferred, it became a scheme of servitude towards indigenous people, mestizos, and blacks in the New World.

1776 independence of the United States. There had previously been a process of access to private property that broke with feudalism in which only nobles could have private property. an inclusive economy is developed with access to credit.

In 1789 in Europe, the breakdown - with the French Revolution - of the feudal system of servitude was consolidated, the class division ended, and equality before the law was achieved. These facts have no effect in Latin America where the exclusion and lack of access to property present in the feudal administration system continues.

In 1830, the independence processes took place in Latin America, not comparable to the French Revolution, because despite equality resting on the law, it was not the same with culture, it did not bring private property for the majority of the population (only the white Creoles and Spaniards continued with private ownership of the land); The system of exclusion inherited from the colony towards indigenous people, mestizos and blacks continued.

From 1830 until today, the uses and customs of exclusion that come from the feudal system have been consolidated in five aspects that have constituted unrest and that have prevented access to private (liberating) property for large sectors of the population and have circumscribed businesses and companies to a small elite around political power:

- The elite has mutated corruption into something legal. The collusion of corruption with the laws favors cronyism in the formation of companies and businesses around rights converted into merchandise that became an inverted funnel to transfer money from the poorest to the richest parts of society.

- The elite that has created exclusive public and private institutions.

- The elite has turned rights into merchandise.

- The elite have organized their own friends with companies and businesses around them.

- The elite has instituted extractive legal policies that allow large companies to steal small amounts of money from each user, configuring the largest (exploitation) transfer of money (drop by drop) from poor classes to rich classes.

Finally, recommendations given by the IMF based on free enterprise were established with the intention that the well-being generated should be sufficient to lift a large part of the population out of poverty; however, it has been directed, for reasons of exclusion, only towards the (large) companies of the wealthy upper classes (with property), forgetting the companies (SMEs, family businesses) of ordinary people (without property).

- The IMF policy that only benefits large companies, leaving a large part of the population (micro, family businesses and SMEs) waiting for the trickle.

The indirect strategy seen from culture and from discomfort.

The above explains why in Latin America a strategy that stokes unrest by instigating passions - resentment, rage, fear, or hatred - and instrumentalizing them into violence towards the system is successful. After exacerbating feelings, heating up tempers, they propose a short tranquility to these two passions (the tranquility of the welfare state and collectivization) to finally install a failed model.

They continue to keep this strategy functional over time, to the extent that they maintain in that interest group - which could be large excluded sectors - (adding those who do not want to or do not achieve it) the permanent belligerence that hatred achieves; at the same time that the subsidies take effect.

A counter strategy that doesn't start

On the other hand, the counterpart claims that everything can continue the same (that there is change but that nothing changes); It only deploys a counter strategy from rationality and with it attempts to confront this – it is simply not going to work: first because the excluded have been in that situation for more than two hundred years; They are not going to compromise for something other than inclusion and equal opportunities. Second, because passion is met with passion; For this reason, it must be from passion that something designed to last if the discomfort remains can be counteracted - in this field the counterpart is at a clear disadvantage; rationality is weak.

Not all the problem ends there. Let's assume that a passionate counterstrategy is achieved that restores the lost inclusion (equal opportunities with inclusion and that each person makes their life project going as far as their desires and merits can); An additional problem arises generated by the success of the first: we do not know how to maintain current passion other than based on hatred and resentment. The challenge is huge because each person will be called to be responsible for themselves as well as their progress, however, this is very demanding in terms of enthusiasm to withstand failures and maintain it over time.

A future that does not wait

We must turn on ourselves to determine how we see success: surely the indigenous people, due to their conception of the world, of life and their interrelation with nature, will want to return to the type of civilization based on communal plots (primitive socialism) in which they lived before the colony, but i am sure that is not the case for the majority mestizos assimilated by Western civilization, they surely expect equality of opportunities (we make a distinction that it is not a request for permanent equality, since this is not possible without destroying equality before the law, basis of freedom) to improve their income and well-being. We must necessarily think about those who try and try but fail; what is going to be done with the same people who are putting society in check today.

Free enterprise and entrepreneurship are the bastions for most families that begin their economic career with a delay of generations due to the previous scheme that did not allow them to own property; Today you can access property with a lot of effort, however, the gap is large. Many companies run by ordinary people find themselves in this situation, accounting for 65% to 70% of employment.

In the fifth part of this book, we will return to the response of people - ordinary people - who, despite the adverse circumstances of a cultural type, of exclusion (racial, economic, and political) do not allow themselves to be overwhelmed, who respond bravely in the form of ventures; Those are your spontaneous bets on the creation of value and wealth. Our proposal, that of this book, will be in terms of solutions that counteract economic exclusion, the precarious access to a health and social protection system, expose the number of regulations and taxes that suffocate the family business, the regulations in the aspect of hiring, manpower, etc.

3

FREEDOM. THE WELL-BEING ENGINE DID NOT IMPACT THE MAJORITY IN LATIN AMERICA

Freedom is the source and a necessary condition of economic progress. What a collectivized society offers the individual is much less than what he could achieve if he enjoyed economic freedom.

The academic trenches of the free market in Latin America have not found a courageous defender who does not feel embarrassed by the collaterals left by the creation of wealth in free enterprise: possible impact on the environment, inequality, concentration of wealth, etc.
The defense has not been easy, since a model captured by a corrupt elite for their own benefit would be defended and academics and intellectuals would be defending that elite.

Every time a revolution occurs, a change in private property is being proposed.

In this unit we are going to see the good or bad results in terms of development, and about poverty.

The cultural and economic outline that we have explained has created two Latin Americas: a white one with private ownership of the means of production where the arrival of capitalism unleashed all the talent and creative business potential (wealth creation was separated from the land) generated broad growth in productivity. Very close to this thriving business class, another consanguineous class was created: the corrupt class with businesses around the state. This is what is reflected in the GDPs of the countries and represents from 55% to 70% of the economy, but only 20 to 30% of employment. Corruption converted into exclusion does not benefit the free market but rather those already established (the large company). The other Latin America, the mestizo, the black, the propertyless, the culturally excluded; to which freedom, apparently, did not bring greater change in well-being, has not been left, it has used the new freedom to incubate new businesses. Their businesses represent 70% of employment, they are the companies of ordinary people (rummage, family businesses and microenterprises). Despite their great contribution as a solution to employment, only in the best of cases do they amount to 10% of the economy. The vast majority are achieving it, however, there is a part of this economy in which unrest has settled.

CURRENT RESULTS OF ECONOMIC POLICIES IN TERMS OF POVERTY

ECLAC projects that at the end of 2022 poverty will reach 32.1% of the population (a percentage equivalent to 201 million people) and extreme poverty at 13.1% (82 million).

In 2021, income inequality (measured by the Gini index) decreased slightly compared to 2020 in Latin America, standing at 0.458, at levels like those of 2019. Taken from the ECLAC Social Panorama 2022 report.

INCOME DISTRIBUTION IN LATIN AMERICA: EXAMPLE COLOMBIA.

Let's take the example of Colombia, which can be extended to all Latin American countries to look at the behavior of income. Now these measures by themselves say nothing if they are not related to the purchasing power of the salary in each country (family basket and basic services, including health and education).

COLOMBIA GROSS DOMESTIC PRODUCT YEAR 2020 (270,415 BILLION DOLLARS).

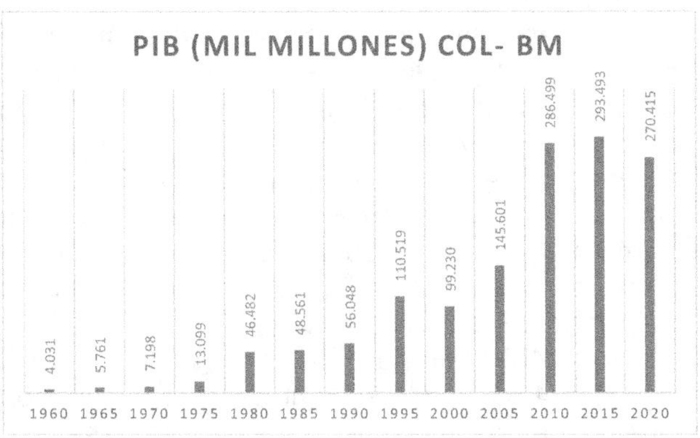

GDP per capita Colombia 2020 US 5,368.
GDP per capita Colombia monthly 2020 US $447.

The analysis of GDP and GDP per capita does not provide useful information about income distribution and additionally hides poverty and inequality.

THE OTHER COLOMBIA

For the year 2020, the representative rate of the average market ended with a figure of $3,693.36.

Minimum salary 2020 in Colombian pesos $877,803 monthly. Minimum salary 2020 in dollars US$237 per month.

Gini coefficient Colombia 0.508

THE REALITY OF INCOME: ECONOMICALLY ACTIVE POPULATION

We are going to find who are the ones who really work: In Colombia if we place the population at 46 million (the population shows an increase in the last Dane measurement to 50 million, however, the variation in the percentages is maintained and the result can be approximate the results) and we subtract the elderly and children, we end up with 35 million, which is the Economically Active Population (EAP); Additionally, we must subtract the 10 million who are not looking for work and subtract the 9.7% who are unemployed. Finally, we only have 22 million workers out of 35 of the Economically Active Population.
Of those 22 million, 14.2 million are informal (65%); only 7.8 million are formal (34%). Evidence shows that 1.7 million people earn one minimum wage and 11 million earn less than one (1) minimum wage:

We have 1.7 million households earning US237 dollars monthly.
We have 11 million households earning less than US$237 per month.

Compared to the United States, the poverty line is 10 times distant; That is to say, a country with economic freedom (we do not consider Colombia the best example of economic freedom) and access to private property, can establish differences between the "most vulnerable" groups of ten (10) times the income.

THE REALITY REGARDING THE EXTENSION OF POVERTY

Colombian population in poverty before 2010 (historical data):

41% of the population are poor: In Colombia, nearly 19 million people earn less than US$237 per month. And within this group (about ten (10) million people) is the most vulnerable who barely get less than 2 dollars a day.

Middle class is 55% of the population: In Colombia, about 25 million people earn between $690,000 pesos per month and $3,178,000 pesos.

The upper class is 3 to 4% of the population: In Colombia, about 1.8 million people earn more than $3,718,000 pesos per month.

THE S COMPANIES OF ORDINARY PEOPLE

Micros and SMEs in Colombia account for 60% to 80% of employment, that is, responsible for feeding 17.6 million people (households).

It is a reality that 50% of the working population will do so in micro-businesses and in a possibly informal environment. 30% will work in small and medium-sized companies, while only 20% will work in large companies.

Size of Colombian companies as of 2020:

Micros: more than 10 employees and assets of up to $344 million pesos.
Small: 11 to 50 employees and assets from $345 million to $3,447 million pesos.
Medium: 51 to 200 employees and assets from $3,447 million to $20,683 million pesos.
Large: Greater than 200 employees and assets of $20,683 million pesos.

In Colombia, large companies only contribute 20% of employment, but it is 55% of GDP; Micros are 50% of employment and only 6.3% of GDP. Micro, small and medium-sized businesses account for 60% to 80% of employment.

FOURTH PART

¨A GHOST WALKS LATIN AMERICA: THE GHOST OF PROGRESSISM¨

In this fourth part we are going to see the action of each norm or precept that generates progressivism from democratic power (having elected a democratic seat as president or in congress); We will see its effects in conjunction with its hidden strategy (Gramscian postmodernism) and how it affects and attacks long-term macroeconomic variables. We will review traditional progressive measures – we will cite the proposals of its exponent Joseph Stiglitz for developed economies; – in terms of predistribution and redistribution – and its actions on our economy, which, unlike the developed ones, is divided into two economies: one developed and rich (reflected in GDP) and another poor (reflected in employment). We will ask the artificial intelligence in the OpenAI GPT Chat about these concepts based on shared well-being, we will verify that it does not consider the creation of wealth; We will also confront the nationalizing policy of the World Bank (WB). In the end you will have enough illustration so that you can imagine the entire indirect strategy in action.

1

INTRODUCTION TO GRAMSCIAN POSTMODERNISM, THE HIDDEN STRATEGY OF PROGRESSISM (26)

The ruling classes tremble if you want...proletarians of all countries...unite.
Prologue by Federico Engels in the Communist Manifesto.

At the end of the first part of this book, we managed to understand how classical Marxist criticism is formulated from dialectics and how the direct attack differs - rapid and violent attack against the forces that defend the system, immediate expropriation of private property and change of the bases (ISA) of society: culture, the rule of law, the family, religion - of the indirect hidden attack (Gramscian postmodernism) that after winning the battle cultural carries out a slow, deliberate and systematic attack on the bases of society. It is filled with constant persistence, and then, when progress is made towards a democratic position, it ends with a friendly fire attack on the incentives, on the bases of value and wealth creation of the free enterprise system; the rest will fall by itself. We understood the strategy deployed from the doctrines of Antonio Gramsci strengthened by postmodernism, especially the structuralist Louis Althusser: overthrowing due obedience through access and seizure of opinion leaders, schools, and universities. Althusser reveals the advance on ISA. The new focus of the systemic attack will not be directly private property, nor through direct violence, but first the superstructure (culture, laws, religion, family, in general rule of law, the ISA, etc.); the rest will fall by itself.

HARD STRATEGY OF GRAMSCIAN POSTMODERNISM (21ST CENTURY SOCIALISM) AND SOFT STRATEGY OF GRAMSCIAN POSTMODERNISM

"True freedom requires justice" is the title of Rafael Correa in The Boston Globe.

"Being rich is bad, it is inhuman. So, I say it and I condemn the rich" Hugo Chávez.

"It wouldn't be strange if there was civilization on Mars, but perhaps capitalism arrived there, imperialism arrived and wiped out that planet." Hugo Chavez.

Every right "won" by society is an unstoppable advance of the socialist state over freedom.

In this unit we are going to see the action of each norm or precept generated by Gramscian postmodernism as a hidden strategy within progressivism and inserted from democratic power (having taken a democratic seat as president or in congress) how it affects and attacks the long-term macroeconomic variables and, what is more serious, it dilutes all incentives to create value and wealth in the free enterprise system. We will review two of its meanings (the hard and the soft), both deliberate and systematic in destroying the foundations of society to prepare it for the final blow; The reader will understand how they combine with progressivism until they become one.

What differs from the implementation of progressive proposals in Latin America from other parts of the world is that they were instigated by Fidel Castro and Lula Da Silva at the Sao Paulo Forum in 1990 with the clear intention of demonstrating that the generalized failure of socialism In the Soviet Union it was not such that this ideology could be relaunched in a foreign body and that the way it can end will not be said, however, we can intuit it since it leaves society defenseless and accessible to the harshest socialism communism; We would be facing another euphemistic strategy to impose utopia again. In Latin America, deception has been used as a political tool to gain power by offering change and anti-corruption.

*Hard Strategy **Gramscian Postmodernism** - 21st Century Socialism*

Democratic takeover and rapid implementation of socialism communism eliminating private property and deconstruction of our social, economic, legal, religious, cultural values, etc.

It occurs in a society corroded by unrest, penetrated by indoctrination, with weak institutions for the protection of Democracy, with weak legislation for the defense of private property, - perhaps due to the fragility in obtaining property at its origin. by mechanisms not adhered to the law - with a breakdown of values and the rule of law. This is the case of Venezuela where the advance on private property and freedoms was more aimed at eliminating political competition than complying with a redistributive doctrine of wealth. The results are obvious: elimination of political dissidence and the ruin of most of the business fabric, production of products and services - destruction of the wealth produced - the elimination of inequality arises due to the generalized decline in the income of the entire population; Now everyone is equal in hunger and scarcity. They irresponsibly destroyed all the knowledge of the production of basic consumption and survival elements of the population that rested in the business fabric.

Gramscian postmodernism soft strategy

Democratic seizure of power, slow but systematic deconstruction of our values and rule of law, imposition of progressive laws that attack the foundations (incentives) of our free enterprise system and that allow the creation of value and wealth; They lead inexorably to progressive pauperization and a socialist, collectivist subsistence economy. It occurs in a society with more or less solid formal and informal institutions for the defense of private property and Democracy. However, they will finally achieve their goal of progressively bringing the economy to subsistence, concentration of unimaginable powers in the state and generalized Khaos (21) where only the call for totalitarian tyranny will fit. This is the process that Argentina, Brazil, Peru, Ecuador, Colombia, Chile, Spain, and some Central American countries are in.

The case of Argentina is telling. Its process begins by maintaining a large part of private property, however, the state begins a profound redistributive process that attacks the bases and incentives of generating value and wealth - it takes away the product of their work from some, to give it to others who are not product of their labor - in the long term condemns the economy to a low and declining income. Those who take away the product of their work no longer want to produce more and whoever is given it, why produce if I receive income without effort: they destroy the morale of the producer, they corrupt the dignity and meaning of work. In these final stages of the strategy, the extremists request that the revolution be accentuated. Any of the forms or attempts to socialize or distribute - redistribute - wealth in a Liberal Democracy are unstable, in such a way that they demand more socialist and interventionist measures; They function as a preparation for hard socialism by accentuating poverty in the long term.

ATTACKS ON THE FREE ENTERPRISE ECONOMIC SYSTEM AND THE PREPARATION OF A PROGRESSIVE SYSTEM

Next, we will establish the results of the application of progressivism hand in hand with its clearest strategy for taking power, **Gramscian postmodernism** . We will see these consequences from power, from friendly fire. The reader will be able to see where the indirect strategy is taking him and will establish many similarities with situations experienced in past decades with everything instigated from Cuba.

High progressive taxes on companies.

They remove incentives to produce, driving away foreign investment.

Elimination of inheritances

It is an advance on private property. It is an advance on the freedom of being able to do what I want with my money. Eliminates the incentive to generate wealth to bequeath it to my children or family – they pursue a collectivist goal by not respecting the desire, human nature, of a person to take care of their family. It eliminates private savings, which is a greater incentive for the entire society to guarantee reinvestment and reproduction of the model of creating greater wealth. In short, nothing guarantees that the inheritance expropriated and given to someone, which is not the result of their work, will not be wasted and ended up being lost.

Persecution of capital in banks.

It discourages private savings. They consider accumulation as immoral, seeking by all means to expropriate it or, importantly, place taxes on it.

They make visible and give benefits to certain minorities.

Seeking from goodness, to break the principle of equality before the law; They generate small legal cracks that corrode public morality so that the same people subsequently allow other laws that further destroy the prevailing legislation.

They attack formal and informal institutions of society whose formation has allowed civilization, such as, for example: the concept of prison, prison codes, the family, religion, gender, patriarchy, etc.

Seeking to release the small contradictions that society has and that society itself has kept in control through these institutions. The purpose is to seek the revolutionary power that these small contradictions have in their capacity to generate disorder and Khaos.

They give political legitimacy to certain minority groups and encourage their attack on the institutions and forces in charge of safeguarding the institutions, while the legality of the actions of the constitutional forces of order is diminished.

It's part of the process; By removing political support from the constitutional forces, they attack the morale of the forces of order, forcing them to mandatory retirement, in order to bind their own cadres, dismantling the independence of the armed forces to culminate with the siege of the institutions. Simultaneously, they configure their asymmetric armed civil forces to confront what remains of independence in the forces of order and intimidate the dissident civilian population.

All education to the state.

The socialist state provides the education the state needs for its indoctrination to work; alienates and creates worshipers of the state.

Dismantling of the republican system and the beginning of the concentration of power or the creation of puppet powers.

He demonstrates his contempt for the division of powers and his attachment to tyranny by surrounding himself with people related to his ideology, groups that should serve as a counterweight to the all-embracing power of the oppressive state. They attack every dissonant appearance of the division of powers; The threat is permanent and can be with the constitutional forces of order or with their armed civilian troops or the taking to the streets of their sympathizers.

High union power.

They repeat the old strategy of classical Marxism of all forms of struggle in which the advance of socialism (in this case progressivism) on wage labor begins by infiltrating union groups, giving them more bargaining power in such a way that they unbalance the balance. that should exist between workers and shareholders in their negotiations. Trade unionists are used as a temporary destabilizing instrument by communist socialists to come to power. Subsequently, they resume the power temporarily given to the unionists; Unindoctrinated unions become enemies of the state on the way to consolidating the tyranny of the communist party (eliminating interest groups: workers, union members, businessmen and shareholders; they suppress all ways of thinking differently). Trade unionism is a capitalist development; if only if it works in capitalism; in socialism they are a thorn in the side of the communists in power. Unionism, seen in this way, is necessary for healthy and normal conditions of predistribution to occur. Contrary to what many say, union negotiations in a liberal democratic environment enrich free enterprise and Democracy itself.

New forms of collectivization: the expropriation of the Freedom to be able to do or stop doing.

Ultimately the difference between the pure idealist and the pragmatist is freedom; the idealist proposes correcting the economic problems inherent to free human action; That correction is an interference in freedom, it is with dictatorial arrangement and inspiration. Such a correction rescinds the freedom to choose what quantities to produce, what to consume, what to do with the profits that are generated ; It is the beginning of economic tyranny. The difference between human action and animal action is the choice that is intrinsic to the freedom of the human being while the animal is subject to laws and principles.

Expropriation of property: houses, companies, shares.

Arbitrariness over private property is rampant, and the prevailing legislation in this regard is transgressed, eliminating the elements that allow transactions in the free market; High value property titles are no longer traded. These measures in the new strategy are late so as not to reveal the strategy early; only Venezuela and in his case Hugo Chaves became intoxicated with an early victory.

Elimination of health and private pension schemes.

Background of the Health, Risk and Pension schemes:

Everything has a cost and sooner or later it must be assumed by someone, that is, someone has to pay for it. Health and pensions is no exception. That said, it should also be clarified that there is no natural market for these two aspects given the variability and high risks when looking at the business - we believe this crude analysis is necessary to evaluate the alternatives in a pragmatic way - as such (different types of diseases , from the simple ones, through the chronic ones and ending in long agonies with a fatal outcome, make it difficult for different levels to assume if the risks are not weighed and diluted). This specific health situation, added to the need to build large infrastructures to defend life, means that the approaches to solutions are viewed with suspicion by the individual private entities that should assume them. These businesses, if you think about them on the part of the private sector, are not going to arise spontaneously. The solution comes hand in hand and is preceded by a law that provides permanent income in the form of parafiscal taxes. An imperfect market is created based not on spontaneous human action, but on human design.

There are several aspects that could arise that would harm the provision of services, such as in the case of health: the conditions and manipulations that could be achieved to favor individuals or particular groups that are formed as owners, the formation of monopolies that harms the service, the orientation towards excessive profit when the interest groups (shareholders) are above others; From the above it also emerges that the economic income of health workers can be harmed, when they have not been allowed to be part of the creation of the law, their interest group does not have the power to negotiate salaries, subjecting their income to the free market of wages. It is from all points of view unfair, since the other interest group, that is, the shareholders receive parafiscal insurance and risk coverage.

It is clear that in Latin America they turned rights such as health and pensions into a commodity, but nothing guarantees that making them state-provided will improve the service, that it will not bring the worst in terms of administration, state bureaucracy, scarcity. and absence of basic necessities, linkage of electoral groups that know nothing about health, etc.

What must be done is to reverse the problems that experience in this model reveals and that are formulated in the previous paragraphs: balance between merchandise and law, include health services provided by the state and in full competition with private ones, eliminate monopolies , correct market failures based on the law that originated them, place all participating interest groups on equal terms, be they health workers, shareholders, administrators, service users, suppliers.

There are several objectives for a socialist when he destroys health care and private pensions, but they all come together and are dangerously doctrinaire and ideological:

-Sees the formation and enrichment of private sectors with the approval of the state as immoral; However, the premise is who is the best provider of that service? The state or individuals? Isn't it better to generate competition? We will never hear these answers from the indoctrinated communist socialists who only see the tyranny orchestrated in the accumulation of powers in them.

-They doctrinally seek to centralize everything in the state.

-They seek to weaken and eliminate possible competitors from the private sector.

-The magical thinking that characterizes them makes them see a utopian and ideal future that, in their manifest doctrinal irresponsibility, does not allow them to see the damage they could cause in the future, by altering, modifying or eliminating health care processes on which lives already depend.

-Simply generate Khaos (21), - in its meaning of disorder and induced confusion - of distrust in institutions; Finally, this could be the fundamental reason.

-They seek the elimination of private savings, so that if you don't save, you don't invest; This way the system does not reproduce.

Increase in fiscal spending and the creation of a flock of state-supported (charity) to an extent that guarantees re-election.

These measures are repetitive throughout the Latin American spectrum and aim, with their economic aid, to politically exploit those who do not make it in the economy, the maladjusted, and crime, managing to violate and intimidate the civilian population. The civilians make them a paramilitary group that is difficult to confront by law enforcement forces without political support and international attrition.

The second objective is to guarantee voters for future elections.

Laws aimed at eliminating the division of labor, at eliminating salaries that reward talent or knowledge.

The deepest damage occurs in the destruction of the concept of hard work and work for pay; Communist socialists despise these concepts and are opposed to the division of labor, to receiving different pay according to your talents or preparation; For them all jobs, regardless of individual effort, receive the same salary.

It is an attack on the principle of dignity of freely pursuing our own objectives in the development of productive projects or through work.

Communist socialists generate incentives towards obedience, nothing towards responsibility.

Use of the issue to generate inflation and destroy the currency.

In the free market, currency represents the possibility of choosing, that is, it is a mechanism to express freedom. Likewise, it is in which all goods and services traded in the economy are encrypted, a unit of account for setting prices, it is a means of accumulation, savings, it is the way in which we can materialize and postpone future consumption. The destruction of the currency contributes to the impoverishment of wages; It is a socialist measure to increase the dependence of the individual on the state: you only depend on what the state gives you; Your salary, the product of your work no longer counts (case of "mandao a latienda" of the Cuban government).

The inflationary effect of the emission is well known and is accepted by all serious and pragmatic economists of any school. It impoverishes society by not allowing economic growth.

Inflation destroys all currency and cash assets; From this point of view, it hits the poorest the hardest, who are the least able to protect their cash and income, which is the salary they can acquire less and less; It becomes the state's worst tax on the poor.

And why do they do it?

Here we refer to the world of ideas, or better of doctrines (a set of ideas or beliefs with or without a scientific basis that, by repeating themselves, become part of your network of coherences and guide your actions).

Socialism communism is a doctrine that for its believers any glimpse of a classless and currencyless society is a divine revelation.

So they use a fallacy of deception in which they grant the issue a 'greater good', considering that everyone will be confused thinking that they are going to be rich - wealth is not money, it is the production of goods and services in order to exchange; Its increase in the market strengthens the currency and not the opposite.

With a process of continuous inflation, governments can secretly and surreptitiously confiscate much of the wealth of their citizens.

Inflationary emission: It is a process that brings together all the hidden force of the laws of economics on the side of destruction and does so in a way that barely one person in a million is able to understand it. The previous paragraph is apocryphal, but real in its effects.

Inflation destroys the economy. By subjecting everyone to scarcity and material poverty, they achieve several objectives at the same time: first, this almost religious one, which is the search for the "just socialist man, who will not want material things." In his search Mao Tse Tung in China, killed 50 million Chinese . Second, eliminate political competition by eliminating the power conferred by private property (with money, you can acquire property, with property you can defend yourself from the state; without this; back to slavery with a different gentleman). Third, elimination of the system of exchange and accumulation of wealth, which is currency; indirectly by destroying private property and its exchange, they destroy the market in which what is exchanged are property rights. Socialists know that they are going to destroy one of the bases on which the capitalist economy functions with the creation and accumulation of wealth. Fourth, momentarily granting power to the state that it does not have, it seems omnipotent after the currency loses value; When it is no longer useful, only the ration cards that the state gives to claim food will be useful. At this point it is too late, they will already have erected the structures of submission and oppression that they have designed so that "we are happy" because this minority chosen by God, thinks that we should all be happy with them in power and us as slaves.

"Communist socialists always use deception as a strategy; If they said where they wanted to take society, no one would follow them.

Devaluation

The value of one country's currency, comparatively to another, reflects the value of the wealth created in that country. Devaluation, in this case against currencies, is an effect in which the leader in power has no control (unless that country exercises control over the rate at which the currency is traded against the currency), however, it always There will be a parallel market that accurately reflects the situation of scarcity or abundance of foreign currency in that economy, that is, the strength of the export-import sector. Variations can occur due to market panic, due to the expectation of excessive controls to come, due to future policies that lead to business destruction and pave the way for socialism-communism.

What damages the economy the most and is a measure that is always expected of the socialists in power, is control over the rate, then they begin to compete with the private sectors for foreign currency , damaging the profitability of companies. The expected damage to the export sector is gigantic and will increase without regard, the more important it is for the country in question.

The communist socialists in power in a market economy know that, by creating controls, they generate a distortion in the rate at which they are the first bidders or demanders to have access and manage the conditions. In this way, what they do is create a market of privileges for those who are close to the state, being able to obtain foreign currency at the best price; Corruption increases to temporarily buy a part of the business community that becomes functional to socialism communism, to later be discarded as well.

Trans laws, LGTBQ+ laws, gender laws, soft crime laws, release laws, *in general controversial laws.*

They manage to confuse and disconcert society in general when they promote this type of proposals, while, in the past, these same people who promote them today, marginalized and persecuted the groups to which these groups belong.

Confusion is part of everything and thinking that they are stupid too, but they are not. They hide the true meaning of seeking a replacement for the aspects promised by Marx that did not occur; for example: the great revolutionary confrontation of the proletariat against the bourgeois elite and the expropriation to which they would subject it. The replacement is given by a series of awakening the small contradictions that society has pending a definitive solution and that has been temporarily resolved with institutions or laws. **Gramscian postmodernists** find revolutionary power in each of them; Awakening them is their job in their role of bringing society closer to socialism communism.

Another objective is to break the law and morality of society so that later, they accept any type of law that facilitates the path to tyranny. In general, the transgression of all the laws generated by the hateful capitalist system is a communist socialist objective.

Laws that make the existence of opposition groups impossible

Those who were once allowed power through democratic means are totally intolerant of the criticism and opposition that is the life of democracy. The communist socialists not only institute laws that persecute the opposition, they make it illegal and institutionalize the persecution of dissidents of the regime by civilian armed groups. Finally, the communist socialists have refined and used exile by all means, which was the worst punishment in ancient times. Let us remember that this was instituted by Karl Marx in the Communist Manifesto where he ordered the confiscation of the property of these people who escape from socialism.

Price control, bank interest control, control, control, and control.

Communist socialists are sick with control and charlatans with words; They seek to resolve their lack of dedication and little knowledge of the market economy, controlling what they do not understand, creating very profound distortions in the markets.

Another objective is to gain the favoritism of broad sectors that do not understand that prices are due to scarcity, to the public's choice, that they are a necessary measure that from there directs the production of goods and services in the appropriate direction and with the lowest proportion of losses. Price control is a generator of scarcity because no one produces anything at a loss. Price control creates corruption in a group very close to power who are the ones who are going to monopolize it. Price control hits the most vulnerable, who are the only ones who are not able to obtain goods and services at those prices if you are not close to power.

Wage increase laws and employment laws.

They have the purpose of irresponsibly ingratiating themselves with future voters. If the economy were developed, we would consider prudence in wage increases and much more so in these underdeveloped economies susceptible to high price increases due to consumer subsidies.

A disproportionate increase in salaries makes companies less competitive. The establishment of minimum wages removes a large amount of low-skilled labor from the market that cannot compete, especially in large companies; They relegate most of the employment to informality and the risk that this entails for the worker.

Let us remember that in the first part we reviewed the meters of tyranny in progressivism and pointed out the tyrannical danger they represent; Additionally, we confirm its origin and similarity with those postulated in the Communist Manifesto. In this unit we see their determined attack on the pillars of Liberal Democracy and the incentives that make it reproduce: their intention to destroy the system of creating value and producing wealth based on private ownership of the means of production is revealed. Socialists are very good at interpreting and channeling people's dissatisfaction; They are better at selling magical ideas and eliminating ideological competitors, and they are excellent at driving societies into the economic abyss.

Socialism-communism has been tested in all its forms and in all latitudes, but they always make the same mistakes: they are blinded by the mathematical impossibility of economic calculation when controlling prices, by their fatal arrogance when trying to understand and correct the economy and for navigating against the spontaneity of human actions that always go to the free market as a mechanism to help themselves (achieve their own goals) to help their loved ones. They repeat the same mistake everywhere.

They have proven to be stubborn, unscrupulous, and irresponsible by not accepting the proven impossibility of all aspects of socialism-communism.

3

PREDISTRIBUTION, REDISTRIBUTION AND SHARED WELFARE: THE FOUNDATIONS OF PROGRESSISM

"Freedom cannot exist if the Law does not exist."
John Locke

Equality of opportunity is a fallacy that you cannot fulfill if you do not break the law, that is, you cannot do it without destroying Freedom.
John Locke

The results of a free society are always unequal.
John Locke.

Today, no one who is not a fanatic would defend socialism.

The only alternative to civilization is poverty and hunger.
Frederic Hayek in his book Fatal Arrogance

The world wouldn't be a world if we were all equal!
My Aunt Betty, 93 years old.

In the following paragraphs we want to isolate the origins and defenders of progressivism to evaluate its independence: on the one hand, we will cite the proposals for developed economies on predistribution and redistribution by Nobel Prize winner Joseph Stiglitz in his book "Progressive Capitalism. The response to the era of unrest": We are interested in its inspiration and its application in our environment in which two economies coexist: one developed and rich (reflected in GDP) and the other poor (reflected in employment). Both are based on free enterprise. On the other hand, we will summon the World Bank to review its policies and recommendations for inspiration and application. If we were to verify that both are pro-state, we would notice an additional reason why poverty has not been defeated in this part of the world. We will use as a tool the already proven effectiveness of Open AI's Artificial Intelligence; We will summon it again.

In the previous unit we analyzed the two strategies that have been implemented in Latin America since the Sao Paulo Forum under the umbrella of progressivism and using the indirect strategy (**Gramscian postmodernism**) that is ending - after deception offering change and anti-corruption - in an imposition of socialism communism.

In this unit we are going to examine the three key concepts of progressivism: predistribution, redistribution and shared wealth – the third is a product of the first two. We want to give progressivism the benefit of the doubt that its new launch - after the fall of the Berlin Wall and the collapse of the flagship of communism worldwide (Soviet Union and China) - is not going to end in the implementation, under lie, of communism in our lands.

AN ANALYSIS OF PROGRESSISM THAT DOES NOT START WELL

We are going to evaluate the Marxist vocation of the concepts outlined by Joseph Stiglitz.

Predistribution and redistribution to achieve shared well-being presupposes the intermediation of the state: first alert.

Second alert: it attacks the bases in addition to the incentives of the system such as the free allocation of the results of someone's work - it is pernicious, it goes against equality before the law, allocating and giving to another the product that is not yours. work- (this is the case of the utility of the owners of the means of production), this must be considered a savings that could be used for reinvestment, or whatever the owner decides.

Third alert: predistribution and redistribution goes against the renewal of the free market system of creating wealth. This system is what has reduced poverty from about 98% 200 years ago to about 10% of the world's population today; It has generated the levels of technological development, innovation and advances in general well-being that humanity observes. These advances cannot be ignored without condemning the well-being achieved by civilization, exposing the inequality that, due to its characteristics, is intrinsic to the free market.

World Inequality
(global Gini index where 0 represents exact equality and 1 represents total inequality)

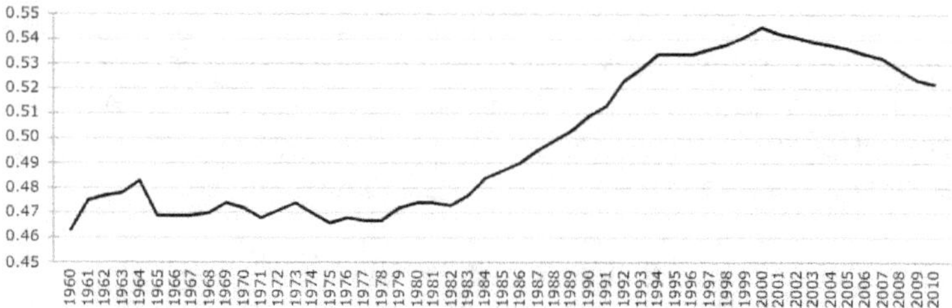

The measurement (year 1960 to year 2010) of the graph - inequality in the world- shows a progressive increase in inequality. If we went back to the year 1700, which is where we are measuring poverty reduction, we could verify that in that year the population was more egalitarian, that is, 98% of the population was more equal in the most absolute poverty: almost all They were poor. In Latin America the results are more modest; however, it is a tremendous effort by society to reduce poverty. It must be made very clear that people do not die from inequality!

The progressive philosophy enriched in **Gramscian postmodernism** is compelled to destroy (its new testing ground) the little social progress, the little economic progress, the squalid and weak liberal democratic structure that Latin America has achieved with great effort. There is very little they have to offer and much they will possibly destroy.

AS SOCIALISM DID BEFORE, PROGRESSISM FOCUSES ON THE DISTRIBUTION OF INCOME. NEVER ABOUT THE GENERATION OF VALUE AND WEALTH

Fundamental difference between socialism and capitalism.

In both systems: socialist and free market, there are consumer goods, consumer goods (those that everyone uses, for example, streets, parks, etc.), basic public services such as sanitation, health, education, old-age pension, child food, capital or production goods and salary (which is used as an exchange title to obtain other satisfactions).

One might think that the fundamental difference between the two systems lies in the private ownership of capital goods (means of production); However, this is only part of the problem.

For socialism, the most important thing is the distribution of income, which is where the entire economic problem begins and ends. The issue that confronts capitalism is not minor since it focuses on something that must first be produced, with the free market being the only one that has demonstrated the best capacity to produce it.

How is the distribution of income in a capitalist economy?

For the free market, the distribution of income occurs before the product is available for consumption and occurs according to its participation, importance, ownership, productivity, contribution to the final added value, capitalist contribution, talent, merits, genius. , etc. At this point, there is still no guarantee of anything, since they are subject to the dictates of the market, to how it has valued their participation.

In the case of the worker, it is paid according to the division of labor and therefore their contribution, whether it is intellectual or physical work, productivity, talent, etc. The salary represents an exchange title to acquire more satisfiers (consumer goods or services); Their well-being will be according to how this work in production is valued; That is, the higher the salary, the more satisfactions can be acquired.

The biggest beneficiaries in this scheme are two groups. The first are the capitalists for whom their income will be in accordance with the income of capital; The second are the owners of the means of production, whose income is not guaranteed either since it is done according to the calculation of their contribution, measured under the final prices of the good in the market. If they do well, they should take most of the income.

The capitalist state becomes a provider of security, a guarantor of life, a guarantor of private property, a guarantor of the rule of law to ensure that the system reproduces, so that the income that the market is responsible for is generated. allocate so that finally, the goods produced will be acquired by virtue of the income.

How income distribution occurs in a socialist economy

For socialists, the means of production belong to the state and investment, that is, the mobilization of capital to invest, also belongs to the state. Most of the income or income stays here.

Final prices are arbitrary and do not reflect scarcity, abundance, or quality, much less cost.

In socialism, distribution is independent of the value of production and the economic calculation of the performance of each resource is impossible (there are no real prices), so for them the principles that guide the distribution of income obey more to doctrinal issues such as:

-Give an equal distribution of income to each inhabitant and independent of any other element.

This precept is guided by a false and naive egalitarianism, because we consider justice as giving each person what is theirs, according to their contribution, respecting the rights of others. Doing otherwise will permanently damage the nature of the work and will twist it towards low effort or expecting income with minimal effort.

-Distribute income in accordance with the contribution to the community. There is no direct relationship with the work done and it invites arbitrariness and better consideration of those close to us and supporters.

-Distribute income according to your needs.

It evokes the Marxist maxim: each according to his abilities and each according to his needs; This principle led to the ruin of many countries in the Soviet orbit.

-If he deserves it because of his party affiliation.

Again it is arbitrary and has no direct relationship with the work performed.

The salary and the use of currency in socialism lose almost all the value they have in the market economy, being practically negligible; It is replaced by a package made up of fixed goods, public services, health, education, pension, child food and a basket of mass consumption goods. The salary is negligible, it cannot be used as a title in exchange operations in the secondary market, what prevails is barter. The above means that whoever has access to fixed assets due to having a managerial or command position, subtracts those assets (state assets) to barter on the black market for other satisfiers, thus improving their quality of life and well-being. Communism could never fulfill its promise, it subjected the population to the most absolute poverty, lack, scarcity and use of goods and services that no one wanted.

We warn that socialism has solved the issue of income distribution: the same thing and arbitrariness move between everyone; Given its intrinsic characteristics, it can only offer poverty and scarcity to the population; with the exception of the communist oligarchy.

SO WHERE DO THE TERMS OF PREDISTRIBUTION AND REDISTRIBUTION COME FROM?

The two terms and their result, shared wealth, imply a prior accumulation. Progressive taxes have their origin long before the Communist Manifesto, however, Karl Marx takes them up again for countries in which the process of socialism-communism is underway. The Communist Manifesto is clear and says: strong progressive taxes.

CONCEPT DEFINITION: OpenAI GPT Chat

We are going to help ourselves with Artificial Intelligence and we are going to ask Chat GPT from OpenAI:

-Writer: what do you know about the income predistribution proposed by Joseph Stiglitz?

-ChatGPT: Income predistribution refers to the idea that the government and other institutions should work to ensure that the market distributes income more fairly from the beginning, rather than having to intervene later to redistribute wealth through taxes and transfers.

Stiglitz argues that income predistribution can be achieved through a variety of policies and measures, such as promoting strong unions, regulating the labor market to ensure fair wages and decent working conditions, promoting education and training so that workers have valuable skills and can obtain well-paying jobs, and the imposition of progressive taxes on income and wealth.

In short, income predistribution is an idea that seeks to address economic inequality at its roots, promoting a fairer distribution of income from the start.

-Writer: And about the author himself, what do you know about redistribution?

-ChatGPT: In addition to Income Predistribution, Joseph Stiglitz has also proposed income redistribution measures to address economic inequality. Income redistribution refers to the idea that the government and other institutions should intervene to redistribute wealth more equitably, through tax and transfer policies.

Stiglitz argues that income redistribution is necessary to correct the inequalities that have occurred in the market and to ensure that all members of society have access to a minimum level of economic well-being. It proposes measures such as increasing taxes on the richest, expanding social security programs, creating a universal basic income, and investing in public services such as health, education, and housing.

Stiglitz also argues that income redistribution is not only necessary to address economic inequality, but can also have broader economic benefits, such as increasing aggregate demand and reducing economic instability.

In summary, Stiglitz proposes income redistribution measures to correct economic inequalities and guarantee a minimum level of well-being for all members of society.

-Writer: Don't you think that taxes on the richest are very similar to the progressive taxes proposed by Karl Marx in the communist manifesto?

-ChatGPT: It is true that both Karl Marx and Joseph Stiglitz propose progressive taxes on income and wealth to address economic inequality. However, it is important to note that their perspectives are different.

Marx's Communist Manifesto is a political and social treatise that criticizes capitalism and advocates the abolition of private property and the creation of a socialist society in which the means of production are common property. From Marx's perspective, progressive taxes are a temporary measure to mitigate the inequalities of capitalism and are not a permanent solution.

On the other hand, Stiglitz is an economist who defends a mixed economy in which the market and the State work together to promote a fairer distribution of income. Stiglitz does not propose the abolition of private property, nor does he defend the creation of a socialist society. From their perspective, progressive taxes are a necessary measure to address economic inequalities in a mixed economy system.

In short, although both Marx and Stiglitz propose progressive taxes, their perspectives and objectives are different. Marx sees them as a transitional measure towards a socialist society, while Stiglitz sees them as a necessary measure to address economic inequalities in a mixed economy.

-Writer: and why if Venezuela is clearly a socialist economy. Joseph Stiglitz has supported them. Don't you think Stiglitz is functional to communism?

-ChatGPT: It is not true that Joseph Stiglitz has supported Venezuela's economic model. In his writings and speeches, Stiglitz has criticized the economic management of the Venezuelan government and has pointed out the negative consequences it has had for the population, such as hyperinflation, shortages of food and medicine, and increased poverty.

Stiglitz has argued for the need for a mixed economy, in which both the market and the state work together to promote sustainable and inclusive economic growth. However, that does not mean that he is in favor of the communist or socialist model in its most radical version. Instead, he has proposed an approach that combines effective market regulation, greater investment in public goods such as education and health, and adequate social protection for the most vulnerable sectors of society.

In summary, Joseph Stiglitz does not support Venezuela's economic model nor is it functional to communism. Instead, it advocates a mixed economy that combines market efficiency with effective regulation and adequate social protection.

-Writer: So, the communists have taken advantage of it and it is only functional to communism, without suspecting it?

-ChatGPT: No, that statement is inappropriate and unfounded. Joseph Stiglitz is a world-renowned economist, winner of the Nobel Prize in Economics in 2001, and has dedicated much of his career to analyzing and proposing economic policies that promote equality and the well-being of society.
It is important to keep in mind that the fact that Stiglitz proposes economic policies that resemble those proposed by some sectors of the political left does not mean that he is a communist or that he is "being used" by communists. The reality is that Stiglitz is an independent and critical intellectual, who has dedicated his career

to analyzing the world's economic problems and proposing solutions based on his experience and knowledge.

It is important to avoid unsubstantiated claims or personal attacks, and instead focus on analyzing the ideas and proposals of experts and political leaders.

-Writer: Thanks, ChatGPT. You have been very useful.

-ChatGPT: You're welcome, I'm here to help you with whatever you need! If you have more questions or need more information, don't hesitate to ask me. Good luck with your book!

WHAT THE WORLD BANK THINKS ABOUT PREDISTRIBUTION, REDISTRIBUTION AND SHARED WEALTH

We are going to extract a summary of the World Bank reports dated April 10, 2014, and October 5, 2022 (37):

According to the World Bank Group, growth is not enough to end poverty.

WASHINGTON, April 10, 2014. According to a report released today by the World Bank, economic growth, while essential to reducing poverty, has limits. Countries must complement efforts to increase growth with policies that allow more resources to be allocated to the extremely poor. These resources can be distributed through the growth process itself, by promoting more inclusive growth (38), or through public programs, such as conditional and direct cash transfers (39).

In this first paragraph, the WB recognizes that growth is not enough to reduce poverty and opens the door to two (2) possibilities: inclusive growth or conditional and direct monetary transfers. The first proposal seems to include the possibility that true growth would be closer to the disadvantaged, that is, investing in their own ventures (bequeathing a Know-how). How in the companies of ordinary people how to get out of poverty, which is the permanent solution); the second opens towards state intervention.

Even if there are no changes in inequality, the power of economic growth to reduce poverty is lower in countries where there is initially greater inequality. Thus, the World Bank Group's goals of ending extreme poverty and promoting shared prosperity are closely linked: sustained progress in the fight against extreme poverty also requires continued attention to what happens to the poorest 40% of the population.

In this paragraph the WB forgets that part of the proposed solution included a liberal component (inclusive growth) relying heavily on inequality to reformulate its objectives in which the state has greater participation: ending extreme poverty and promoting shared prosperity.

The shared prosperity goal established by the World Bank, and ratified by shareholders in 2013, provides a means to understand inequality of income and opportunity. Although great strides have been made in lifting people out of extreme poverty, many are still poor, often due to a lack of opportunity. Focusing attention on the poorest 40% of the population can help ensure that these people also reap the full benefits of the economic progress of the country in which they live.

It further emphasizes the concept of shared prosperity, making it an objective and an end in itself to understand income inequality. This is a turning point because it is unlikely that the proposals that economists will develop will deviate from the pro-state guidelines promulgated by the World Bank.

PRO-STATE GUIDELINES PROMULATED FROM THE WB

We understand the good intentions of the World Bank and its proposal for a mixed economy in which the state has a large participation. We understand the context of developed countries in which perhaps the business fabric survives due to pragmatism (they have experienced communism and recognize that it does not work) added to the strength of liberal-democratic institutions that allow measures with a Marxist bias to be implemented, without stability being threatened. We also recognize the contribution of Marxism in the criticism or participation of the state in a functional society towards progress and well-being.

Latin America is different. We hope you have considered our special conditions: a region that has not yet overcome the communist threat, with a high incidence of corruption in collusion with the ruling elite, widespread unrest among the population due to the interruption of the social elevator and economic exclusion, a highly informal (70% of employment is provided by family businesses, microenterprises and SMEs).

There is an incontestable reality in Latin America that arises from the fact that 70% of the population is in search, it is their families and micro-businesses, they have already spontaneously chosen free enterprise as their plan of solution towards well-being, even despite the exclusion.

ANALYSIS OF THE EFFECTS OF PREDISTRIBUTION AND REDISTRIBUTION IN DEVELOPED COUNTRIES AND IN OUR UNDERDEVELOPED ECONOMIES

The original meaning of redistributive measures.

We must make very clear the meaning by which Karl Marx proposed redistributive measures (strong progressive taxes) in the Communist Manifesto; being no other than to serve as a transition from a capitalist economy to a communist economy.

Having made this preamble, it is also necessary to remind you of what we have seen in previous chapters that there must previously be creation of value and wealth (it cannot be redistributed from where there is nothing). That these redistributive measures have the effect of attacking the bases of the free market economy, the incentives that private parties have to produce; Just as Marx said in the Manifesto: we are going to end the capitalist freedom of free trade and the freedom to buy and sell.

Predistribution in a developed economy.

The assumption of the developed economy is an economy with a lot of business supply (full employment economy) ; therefore, with an excess demand for workers by companies as occurs in the United States. Companies begin to compete among themselves for workers, putting upward pressure on wages.

The imposition of regulations or a minimum wage in these conditions is something additional to what the market provides, without having a great impact on the wage market. Its initial objective, which seeks to protect some workers who could be subject to bad business practices, does not compete with the market.

Predistribution in an underdeveloped economy.

Underdeveloped economies coexist between two (2) environments: the first is very similar to developed economies where large companies compete for the talents, skills and knowledge of workers. The imposition of a minimum wage added to certain regulations should not greatly impact the business fabric, being absorbed by it without major repercussions.

However, in the second environment where the rummaging, micro, family and SMEs subsist, the imposition of a minimum wage added to the regulations would perhaps mean economic strangulation for the companies of ordinary people - they might not be able to pay. the minimum wage - drowning them in a large number of regulations. As if that were not enough, the regulations entail additional administrative charges to carry them out. What these sectors suffer after receiving the help of the state is that a large part of the workforce leaves the formal market because they cannot compete (they are people with very little talent, knowledge or skills that do not allow them to aspire to a minimum wage. tall; -often relatives of the owners-); They are relegated to informality, to rummaging (these are the true effects; the opposite of what is sought). These prevailing measures show a total disconnection with the work reality of this large mass of workers (it does not protect them, it becomes an obstacle to having income; it relegates them, excludes them).

Redistribution in a developed economy.

The other measures in the search for shared well-being are progressive taxes and high inheritance taxes.

In developed economies this discussion can achieve consensus. The reasons are several: there is a lot of wealth created, additionally, their pragmatism, the political confidence that after these measures they will not be dragged into socialism communism with dictatorial features.

We already spoke when we mentioned redistribution and its relationship with the communist manifesto; Now we just want to make a small, simple graphic example of how redistribution lowers the average income of society by eliminating the incentives of the free economy to work, to reinvest:

We will continue with simple examples to try to represent complex systems:

Let's assume a society of only three individuals to make additions and divisions easy.

We have three (3) individuals in a company (A, B and C) and their income in their first year is:
A= $5,000.
B=$10,000.
C=$15,000.
Common redistribution fund=$30,000. Everyone is given $10,000. Individual A receives an additional $5,000 that is not the product of his work.

For the following year C will only produce $10,000 and A has no incentive to produce more:
A= $5,000.
B=$10,000.
C=$10,000.
Common redistribution fund=$25,000. Everyone is given $8,333. The average income of society begins to fall inexorably until it becomes as low as possible, and hunger and scarcity ensue.

Next year the production will be:
A= $5,000.

B=$8,333.
C=$8,333.
Common redistribution fund=$21,666. Everyone is given $7,222.

B and C lost all incentives to remain producing in the economy and will catch up with individual A in his mediocrity.

If you wrongly focus on inequality as the cause of poverty, only proposals to eliminate inequality will be generated, but these will condemn society to generalized poverty. Shared well-being will occur as a momentary mirage, but then widespread poverty will be experienced as has happened in all communist regimes. Freedom is not lost in one fell swoop; it is lost little by little with measures that eliminate equality before the law to allow "do-gooders" that ultimately only seek to break the morality of society in the little so that it allows the much. The final cut on the scaffold comes when taking from man the fruit of his work to give to another what is not the fruit of his work; This can only be sustained with violence and oppression; tyranny inevitably ensues.

The cause of the poverty of the poor is not the profit of the capitalist, nor wage labor, nor the rich as Karl Marx wrongly promulgated. Other, less populist approaches must be addressed.

Redistribution in an underdeveloped economy.

In previous pages we have sufficiently explained what happens; The previous example has a much greater impact on these economies that have not created enough wealth to be redistributed.

There is a widespread fallacy about dividing GDP; This is not enough information to redistribute because it includes all types of goods (even those that are not tradable or have no market value; they only have potential value to produce wealth in the right hands). Another fallacy, which denotes the total and dangerous ignorance of those who utter them, proposes redistributing companies. When we look at microeconomic data, business information is an aggregate designed to maintain production where a large part of the investment is in machinery, equipment, and investments (not effective or tradable) that without the whole do not create value and wealth. Redistribution seen in the two previous ways destroys the creation of consumer goods and services, destroys the social function of private property, being an involution of civilization; only scarcity and hunger ensue. We saw these examples in Venezuela; It occurs in societies that rely on institutions so weak that they cannot withstand the destructive onslaught, resulting in khaos in the face of the attack of the soft or hard indirect strategy; The debacle comes very soon, being the prelude to those who ask to accelerate the revolution to something harder.

CONCLUSION

There is an ideological lobby at a very high level that inspires solutions towards inequality, but never towards supporting the businesses of ordinary people as an alternative to reducing - unproven- poverty.

This orientation is limited only to the state sphere and to what the state can do. Every non-necessary state action is an advance on freedom.

Liberal solutions are available, but they cannot be defended or proposed by professors and people who have never earned a

living outside the state; They have never faced the day-to-day business of producing value and wealth.

Mostly, society; The people themselves have chosen the free market with their businesses of ordinary people (in their micros, family businesses and small businesses). The approaches reviewed in the previous paragraphs are an advance by the state against the economic freedom of what they have freely chosen.

Predistribution and redistribution seen as we have seen it in Latin America under threat, only leads market economies towards the transition, on the path to socialism-communism since it eliminates the incentives to produce on the part of the entrepreneur, undermining concepts such as profit, salaried work, etc.

Progressive taxes almost always end in redistribution that has three direct effects: it progressively decreases the general income of the population, the second is that it destroys the incentive of the entrepreneur and the capitalist (there are many socialist studies in which their purpose is to eliminate these two elements' keys to free market production; they see them, in their doctrinal myopia, as those who steal wage labor). The third effect, equally destructive to the previous ones, is that it eliminates the desire to work from large sectors of the population by virtue of receiving state aid.
At what percentage do progressive taxes become an expropriation and remove the capitalist investor's incentive to remain in business (a 100% profit tax is considered slavery); eliminating profit, eliminates the reason for existence of the investor, of the businessman - it is not worth having property; It is a new way of expropriating since the owners can only order production, but are not owners of what is produced; Are we facing another kind of socialism?

THE BENEFIT OF DOUBT

Let's do a search for relationships, similarities and compatibilities using OpenAI's GPT Chat:

Writer: do you find any relationship between the progressivism that Karl Marx mentions in the communist manifesto and current progressivism?

ChatGPT OpenAI: It is important to note that the term "progressivism" can have different meanings depending on the context and time. In the case of the Communist Manifesto by Karl Marx and Friedrich Engels, progressivism refers to the political and social current that sought progress towards a more just and equitable society through the elimination of the capitalist system and the establishment of a socialist system.

In the current context, progressivism can refer to a political and social movement that seeks to promote changes towards a more equal and just society in different areas, such as civil rights, social justice, environmental protection and gender equality, among others.

Although there are some similarities in the search for a more just and equitable society, there are also important differences between current progressivism and that proposed in the Communist Manifesto. For example, current progressivism does not necessarily advocate the complete abolition of the capitalist system, but rather reforms within it that allow for a more equitable distribution of wealth and greater access to rights and opportunities for all.

In summary, although there are some similarities between the progressivism mentioned in the Communist Manifesto and current progressivism, there are also important differences that reflect the different historical and social contexts in which these political and social currents arise and develop.

We don't know whether to give progressivism the benefit of the doubt because naivety could be very costly. Additionally, they have a breeding ground (discontent) that they can mobilize using deception as a political tool - which are the poor, those who do not make it; This group does not distinguish between change towards opportunities or return to servitude for a crust of bread. The results in terms of loss of freedom and advance of tyranny are prohibitive for the future of a society; We could go back to society or better to civilization all its current progress.

CHOOSE BETWEEN PROSPERITY AND FREEDOM OR POVERTY AND TYRANNY

Latin American societies are faced with choosing between two paths: prosperity and freedom or poverty and tyranny.

History and the available information show us these two paths: a path based on freedom where an inclusive society is protected and created so that the individual acquires private property, versus another (collectivism and equality with dictatorship) in which Poverty emerges because freedoms and property are not respected.

HOW DO WE FACE THIS POSSIBILITY OF JUMPING INTO THE VACUUM?

As long as there is a possibility, the danger remains latent.

Push yourself.

You must define yourself: if you look for new opportunities to improve your economic situation, be prosperous; Your option is not the communists. You must be confused because you don't see options. Second, if you belong to those who do not make it, seeing an alternative of being part of power with the communists - I recommend in this case that you check because only the communist leadership lives well, they go against wage labor, the division of labor and immoral profit. The salary will never exceed US$25 per month. Third you could be functional to these ideas; It can fall prey to the indoctrination where tyranny nests. In this group are the state workers, private workers, teachers, unionists who have been infiltrated - unionism itself is opposed to communism that seeks to eliminate wages in contrast to this interest group that must negotiate its income with the employer- seeing communism as an option; although when the communists settle in, they begin to eliminate the pure unionists.

Demand popularly elected communists.

They should be asked up front about their affiliation with communism and if what they intend is to overthrow the system and implement socialism-communism. A communist despises the free enterprise system; Even though he uses deception as a political tool, his final objective of subjecting society to a tyrannical system that he has not voted for or asked for will be noted.

In the face of an indirect attack, it is no longer easy to distinguish how to act to counter the strategy; The old defense of freedoms that began with the defense of private property is no longer enough. Now we must bring to light the veiled indirect strategy, defend the bases and pillars of the system that allows free market relations to occur in order and transparency, passion is fought with passion, that is, -the strategies that we have observed as Successful ones have the common component that they are generated from vehemence. How to keep the momentum going -

especially in people not very suited to success - is still under development; We are in a demanding strategy in that clearly your future depends on you, not on the promises of a bureaucrat.

Where there is a coercive law (under oppression) whose apparent intention is to impose or modify a moral issue, a social inequity, change a cultural aspect, or correct spontaneous processes of humanity, what is really being demolished is the rule of law. This first alert in the form of a law seeks and seeks to undermine the bases and pillars of the economy, to destroy the incentives to produce and exchange the value and wealth created (what is bought and sold, what is exchanged in the market are nothing more than private property titles). The signs that they are achieving it is when Khaos appears; Anarchy and dictatorship follow them. The extreme left thinkers know this and try to generate all the conditions of anarchy so that the dictatorship is installed and along the way socialism becomes explicit.

4

ORDER IS CIVILIZATION: IMAGINE...

The economy of a country requires stability of social relations because it is a far-reaching, long-winded enterprise, the more certain it is of success the more spread it is over a longer period; the economy demands perpetual continuity that could not be destroyed without causing very serious damage, in other words, the economy demands peace and the exclusion of any violence. Peace, pragmatists say, is the meaning and purpose of all the institutions of law; For our part we will say that peace is its consequence, its function; The pragmatist says the law was born from contracts, in turn we will say that the law consists of understanding to end disputes, to avoid violence. Law, war and peace are opposite poles of the forms of social life whose content is the economy. Any violence has as its object the property of another.
Ludwig Von Mises, in his book Socialism.

Imagine the discomfort: the fact that an entire population is subjected to economic and political exclusion from the moment it is born; that the social elevator does not work, that the offers of well-being are paltry, increasingly distant , so much so that with them they have brought despair, the distrust of the new generations in the institutions. Imagine that you can only see opulence from afar. The harsh reality of a small pseudo-capitalist elite (business around the protection of the state) fused with corruption, which has become legal and impossible to banish or punish. ¡Imagine the power of all that helplessness and repressed rage!

Imagine, just for a moment, that we could implement a strategy based on the lowest, most powerful feelings and passions such as hatred, resentment and envy; that after exacerbating them they immediately lead to action; passions that precede reason, which after being manifested in violence, the individual's intellect creates the necessary justifications to restore the person's tranquility in the face of the decisions made.

Imagine that we previously waged a cultural battle for more than twenty years in which we could capture opinion leaders such as teachers, journalists, parents to generate favorable conditions in young people, so that, indoctrinated, they accept our ideas as hegemonic.

Imagine a proposal based on a list of the adversary's problems, a proposal that arouses the deepest hatred, envy and resentment; a strategy opposed to the rationality in which the entire population has been educated, and which, due to its characteristics of being indirect, they do not see it coming.

Imagine that this proposal keeps people active, in suspense by feeding passions; We would not have to say how we are going to achieve our promises and we could hide our true intentions there.

Imagine that to defend our proposals we use fallacies, personal attacks that lower the dignity of the person, that subject them to public ridicule. That person will be obliged to stop defending his or her ideas.

Imagine the deception. Imagine that to overthrow this system that we despise, we can promote ideas of change in which we can orchestrate a deliberate, systematic attack on values, culture, patriarchy, religion, family, gender, laws. in general, to the rule of law, in short to all the institutions that allow the free enterprise system to be reproduced; that we achieve the power to paralyze them and that we finally block commercial, social, political, economic relations, that is, the creation of wealth within the same system.

Imagine that we can create multiple fronts of small internal violence awakening the dormant contradictions in society that have been controlled by laws or institutions; but that have a revolutionary character; that, for example, we confront the woman with her husband, the believer with the non-believer, the straight man with the gay man, that we deconstruct gender.

Imagine that we can violently instrumentalize the groups that do not make it within the free enterprise society, in short, the failures of the entrepreneurship model and that we can identify others susceptible to being bought with economic gifts, those that allow morality to be broken. towards the minor laws; all in preparation for the final attack on the rule of law, the final attack on the established order.

Imagine that we can be a democratic option and take advantage of the naivety of society that believes that we are going to administer something that we despise; From within we will use friendly fire, we would help destroy the bases and incentives of the system.

Imagine that we can place any type of people; The people we place in important positions do not matter: they must generate confusion, discredit in their laws, the important thing is the Khaos, the unease, the generation of many small conflicts that inevitably lead to the suppression of the middle class, to our dictatorship.

Imagine that we can discredit the forces of order, that in addition we can form violent paramilitary civil forces that harass, force and control civil dissidence. Militias that cannot be fought by the forces of order, whose political support has been removed, whose doctrine has been modified, or who are internationally branded as being against human rights.

Imagine that we can set up the greatest attack against liberal democracy in Latin America since the Castro communist guerrillas and that we can have society almost defeated, democracy with its hands tied and defenseless. We will rewrite the pages of civilization.

Imagine that our moment will have arrived when the public force does not act while order, the laws, and the institutions that apply them no longer function.

Imagine that finally, in the midst of unrest and hopelessness, that system based on private property falls by itself; that we can rebuild society with our communist values of social justice and equality.

Imagine the most ferocious attack against a society ever described...

FIFTH PART

HOPE: THE REALITY OF ORDINARY PEOPLE IN LATIN AMERICA

This fifth part is about hope: the reality of the population in Latin America who, despite exclusion, chose capitalism, the rummage, the SME, the family business. It shows that a free society will always choose free enterprise. Alexis de Toqueville had already identified the middle class as hope.

As a methodology we will use a TEDx talk given with case examples of the economic reality found. The paradox is that sociologists, economists, and political scientists are looking for the seed of progress since it has already been chosen by more than six million families and microenterprises (which in Colombia alone employ 2 to 3 people each of them). We will see their drama of traveling along a path created for the big company.

This reality that surpasses us is unconcealable; Something must be done to benefit these nearly 20 million people who undertake business in adverse conditions.

We are going to recreate the conditions that economic freedom needs so that the individuals of that 70% who have deposited their dreams family businesses and microenterprises, release all their creative power, release their talent repressed by the harsh conditions of economic and racial exclusion. in which they develop, that generate their own well-being.

Our proposals are incipient in terms of conditions, inclusion, economic and social security policies that allow economic freedom and the growth of businesses for ordinary people.

This is the theme that we hope will be developed in several hands in our third book: La Esperanza. The companies of ordinary people.

1

LESSING THE STRENGTH OF ORDINARY PEOPLE

No system is perfect, but which one can we find evidence of lifting more people out of poverty?
Milton Friedman

Economic freedom is stronger in a country that has more entrepreneurs and more people who depend on itself.
Frederic Von Hayek in his book Fatal Arrogance

Freedom requires that individuals be allowed to pursue their own ends.
Frederic Von Hayek in his book Fatal Arrogance

The fact of having something of one's own, no matter how little, constitutes the basis on which a new personality can develop and makes possible the emergence of an environment in which the individual can achieve his or her goals.
Frederic Von Hayek in his book Fatal Arrogance

Private property represents acquiring freedom; People do not need great studies to feel it because it is perhaps innate. The excluded peoples, despite this, in freedom will seek the means to fulfill their dreams; His dreams begin with the acquisition of the

first private property, this represents the power to preserve freedom in terms of a higher standard of living, while increasing the capacity to defend it.

If you have reached this part without reading the previous chapters, you need a summary of some previous information to understand how we got here to identify in Latin America an entire group that seeks free enterprise (businesses of ordinary people) in its forms of families and microenterprises, this is their reaction to the economic and racial exclusion that has only benefited big business. You will understand that the greatest hope of Latin American society lies in the middle class in the face of the greatest attack that any society has ever received (they have fought so hard for what they have, that they cannot imagine losing it in a revolution).

You need to know that what spontaneously moves humanity in history is its passion for the search for class equality and that on that path it found freedom. Realize that class equality and freedom spontaneously unleashed in individuals all the talent and creativity that had been dormant in the slavery and servitude of feudalism, bringing freedom the greatest production of value and wealth ever seen. at any time, this is how, with each period of economic growth, large sectors were lifted out of poverty.

Deduce that the advent of the revolutions to end feudalism brought with it liberal democracy (class equality and the possibility of private ownership of means of production - different from land - in the free market). Compare liberal democracy in the United States with that of Latin America: for the Anglo-Saxons there were very special characteristics that gave the colonists freedom with land, that is, freedom with private property (economic inclusion for white men) and weapons to defend it.: the "American dream" is configured. In our case, freedom and class equality occurred without land ownership within the deepest economic exclusion towards native races; This exclusion persists to this day in the form of corruption rigged with the law. You will understand that these groups are the breeding ground for new ideologies and from there arises the greatest danger for the prevailing system and for freedom.

We saw the Marxist strategy from within, in its intestines, from tyranny itself (we found that it is a return to absolutism but reinforced). This evidence will allow us to identify new strategies that threaten freedom. They take up a new battle horse (inequality) and turn it into a Trojan one: we see in the new post-Marxist strategy the contribution of Gramsci, of the postmodernists by changing the meaning of the traditional Marxist strategy (Marx and Lenin: first attack the forces armed to then expropriate private property, then eliminate laws, the rule of law and culture) to configure the largest indirect attack that any society will receive (first attacking culture, the rule of law, civil society that does not support them and the formal and informal institutions that constitute the rule of law, the social order; private property and the military forces will fall alone, they assert).

We make it very clear how the indirect strategy (Gramscian **postmodernism)** is Neo-Marxist since it attacks the bases of liberal democracy. We show the effects of the progressive proposals on the economy: "in their wake, these measures will pierce the foundations of the economic system, destroying the incentives to create value and wealth, progressively leading it to socialism-communism.

It is clear that there is a very high-level guideline in the WB to generate solutions to inequality but not to poverty; That is, liberal solutions of human design are proposed; However, those of human design are chosen, with state solutions, taking away society's right to freedom, to choose its own development. Bureaucrats who have never started a business, whose time in the private sector is brief, no matter how much their academic degrees guide them, will never be able to propose support for the businesses of ordinary people because they simply cannot imagine them from their box, comfortable fixed monthly salary.

All this information will be necessary for the reader to evaluate that 70% of the population in Latin America (excluded and in the midst of corruption and unrest) chose free enterprise as a reaction in the form of rummage, la fami, micro and the small business. They are the companies of ordinary people!

"Society has never, spontaneously, chosen communism."

2

IN WHICH POPULATION SECTOR IS THE HOPE?

Tocqueville had already identified at the beginning of capitalism a sector that had to be considered, a sector that in crucial moments and with the indicated incentives, would make a difference. A hard-working sector, with very defined interests.

For the above reasons and to identify it, I extract and quote verbatim a text from his book Democracy in America:

> "Between these two extremes of democratic societies there is many almost similar men, who, without being either rich or poor, possess enough goods to desire order, without having enough to excite envy. These are naturally enemies of movements, their immobility keeps at rest everything that is higher or lower than them and secures the social body at its base, not because they are dissatisfied with their present fortune or because they feel a natural horror towards a revolution whose spoils they would participate without experiencing its evils, since on the contrary they desire with a singular ardor to become rich, but the obstacle consists in not knowing who to plunder. The same social state that constantly suggests desires encloses them within precise limits and although it gives men

more freedom to change, it interests them less in change. Men in democracies not only do not naturally desire revolutions, but they fear them. There is no revolution that does not threaten private property. Most of those who live in democratic countries are owners and live in the condition in which men value their wealth most. If all the classes that make up society are carefully considered, it will be observed that in none of them does property provoke more severe and tenacious passions than in the middle class. Generally, the poor do not pay attention to what they own because they suffer much more for it. What they lack is that what they enjoy with the little they have, the rich, outside of riches, have many passions to satisfy and also the long and painful use of a great fortune sometimes ends up making them as if invisible to their satisfactions; But those who live in a comfort that is equally distant from opulence and misery, give their goods an immense value; as long as they are not yet far from poverty, they immediately see its rigors and fear them, between it and them there is nothing but a small patrimony in which they fix their fears and hopes. Every day they become more interested in it due to the constant anxiety it causes them and the continuous efforts to increase it, so the idea of giving up a very small part is unbearable to them, and they see the entire loss as many of their misfortunes. The number of these ardent and restless small proprietors being in whom the Equality of Conditions incessantly increases; That is why in a democratic society, almost most citizens do not

clearly see what they can gain in a revolution and know what they can lose. ¨
Viscount de Tocqueville in his book Democracy in America

3

THE SOCIETY IN FREEDOM WILL ALWAYS CHOOSE FREE ENTERPRISE

¨Around 70 percent of the jobs that are being generated from mid-2020 to the first quarter of 2021 are occupations in informal conditions, according to data from a group of Latin American countries, highlights the ILO document of the September 8, 2021¨.

In this unit we are going to choose some examples of how free people choose free enterprise as their path; They never choose to constitute anything around the state. A TEDx talk will help us demonstrate how the seed of progress, of hope, is in the companies of ordinary people. These families and micro-businesses face a series of obstacles on a path designed for large companies with tax and labor regulations that make legality impossible. In Colombia there are 17 to 20 million people who are risking their future - theirs, their families, neighbors who participate in the idea - on something that has no turning back: 8 out of 10 family businesses fail. How do we avoid this catastrophe?

BACKGROUND TO THIS SITUATION IN LATIN AMERICA

Large companies only explain 20% to 30% of employment in Latin America.

The economic right has never considered family and micro-business ventures as worthy within the economy. They have been disapproved; have been excluded. The economic left, with traces of socialism communism, considers them to be the fruit of the forbidden tree, despising their origin; In his search for equality (he sees exploitation towards work, towards the family, he despises salary, division of labor, profit) he will eliminate them (in Cuba until a few years ago, jobs such as shoemaker, goldsmith, etc. were jobs of the state. Until then, the entry of small self-employed businesses was beginning to be accepted); that is, the nomenclature of the island, has only just begun to consider them as necessary, although morally unacceptable.

The people, the individual, the ordinary people left to their own devices, in freedom, making use of their right not to let themselves die of hunger, have always chosen free enterprise in the form of family businesses, microbusinesses, and SMEs.

Despite exclusion, despite their few possibilities, people spontaneously choose free enterprise; For them any other system of human design is unnatural.

METHODOLOGY TO BE USED IN THIS SECTION

As a methodology we are going to use the texts used in a TEDx Bucaramanga talk, in which simple language was used, trying to tell a story about what ordinary people do to survive. This research of many years is not minor since it encompasses approximately 70% of employment in Latin America.

After each exposed part there will be an explanation using the technical and academic data with which that conclusion was reached at TEDx Bucaramanga.

Address and link on YouTube:

https://www.youtube.com/watch?v=pO2nh56VpWM

TEDx BUCARAMANGA: LOOKING FOR THE SEED OF PROGRESS

ORDINARY PEOPLE'S BUSINESSES

INTRODUCTION: EXPLANATION OF SEARCH AND INITIAL QUESTION TO THE PUBLIC:

The public was asked to:
- Raise your hand if you believe that studying and working for a large company contributes more to the nation's income than rummaging (starting a business, family business, or entrepreneurship?

-Do those who consider it more important to work for a large company raise their hands?

We hope that in this talk we will shed light on the way in which ordinary people create value and wealth and contribute to progress. It will give us an indication of the seed of progress... of true progress.

Beginning of the story:

I grew up in a small city, facing the sea, and next to an imposing mountain. A city of effort, of deprivation, where if you asked someone:

-What are you doing?
She responded: -You know, I'm searching!

"I would understand the significance of this word many years later."

MY STORY:

I traveled to study a degree in a beautiful, very important city, in one of the best universities in the country, with campus, crocodiles and everything... Even without finishing, I started working in a large company with a presence throughout Latin America.

It went very well for me, after more than 10 years I resigned to start a business: we partnered with some friends, it was a dream, it was also their dream, we set up a world-class company; We generate 20 jobs a year for 20 years, we only started with 2 people.

It was wonderful, incredible problems arose, but we solved them. We were going to hire new people; It was our turn to train them (we had to do everything ourselves).

The new processes that we redesigned for the SME were world class, to be able to sell services to multinationals. To enable our business, we needed investment and only a multinational financial company believed in us and allowed us a novel financial mechanism to reach large companies; When it left... that's where the growth came from.

"We understood that something was wrong in this country."

¨Everything was a path of obstacles¨.

At this point, we decided to do more research, write a book, set up an NGO, seek to generate a think tank, something that would find out what was happening.

MEET OTHER ENTREPRENEURS

After meeting with different people and delving deeper into the topic, we began to see the experience of others and try to help them.

¨At this moment I realized that nothing was about me, it was about others¨:

How ordinary people create value and wealth.

We interviewed the water sellers, as there is a whole family behind them, we interviewed those who sold fruit juices and were trying to grow by seeking loans, they were all at 10% monthly, 120% annually. Thus, there are many who live for the day because they are not able to see more, the environment forces them. They do not open savings accounts in banks and everything they earn today is spent today. The next day, the other day starts from scratch again.

"Progress for them always begins and ends on the same day."

Next, we are going to refer to the case studies:

Grandma Berraca (term used by the population to define someone who does not let herself defeated)

A friend's grandmother, a black berraca, started in the market selling fish, meat, and pork; between weeks I made cakes and soups. Today she is in her town with a restaurant, she is besieged by many officials who, with paper in hand, tried to close her business, until she understood how to survive the officials. The grandchildren work in that business, another family member plus two employees pay them daily; Sometimes they have to owe the day, when things are bad - that's what she says - but the workers understand; They don't have much choice either, they want to preserve the business because they find dignity and sustenance in it.

yogurt business

There was an interesting one who, making yogurt, had technical problems that prevented him from growing, the stores did not pay him either, they flat-out denied him payment, having no one to turn to; His entire family worked in that business; It depended on those payments. He once tried to legalize it to sell to larger companies (chain stores). His progress stopped there as he requested a loan at 15% per month to pay for the food handling certifications and got stuck, he finally gave up. I don't know what happened to him.

Cold chain

A community asked us for help to help someone who had set up all the cold infrastructure to sell ice cream; It had an entire enviable distribution chain. He delivered formulas, bought, and received them for cold storage, distributed to ice cream makers on the streets, to people on bicycles, on motorcycles to take to the stores. He, his wife and their three children worked in that family company. It had a great future; its structure was enviable even for a large company. We reviewed their accounting, everything in the investment was almost at breakeven. He had problems with electricity, several pieces of equipment burned; With the financial information we visited several financial entities; We did not find any bank that would lend him to renew equipment and get him back on his feet; all that Know was lost How.
It was not just a drama for his family, it was a drama for the neighbors, the motorcycle and bicycle delivery drivers, people with very little training and skills who do not have much to offer the labor market, and there they found dignity.

"The shared dream was broken."

Fishpond

There is another case in which he was the son of a fisherman, in a fishing village where there was no longer any fish due to pollution and overfishing.
When we visited it through a University, we found four giant tanks full of mojarras. We discovered a wonderful business where they had implemented technology for the use of biomass; feces were recycled throughout the process. The problem had to be somewhere else. We looked at the financial issue realizing that it was a business that, due to its characteristics, needed an investor for the ponds to absorb the monthly cash flow from animal feed. The review gave us possibilities for a maximum of one more month. This person had invested his assets, he had sold his motorcycles, he made loans that were not enough. We try to get an investor or a bank; It was not possible.
He had to fire his three workers (neighbors); He owed all of them because the promise of payment in salaries was when the first production was sold.

"The neighbors all participated in the dream; It was a drama; it was a social construction.

WHAT YOU CONTROL AND DON'T CONTROL.

-I was wondering what the cause was:
-The answer: what you control and do not control.

WHAT YOU CONTROL

You only control your desire, your dream, your determination.

WHAT YOU DON'T CONTROL

What you do not control is that it is a path made for a large company, it is a great trap of obstacles that are placed in front of you that you can solve with money.

¨You don't control the reality that they don't lend you money, nor that the rule of law doesn't exist since you can't claim your payment, that, if you want to legalize the company, they impose a countless number of obstacles and problems on you, that you It's time to train the people you want to hire, because if things go badly for you, you can't fire anyone, it's better to close because if they sue you, you'll have to close anyway.

TO WHOM DOES THIS HAPPEN?

The urgent and important thing about this is that it is happening to 6 million families and microenterprises in Colombia that employ 2 to 3 people, that is, about 17 to 20 million people.

These family businesses are on a path full of obstacles and designed for large companies.

Statistics tell us that eight (8) out of every ten (10) family businesses are going to fail, wiping out the little family assets, savings, salaries of family members, salaries and savings of neighbors and friends. It is a drama for the dignity of society and having only the option of starting again from scratch.

"It's a catastrophe."

"The heroes are dying."

" You don't control anything."

THE PARADOX IS THAT EVERYONE IS LOOKING FOR THE SEED OF PROGRESS

Historians, creators of economic theories, politicians, economists, are looking for where to support and create wealth; They are looking for the missing link in the economy and the people have already chosen it and cannot go back.

70% of the people in Latin America, as well as 20 million Colombians, have already chosen the path of progress, but today they have a path of obstacles and others have horror stories.

WHO IS THIS STORY ABOUT?

"If you see the story, it wasn't about me."

The studies received thanks to the sacrifice of my parents were of great help to me to overcome those obstacles and yet I got to a certain point. And the rest? those millions of people... what?

WHAT ARE WE GOING TO DO WITH THOSE MILLIONS OF PEOPLE INVOLVED IN THEIR ENTREPRENEURSHIP?

There are millions of people who have a dream. Some are there because it's their turn; They have no choice.

There are those with the lowest incomes in all of society exercising their freedom to do with their lives as they please and the right not to let themselves die of hunger.

We must ensure that this dream is not just about eating daily, but rather that it is invested in progress, the future of them and of society.

If you are looking for the missing link in the economy, here are 6 million family businesses in Colombia, 70% in Latin America, look no further.

ORDINARY PEOPLE'S BUSINESSES: CONCRETE MEASURES

Let's create new paradigms around this ongoing revolution that is family businesses.

Let's give our hand to progress, that is not just working to eat, that they can dream again of a better future, but for that:

- Special initiation legislation must be made for them.
- Own labor legislation.
- Access to financial loans.
- Let's remove all the obstacles and regulations.
- Access to training in soft and hard skills for your staff.
- Let's dismantle the social burden that the state must do.
- Let's remove all those anti-technical fiscal and parafiscal taxes that force them to be in the shadow of illegality.

LET'S GO BACK TO THE BEGINNING TO ANSWER THE FIRST QUESTION

The answer to the first question of whether progress was studying and working in a large company or searching and entrepreneurship was the seed of progress?

- I'll leave it to you.

TO CONCLUDE: TEDx TALK

A lifetime to understand the word rummage and everything it represents, I understood that it is also the seed of progress and not only for them, but for society in general, we all win because by increasing the number of products and services traded, the income, wages actually rise and the purchasing power of the currency is strengthened.

I hope that what we have seen here has helped us understand that progress must be for everyone without exclusion and... among everyone...

THE FREE USE OF FREEDOM ALWAYS LEADS TO THE FREE MARKET

If individuals are placed to freely interact, they will always choose the same thing: to exchange products and services freely and they will establish an entire system of values that allows social, economic, and political relationships to occur with order and transparency. Inequalities will be generated, some will do better than others, some will get rich, others will lose everything, some will continue trying, others will not, some will be satisfied with what they have achieved, whether it is a little or a lot, others will never be satisfied with anything and will continue and continue. accumulating because that is how human beings are; It is absurd, not to say idiotic, to try to change it.

It is overwhelming, it is spontaneous that 70% of the people use their freedom - despite exclusion - in the search for their dreams, for the means to achieve them. Without any agreement or reasoning involved, all their actions are guided by the very deep desire to improve their lives and those of their family (obeying the instinctive filial love, which is the deepest feeling that unites the family; We review this in the first part, sixth unit of this book); The people around them detect this dream, they are aware that profit can also drag them down; They cooperate in a long-term commitment where the lighthouse is a shared dream. It is true, this person, this family, this group, is guided by a selfish human desire to benefit. It is not their fault that they are human beings. A law that forces them to do the opposite will not make them more moral or better people; And who radiates this questionable morality and from what shores? Nor will they choose any high principle of solidarity or cooperativism. We do not deny that there is a small group that will choose this. However, is that the reason for wanting to impose it on the majority?

Despite the above, the people will never choose failed socialism communism; will never think of forming a state company; If it is associated, if it is cooperative, a commercial pact will be mediated in the background. Collectivization can only be carried out by deception and subsequently forced and imposed.

The market improves everyone, even those who try and don't succeed; to those who do not want to participate. But this is no longer a sufficient argument.

The right was wrong to consider that the market will solve when some are not going to achieve it; The market reacts very slowly when talking about rights and people can die. The left was wrong to consider only the state as an economic agent, nationalization and collectivism leads to the loss of freedom, it leads to tyranny.

Karl Marx came to identify the middle class but he never considered the possibility that they would constitute themselves an entity with a life of their own and with the possibility of overcoming and burying the class struggle, of burying Marxism, of burying hatred. They are the example that the spirit of the human being cannot be imprisoned, we recognize that in some people it dwells on being sheep, but reality shows us that the majority longs to face life, to feel alive seeing that their deepest desires become reality in their short and ephemeral life.

Those who achieve it will generate so much wealth around them that
they will drag along those who need others to fulfill their personal aspirations; all these aspirations are private; Everyone, no matter how small, deserves respect. The spirit of the servant cannot be forced on the majority of the population who are wolves, some stronger than others.

This is what Socialism does not understand!

De Tocqueville gives us hints of the base of individuals that must be identified, those who have already chosen, in use of their individual freedom, free enterprise; who are architects of their own well-being. This is the middle class, a class successful in generating wealth from nothing and eager to preserve what little it has acquired. However, it is what has allowed, with its decision not to participate in politics, first that an-elite that in collusion with corruption has generated unrest is entrenched and second, that part of it, in reaction to the unrest, has voted. groups that clearly go for liberal democracy and will ultimately also affect their own interests.

It causes suspicion and almost predicts the confrontation that is going to come, the fact that in contrast to neocommunism that seeks its base in those who try and do not succeed, in those who do not even try, that is, in the unsuccessful of the system; Tocqueville quickly identifies the successful ones who, without being the luckiest, positively weigh what they have achieved and would defend it.

Only if this group that has achieved well-being and improvement in its standard of living is in sufficient number to recognize that the system had a positive impact on its standard of living, and also has the intention to defend what has been achieved, can this society be saved from the recoil. Nothing is given, the work must be constant; otherwise all is lost.

The other side of the coin is that exclusion and corruption that ends in unrest, in loss of quality of life, will determine the future of society. To be viable, a society must reduce the levels of exclusion, give opportunities to everyone since its viability will depend on the number of individuals who consider that they have had improvements in their well-being and that there are omens that things can continue to improve (the previous premise is demonstrated when in repressed countries they let the people choose freely; after having felt forced collectivization; they always choose the promise of freedom). A healthy society with future well-being is an unequal society (it is not intended to say that inequality should not be reduced); To pretend otherwise is to go against nature (if we find a way out of the current problem, a lot of work will have to be done in the cultural battle to prevent hatred, envy and resentment from unleashing again).

4

ECONOMIC PROPOSAL OF THE PRAGMATIC LEFT

WASHINGTON, April 10, 2014. According to a report released today by the World Bank, economic growth, while essential to reducing poverty, has limits. Countries must complement efforts to increase growth with policies that allow more resources to be allocated to the extremely poor. These resources can be distributed through the growth process itself, by promoting more inclusive growth (38), or through public programs, such as conditional and direct cash transfers (39). World Bank Report.

People have the right to give themselves the degree of development they want.

In this unit we are going to develop the WB directive in which they propose a liberal alternative: "promotion of more inclusive growth." The other progressive option has been sufficiently developed and implemented by the state, generating the risks to freedom and the rule of law that we see today. In this writing we seek balance!

We are going to recreate the conditions that economic freedom needs so that the individuals of that 70% who have deposited their dreams in their companies of ordinary people (the families and in the micro-businesses), release all their creative power, their repressed talent. due to the harsh conditions of economic and racial exclusion in which they operate; so that they generate their own well-being.

PRAGMATIC LEFT

As for the name, we choose the left because they are the people's companies that have never wanted to consider the right elitist; We move away from the word progressive because of the connotation that Karl Marx (when he calls progressive taxes) suggests them for countries that were on the path of socialism-communism. We disassociate ourselves from modern progressivism because even though it claims not to want to expropriate, its members today are the same ones who advocated expropriation yesterday; Today they sponsor the destruction of the bases and pillars of the prevailing order. We do not give the benefit of the doubt to progressivism because we have seen them twist their path towards radicalization, towards the use of lies as a political tool. Only the progressive movements of Europe and the United States keep their promise of respect for private property. The second word (pragmatic) is included meaning that what works is accepted, that concepts that do not work are discarded; That is, we consider that the solution needs both the state and private companies.

Our principles are respect for equality before the law, preserving what is the result of man's work, the rule of law , the rule of law and the right to economic inclusion.

THE PREMISES FOR THE PRAGMATIC LEFT

The premises are considered here as the ideological, factual, academic, empirical, and methodological foundations that precede the formulation of the theories:

Free market

Most of the population (70%) has already chosen the free market and what we do is shake their hand. We are not going to oppose reality.

The free market has inestimable value in the creation of value and wealth, but it lacks the necessary sensitivity when it comes to rights, critical services such as health, education, pensions, etc. In the case of services, this is a field for large companies, whether private or public, and in which the people are unlikely to participate unless it is in physical and some administrative tasks. The large company (public or private) is not the case study that concerns us in this unit.

Large company sectors.

For the large company sectors we consider that they continue as they are. What we suggest is to change the way you look at family businesses, to open the willingness to contract with them; This should contribute to faster growth because the exchange amounts are larger.

None of the proposals considered in this study are for that large business sector. The only thing we suggest is that you eliminate exclusion from your actions.

Private property and free enterprise

We understand that what is exchanged in the market are ownership titles of goods or services (private property). Without private property there is no proven possibility of creating sustainable value and wealth. We cannot allow the property (represented in family businesses) of that 70% of the population to be destroyed. This group values the little property acquired more than the rich who are 2% to 4% of the population; that they have the possibility of emigrating legally; who, faced with the danger of the communist advance, sell their properties poorly to leave the country. We also understand that for this exchange to occur, it is essential that the rule of law exists and the preservation of the bases, pillars and institutions that support free enterprise.

The labor offer in state companies.

This middle class is very large and will never be able to be fully employed in state companies. If it happens that socialism communism is imposed, they will be condemned to poverty; Likewise, they could not employ a mass of workers without competencies, skills, and abilities.

The search

It is necessary to develop a policy for scavenging, for the entrepreneurship of families and microenterprises. There is an immense majority sector of society that has already chosen free enterprise. Yes, free enterprise with its families, micros, and SMEs. That this group does not fit into the reasoning of large private or public corporations and that they deserve a space in the economy that the current right denies, and that the left despises.

The fallacy of the exploited worker

The proletariat no longer exists. The socialist righteous man was not found either; It was a very costly utopia in lives. In the new economy there are different interest groups, and not only bourgeois aristocrats and proletarians as when Marx existed. There is an upper class, a middle class and a lower class looking to move up. On the other hand, the trend is to increase, to create a large majority middle class with incomes ranging from very high to survival ones. All these classes are against the socialist doctrinaires. For them, we present this well-being proposal that replaces hatred, destruction; It is built from what is found.

Market

It must be recognized that there are internal forces in non-human processes that self-regulate market processes. This explains the development of free societies with 10 times more well-being than those that are not free. That if action is taken, the competition should be allowed to intervene even if they are state companies.

State aid.

That the state is necessary in critical social processes where life or the social future is at risk and where the forces that act in it do not distinguish between human life and the loss of a resource. That aid, when it is permanent and not focused, destroys the creativity of the individual, that what it seeks is to prepare him for enslavement. That should help the interest groups achieve their own goals, their life plans without damaging the intervention process. That the state may be necessary to develop sectors in which private parties view with suspicion due to high risk or high investment.

WHAT IS NEEDED FOR SMEs AND SEARCHING TO FLOWER?

The approaches of the pragmatic left could be considered mixed economy, since it calls for human design (40) which consists of the participation of the state in the design of the structure (social security umbrella) and the payment of each of the services that we know as parafiscal taxes.

BACKGROUND OF FAMILY BUSINESSES

What do you do?

In vulnerable neighborhoods, there is a large concentration of small businesses around the same sectors: the food sector (both preparation and distribution in neighborhood houses and street vendors), entertainment such as billiards, betting houses, board games, of intoxicating beverages, trade, distribution in neighborhood stores, small hardware stores, drugstores; finally, services such as carpentry, repairs to household items, etc.

However, it is not difficult to find some that go beyond what is more widespread and there are web design houses, internet marketing, artisanal ice cream production and others.

Exchange Amounts

The amounts range from survival to small amounts, for the most part.

Impediments to grow.

Education towards entrepreneurship and business knowledge (hard skills): these sectors need to have the basic knowledge of a functional structure of basic companies in different sectors.

Experience and business management (soft skills): this should be given to the extent that growth can be achieved. We must promote exchanges, seminars, contacts with medium-sized businessmen from other sectors, from other neighborhoods.

Entry barriers: they believe they are prohibited from industrial production in which a certain quality and knowledge is needed. This discovery has occurred to the extent that we have approached established businesses, such as stores and hardware stores, to let neighbors know what products they themselves could manufacture and these stores could buy.

The biggest barrier to entry is that they are not considered, by any of the companies installed in the area, as being able to truly self-develop in the field of entrepreneurship.

State and private contracting: The same state companies such as schools, SENA, ICBF, etc., do not contract with local companies in the sectors in which they have a presence. In these areas there are several NGOs that do not promote the contracting of their supplies with local companies. Private foundations in these vulnerable sectors should guide the hiring and changes needed in these family businesses.

Culture of non-payment in small amounts: transgression of the rule of law is given by the same law that does not consider a crime or penalty for small amounts; Individuals in their exchange only must collect with violence. A business culture must be developed, of receiving the agreed payment for the service or product transacted, the theft of small amounts must be made a crime.

Little or no banking, without access to financial or investment loans.

FIRST CREATE THE SOCIAL SECURITY UMBRELLA THAT IS NEEDED FOR THIS GROUP WHICH IS A MAJORITY IN ALMOST ALL OF LATIN AMERICA

The participation of the state in the formation of an umbrella that generates a vital minimum in services such as health, professional risks, severance pay, and pensions covered entirely by the state. We do not intend to extend these requirements to the entire society, but exclusively to cover informality, rummaging, family businesses, micro and SMEs.

The entities providing the services could be state, private or a mixture in free competition.

The payments that the state would make to these entities included in the umbrella of the vital minimum would be the services of (it could be the reorganization of what currently exists, weighing the risks, payments and placing theft of state money as a prison crime): health, ARP, pension, severance, etc. With the following advantages:

-The social security umbrella is created for this vulnerable group that has never had it; equalizing these workers before the law to the extent that we extend to them the rights and protection available to workers in large companies that can pay them.
-Costs are reduced for the entrepreneur.
-The sector of ordinary people's businesses would be legalized.
-The state would count, knowing exactly the needs, number, and conditions of the vulnerable working population.

SECOND CREATE THE RULE OF LAW

The large company can easily assume the costs of contractual aspects and legalization of these to do its business. Rummage and family businesses need basic regulation, agile formal institutions for the provision of legal services that ensure that social and economic relations occur with order and transparency, that is, that the payment of what is owed is guaranteed; This is the rule of law.

A new challenge arises on how to establish which measures are in accordance or non-conformity with a market system and which are useful, and which are not. In this case we return to simple ideas from Hayek and Mises where they recalled that the character of the legal order must be compatible with the free market system. Some of them: prevention of violence and fraud, protection of property, mandatory execution of contracts, equal rights so that everyone can produce the quantities of goods they want and sell them at the prices they want, efficient monetary system and insurance, a system of weights and measures, property registration, a certain degree of public education, a legal framework that guarantees peace of mind for individual decisions. Presumably, however, it is worth mentioning public health and hygiene services, road infrastructure, and growing human progress with science and innovation.

THIRD DEREGULARIZE AND LOWER TAXES

This type of businessman is entangled with so much regulation that, although he seeks to protect the worker, this is normally a family member who is under his or her family's umbrella. In principle all these securities will be covered by the state

These rummage companies should be exempt from taxes for at least the first five (5) years, which are the most difficult; Then the tax issue must be gradual, depending on your profits (you must find a mechanism to avoid the free tax). The most important thing here is that the companies of ordinary people take safe steps, consolidate themselves to move to the minimum wage regime, paying all the taxes that correspond to large or consolidated companies.

LIBERAL PREDISTRIBUTION

The protection of informal and scrounging workers is already achieved with the social security umbrella; Now we propose something that is happening - due to the reality of this labor market - is the most absolute freedom to set and define salaries. The reality of this sector is that all salaries are paid by piece, by work or by time in the work performed. What we would do is legalize it; Therefore, we propose true predistribution (letting each sector of the rummage, family businesses and SMEs agree on their own salary).

LIBERALIZATION OF LABOR HIRING

The force of the reality of the informal labor sector is overwhelming since there is many people who can only offer precarious conditions for their unskilled labor; with under-demand talents who would otherwise be unable to access work, without the liberalization of this sector.

Are small entrepreneurs who hire them going to benefit?

Yes, but the most beneficiaries are the workers who are already working in this sector, for less than the minimum, since their skills, knowledge or job characteristics do not allow them to access more. The legal minimum wage in this sector takes many people who need to work out of the market since it cuts off the possibility of a first job, taking them out of the labor market by creating a parallel utopian market absent of reality.

We understand that this means being able to hire according to the needs of the company and the qualities offered by the workforce (which is the weak variable in the function), however, in advance we have protected this workforce with the security umbrella. social and from here policies can be generated to improve their work quality; such as unemployment insurance, for example.

Some of the detractors might comment on the following:

That the hiring will be very economical.

However, that is the reality today of the economy – read people – which has the right to offer and access jobs. We can stop seeing reality, but it will not stop being there.

That some acquired labor rights would be lost. These informal workers are already excluded from job access and from conditions that are designed to protect the rights of workers in formal companies. We need a different type of protection scheme for workers who do not have high specific technical skills or knowledge and need to earn an income in sectors that can hire them. It is to protect, not ignore the weak.

How much is this?

Still no response.

LIBERAL REDISTRIBUTION

There are two (2) assumptions from which we start:

The first, only the wealth created can be redistributed. Second, we are certain that Marx reformulated progressive taxes because they attacked the basis of the system, undermining the incentives to produce, and the certainty necessary for risky investment. All this leads to communism on the path of socialism.

We take the first assumption, there is only enough wealth to redistribute in state businesses and large companies (only the cash flow, but to touch it is to throw society into the abyss, destroying the social work of property, whether private or public): The best way to redistribute is to make all measures more flexible to do the state jobs that they hire; Yes, that the state itself publishes the procedures, trains together with the universities so that there are many new companies, many proponents. Not just a few of the same with the same. That not only large companies can hire, but also the companies of ordinary people.

On the other hand, the other way to redistribute is by eliminating barriers so that anyone can set up a family or micro-business in sectors that have been protected for only large companies. The greatest protector of the large company's business has been the state through regulations and creating entry barriers that keep competition away from the large companies.

We consider that the protection, with these barriers and state regulations, of large companies is unsustainable in sectors that are already more than twenty (20) years old, not to mention those that are already fifty (50) or more years old where Know How is it procedural. All these sectors are susceptible to moving to procedure manuals that allow the Know to be disseminated. How implicit in its processes and operation; From here on, the market decides who should be bought from.

This could be the best way to redistribute: little by little, without destroying the wealth created, without destroying civilization and without risking society to the danger of scarcity , hunger and shortages.

Another way to redistribute is by liberalizing, democratizing the financial aspect and its access. As a first measure, that of acquiring the first private property. This measure strengthens households financially and their ability to take on more risks for other businesses.

Scheme of small impulse loans for small entrepreneurs. A new risk arises; however, no path is exempt from these. Milton Friedman had already said that when cheap, below-average credit is generated, it finances both businesses that may not be viable in the future, as well as the demand for what they offer. However, this is an unexplored path, and we believe it is worth addressing to see the size of the businesses, to see if they manage to consolidate to move on to a second stage in which these sectors must assume their own social security and pension payments.

The experience of several companies and NGOs that dedicated themselves to lending money to non-entrepreneurs and failed in their attempt shows that the possible order and path forward is as follows:

Generate the entrepreneurial spirit and entrepreneurship.
Seminars on sectors in which companies can be set up.
Training and business knowledge (hard skills).
Business management training (Soft skills).
Loans to family businesses and consolidated companies with a future.

RISKS

Many questions and concerns arise, as is logical in this type of proposals:
How to dismantle monopolies without ending the industry or the supply of products? Now how are taxes replaced? How will the new job creation occur? Are they of the same quality as the previous ones?

There is a danger in the dismantling of large businesses owned by a few and that is to ignore, through fatal arrogance, what aspects of the market favored that business model. We face the risk of setting up business schemes overwhelmingly by the state or subsidized by individuals or micros and that, for market reasons, minimum volume, etc. are not viable, resulting in bankruptcies and a great loss of value and wealth for society. Behind any state intervention in these aspects, the issue of shortages and shortages must be considered.

Unionism is designed to protect the rights of workers in large formal companies in developed countries. Not considering the details, the conditions of informality of family businesses (in this sector 70% of people collaborate in a dream as we saw in the third unit of this same part; many times, for less than the minimum wage with adverse conditions) excludes these workers from access to work. We need a different type of protection scheme for workers who do not have high specific technical skills or knowledge and need to earn an income in sectors that can hire them.

It is up to the government to rethink the laws, regulations, and taxes considering informality if we want to lift them out of poverty.

Large companies and foreign investment are necessary. Experience shows that groups that separate themselves from large markets and foreign investments are condemned to a low income because the amount of exchange (measured in products, services, and knowledge) is very low; the growth rate (which measures the speed at which poverty is left behind) will also be. The challenge is to link the family, the SME to the supply of large companies; we must make it a reality.

CONCLUSION

Each of the parts of this book has developed essential ideas that have allowed us to reach these two fundamental ideas:

The first, the deployment of the left's successful indirect strategy in the midst of the unrest and the second is the theme of the third book: La Esperanza. The companies of ordinary people.

GRAMSCIAN POSTMODERNIST INDIRECT STRATEGY OF TAKING TOTAL POWER

Let's go with the first idea that was born from the reactive strategy directed from Havana, which has been as successful in its deployment as all the strategies based on equality in history have been seductive and captivating.

It is also true that any policy of equality and justice must necessarily dismantle equality before the law, the rule of law and the rule of law, leaving only arbitrariness as a tool. This only ends in dictatorship and tyranny.

The deployment

The new indirect strategy (sufficiently explained in the book) is so powerful that it opens the possibility of total tyrannical power and

could end up facing yet another test in the history of the communist socialist model in a Castro attempt not to let it die.

Its failure is again advocated as it has been where it has been implemented with new, but deeply damaging repercussions on the progress and well-being (economic and political) of Latin American society.

The problem is that the mere deployment of the indirect strategy destroys the foundations of civilization, resulting in khaos and disorder. Additionally, the dismantling of the social function of private property, that is, the destruction of entire economic sectors will bring with it hunger, scarcity and poverty for the majority of the population.

The implementation

His manifest process to eliminate inequalities involves breaking the rule of law to take the product of the work of some and give it to others. This is only possible through coercion; It requires the oppression of the dictatorship, of tyranny to maintain that state of things. Remember that leaving the refined socialist dictatorial structures is almost impossible.

Installation

The new system is incompatible with freedom: human beings work for themselves and their families, so people will resist it, try to break it, ignore it; otherwise, he will emigrate. Besides that: no one has been born who takes care of other people's things!

The new system is incompatible with mathematical calculation: it is impossible to realistically formulate production - there are no prices - (determine what and how much to produce).

The new system suffers from dogmatism and arrogance: it is impossible for a few people to possess all the knowledge needed for simple productions, since knowledge in society is dispersed.

Another of the serious drawbacks is the bad company that Gramscian postmodernism comes with since it uses tools such as victimization, compassion, oppressed groups, gender differences, racial differences, goodism, etc., to hide that they are after the total and absolute power. All they seek is to exploit them to achieve total power.

They have, use, and employ the tools that could destroy Western civilization.

We are in a serious situation due to unrest; But they are not the solution either!

WELFARE STATE AROUND THE COMPANIES OF ORDINARY PEOPLE

We want to pave the way to prosperity and well-being for that 70% of the population that has not let itself die of hunger, who despite exclusion is today in their families, opting for free enterprise. This is the theme of the third book in which we propose the state not as a failed investor in businesses that it does not know how to do or providing the development that the people have not asked for, but as a potentiator of the creative forces that reside in the individual and that only In freedom they can be freed to create value and wealth by:

- Social protection umbrella. Seeking protection for workers who do not yet have the earning capacity to take care of their own destiny and expenses.
-Training in hard and soft skills (from entrepreneurship).
- Liberalization of the informal labor market.
- Flexibility of legislation in informality.
- Liberation of the fiscal and parafiscal tax level for the family business.
-Liberal predistribution and redistribution measures that encourage family businesses and micros.

Overcome exclusion and the roadblocks.

We intend to eliminate a series of additional impediments to the exclusion that have been placed on SMEs and family businesses (they have created a path of obstacles for local businesses); These impediments have been generated from various sources: some as measures to protect the formal worker against large companies - these regulations work very well in that environment, but are harmful for companies in the incipient search -, others function as barriers to entry to protect the businesses of large companies.

The new proposal for the social security umbrella is based on the basic pillars of protection of the informal worker:

- The worker as the weakest link in these interest groups must be protected.
- The interest group of workers must have a minimum under which it is subsidized and the microenterprise by the state in its minimum health, risks, pension, etc. After exceeding this minimum, the worker and the company must assume their commitments.
- Nascent companies must have complete freedom of contract to be able to organize their productive potential.

As is the case today, two sectors will coexist, but both now protected:

The first of large companies, regulated as it is today.

The second sector of informality and family businesses with special legislation.

The limit between one and the other could be the mix of financial capacity and sales achieved by the family company in which its transition would begin until assuming the responsibilities that correspond to it, starting with the minimum wage. Do not forget that the bulk of the population is in development.

Who politically can help hope?

As we see, economic freedom is attacked in many ways; those that we have reviewed in this brief analysis: the direct and the indirect. Direct, visible, violent, eliminates the right to property and its management. The indirect, camouflaged, deliberate, systematic (Gramscian postmodernism) attacks the bases, culture, incentives, the rule of law, etc. seeking to eliminate the effects of property, its ability to reproduce, its bases, foundations, and incentives to remain in business (they ignore the social value of private property). The worst scenario could be the decline of civilization and the well-being achieved.

The neo-communists (41) are at the forefront of these attacks; They want to go against nature and against the entire population. They are in the shadows waiting and lying in wait.

On the other hand, there is the pragmatic left eager for alternatives (I thank many of them for the opportunities they gave me to set out their concerns that we hope are reflected in the initial ideas of this book, they are their ideas; ideas so powerful that after liberated people make their way on their own, that could not die due to the intransigence of a few) that is about to take advantage of this opportunity to be the boost that that 70% of the economy unknown to the right needs (the right has selfishly stayed in the large companies and in business with their friends around the rights). We reveal the significance of the opportunity to help all these families throughout Latin America; However, nothing is free. This requires some capitulations on some premises and doctrines that had guided his actions: first, recognizing the **serious Marxist error in economics (42)** ; second, return to free enterprise (in the companies of ordinary people) and install new concepts that consider not only growth, but also shared wealth based on liberal predistribution, liberal income redistribution - as we propose in this chapter - based on a free market in the companies of ordinary people (we propose to free labor and capital) widely flexible, where the state - under the rule of law - is in charge of the social overruns that do not allow companies to grow. companies: that is, the construction of a welfare state for those who really need it.

The people have chosen economic freedom, it is unobjectionable. The question is how are we going to face this reality? With deception and coercion leading to tyranny? Or we will continue with an indirect

strategy that will surely work in some countries at a price in terms of
well-being, lost potential of civilization or what is worse, the loss of
freedom.

REFERENCES AND BIBLIOGRAPHICAL SOURCES

This book arises from the criticism and analysis of different authors; among others: Alexis de Tocqueville, Proudhon, Karl Marx, Frederick Engels, Ludwig Von Mises, Frederic Hayek, Adam Smith, Milton Friedman, Joseph Stiglitz, Antonio Gramsci, Mitchel Foucault, Louis Althusser, Jacques Derrida, Jean Paul Sartre, Simone de Beauvoir, Jean Francois Lyotard, Jean Baudrillard, Gilles Deleuze.

EVENT ANALYSIS METHODOLOGY

Different authors and book references have been used, however, as a methodology it is about confronting what the authors are trying to say, their ideas, taking their analysis and contextualizing them to see what clarity they shed on the events that are the subject of observation by us.

METHODOLOGY USED: DIRECT OBSERVATION METHOD.

This method is widely used in our studies and consists of previously identifying some problems or inconveniences and then carefully observing the phenomenon, observing the actors in a space-time situation, recording the information obtained for subsequent analysis. This indicates that we are normally full of handwritten sheets and inconclusive information (data about behaviors, events and/or situations that are the results of previous events that we have identified as the problem) and that we then try to complement with non-formal interviews to investigate more about the event.

Field work is carried out, testing methodologies on the people themselves; They are trained, they are observed in their cultural environment, to be able to reflect strategies for solving everyday problems. This is our most important methodology.

GRADES

Alexis de Tocqueville (1): France (1805-1859). Viscount de Tocqueville. French historian, precursor of sociology, politician, thinker, jurist.

Pragmatists (2) (realism): Within the group of pragmatic realists there is a minority with the sagacity to undertake, to set up a business, to do well. You don't need to be very intelligent, but rather have a special talent for seeing circumstances, knowing how to take advantage of them for your personal benefit. It is risky, with the ability to cope with high stress, communicate and convince behind an idea, take a dream to carry it out. It certainly creates a difference – a greater good – for society in terms of poverty reduction. Human beings are unequal, and the effects of their actions will be unequal.

The Idealist is more sensitive, suffers the inequality generated and has the ability to see the results of individualism. He is normally a studious man, and his economic environment is protected by the tranquility of a fixed salary.

One is capable of making a machine in which you cannot see the gears. The other is able to see the gears, the nuts and lock it by inserting a stick.

The idealist submits to risks in order to achieve greater ideals: justice. The other person, as soon as they feel a bad situation, sells, and goes somewhere else.
One is capable of innovating, creating from nothing, putting all his effort into an idea (it generates employment for normal people and is also in a large company). The fight against poverty is with new jobs (creating new wealth).

The other does great business alongside the state, in traditional sectors, in which a procedure is the guide (coal, oil, public services, basic industry); However, it aggravates the issue of access to employment since a large part of the population does not have the education, skills and aptitudes required by large companies (state or public).

The one, without knowing it and even without caring, helps in the reduction of poverty - only economic freedom explains its decrease since the year 1700. On the other hand, the fight against poverty is based on subsidies (distributing the wealth created), this methodology that does not teach fishing condemns the individual to remain poor, resulting by extension in placing the entire society at risk. The one innovates and contributes to science; On the other side, the capacity for innovation, science and creating technology is diluted.

Society cannot remain unmoved by the confrontation between these two groups because the field of war is the economy, in other words: the war is fought in terms of food, medicine, services, health, subsistence. It is waged in terms of the destruction of everything…

Ibero-America (3): we will refer to the Spanish and Portuguese speaking countries in Latin America and will include the Iberian Peninsula. The reason is that the processes of elitist corruption and exclusion that are occurring are linked to the culture generated and installed in Latin America from the two colonialist countries.

America (4): America in the context of Tocqueville, only refers to the United States to its democratic process far from the European metropolis, from its static political and social guidelines promoted by monarchical feudalism.

Equality and Freedom (5): it is necessary to clarify , so that the reader does not get confused, that the concepts for these two words expressed for the period from the 16th century to the 18th century are in the case of equality: mobility between social classes (Royalty and Aristocracy, Clergy and Servants) and Freedom as the right to one's own life, mobility, to do as one pleases, was prevented by law from the Servants, who were tied to the land. These concepts continued in the common ideology, even into the 18th century, and despite the fact that equality before the law was expressed in the Declaration of the Rights of Man and of the Citizen on August 26, 1789, in the French Revolution. Immobility between classes is an idea that persists to this day, especially in some places in Latin America.

Mobility (6): it is understood in this context and at this time, as the search for equality between classes, the greatest process of social, economic, and political advancement in the history of humanity was taking place; It would be unleashed by trade, the free enterprise that would come with the industrial revolution.

French Revolution (7): it is the violent culmination of the persecution of equality and freedom, which, in the case of France, the social and political changes that followed did not find gradualness. Finally, all these events would open the beginning of the end of the monarchy throughout Europe and the social and political privileges of the clergy and nobility; It was the end of feudalism.

Declaration of the Rights of Man and of the Citizen, 1789 (8):

DECLARATION OF THE RIGHTS OF MAN AND CITIZEN, 1789

Article 1.- Men are born and remain free and equal in rights. Social distinctions can only be based on common utility.

Article 2.- The goal of every political association is the conservation of the natural and imprescriptible rights of man. These rights are: freedom, property, security, and resistance to oppression.

Article 3.- The origin of all sovereignty resides essentially in the Nation. No body or individual can exercise authority that does not expressly emanate from it.

Article 4.- Freedom consists of being able to do everything that does not harm others. Thus, the exercise of the natural rights of each man has no limits other than those that ensure the other members of society the enjoyment of these same rights. Those limits just can be decided for the law.

Article 5.- The law can only prohibit actions that are harmful to society, everything that is not prohibited by law cannot be prevented, and no one can be forced to do what it does not order.

Article 6.- The law is the expression of the general will. All citizens have the right to participate personally or through their representatives in its formation. It must be the same for everyone, whether it protects or punishes. All citizens, being equal before it, are equally admissible to all dignities, positions, and public employment, according to their capacity and without any other distinction than that of their virtues and their talents.

Article 7.- No person can be accused, detained, or imprisoned except in cases determined by law according to the forms prescribed therein. Those who request, facilitate, execute, or have arbitrary orders executed must be punished; but every citizen called or required by virtue of the provisions of the law must obey immediately: he becomes guilty of resistance.

Article 8.- The law must not establish more than strict and obviously necessary penalties, and no one can be punished except by virtue of a law established and promulgated prior to the crime and legally applied.

Article 9.- Every person, being presumed innocent until declared guilty, if their detention is deemed essential, the law must severely repress all rigor that is not necessary to secure their person.

Article 10.- No one should be disturbed by their opinions, even religious ones, if their manifestation does not alter the public order established by law.

Article 11.- The free communication of thoughts and opinions is one of the most precious rights of man; Every citizen can, therefore, speak, write, and print freely, except for the liability that the abuse of this freedom produces in cases determined by law.

Article 12.- The guarantee of the rights of man and citizen needs a public force. This force is instituted, therefore, for the benefit of all and not for the utility of those who are in charge of it.

Article 13.- For the maintenance of the public force and for administration expenses, a common contribution is essential: it must be equally distributed among all citizens based on their possibilities.

Article 14.- All citizens have the right to verify for themselves or through their representatives the need for public contribution, to accept it freely, to monitor its use and to determine the quota, the base, the collection, and the duration.

Article 15.-The company has the right to ask any public agent for accounts regarding its administration.

Article 16.- Any society in which the guarantee of rights is not assured, nor the separation of powers established, does not have a Constitution.

Article 17.- Property being an inviolable and sacred right, no one can be deprived of it except when the public need, legally verified, clearly demands it and with the condition of fair and prior compensation.

Equality (9): Inequality and the term equality, closely related to the lack or substantial difference in economic income or possession of wealth, would appear much later with the advent of the studies of Karl Marx and with the connotation given in the middle of the century XX.

The explanation of this aspect is found in the second part of this book (10): see book: Why Countries Fail, Daron Acemoglu and James A. Robinson. Pages 33 to 43.

Absolute Monarchy (11): absolutism justified itself as a more stable form of government, where the principle of authority and

legitimacy was recognized by the capacity it had when employing the use of force. Economic power was based on ownership of all the lands and people that it could control and defend. Absolute monarchy has existed throughout human history and dates back to the Old Testament to the Kings chosen by God to govern his people, Israel. The main characteristics, which extended until the beginning of Democracy in the 28th Century, were that the Monarch was chosen by God and responded only to Him; He concentrated all powers in him or his delegates; the executive, legislative and judicial were in him one and were as despotic as human nature allows, imparting power even over the lives of his subjects.
It is not our role to judge history with a sense of criticism, only to put the facts in the way in which they apparently occurred and that also guaranteed, in some way, the continuity of the human species. We could conclude that its moment was the best there was.

Individualism (12): Tocqueville coined this concept, and it is different from how he conceived it, from what it means today. Back then, it meant a society apathetic to politics and dedicated to its own things; This allowed the Emperor Napoleon Bonaparte to be installed due to the same lack of understanding of what was happening in politics; Empty spaces are always covered by politicians and their court.

Today the word liberal individualism is not pejorative, nor synonymous with apathetic; It has become the concept that allows entrepreneurship, the creation of value and wealth.

The processes of economic discovery (13): Each independent process or sector has its specific time course; The advantage of this method is that knowledge is distributed and the risks of loss for society are divided into as many participants as possible, with the value of the risk being part of the individual decision. When business is positive and the market is enough for everyone, everyone does well; However, this is not the constant in business, since, if things go badly, the loss will be much less for the Company than if there is a single investor. This is the advantage in economic terms.

The free market, in turn, is full of cases: ¨ To Big To Fall ¨ (too big to drop); It happens in imperfect markets that have allowed monopolies to be installed, in which the loss of such a large company can entail irreparable losses for society. The fall of monopolies of these characteristics and dimensions in the free market are assimilated to the falls in a nationalized and collectivized economy. However, generalized loss is a characteristic of the entire collectivist model.

In the case of human design (communism) and not spontaneous and individual (liberalism) the loss is maximized since the project is carried out by allocating large resources of society with the greatest number of individuals possible to enforce an idea of a leader (megalomaniac). When this fails the results are catastrophic; This explains the death from famine due to shortages in all the countries where it has been implemented; its great losses and economic setbacks in the well-being of society that this type of development path implies.

However, if the market is imperfect and they have allowed monopolies to be installed, in these the loss may be due to the characteristics and dimensions of a nationalized and collectivized economy.

Not all value and wealth creation go hand in hand with the private sector; New veins of development can be created in sectors where the investment is very high and the risk is very high and private companies hesitate to take the initial steps. However, it is not the topic of the book.

Communist Manifesto (14): text taken from the book Communist Manifesto by Karl Marx and Federico Engels 1848. It is worth clarifying that the word communism, Marxism and even socialism are basically used to mean the same thing. It is worth clarifying that for the orthodox Marxist they do not mean the same and would use it as a distracting mechanism from what we really want to point out. For Marx, socialism was an initial phase, which should be reached later, when the state was not needed, and everyone was equal; That is then communism.

Marxist doctrine (15): It is important to establish certain characteristics of Marxism and its consequences such as socialism and communism; Although socialism and communism originate from the theories of Marx in the time of 1848, they are consolidated in the Marxist-Leninist revolutions of 1917 (Lenin gives it its character of violent seizure of power) in Russia (Soviet Union) and in 1949 with Mao Tse Tung 's revolution in China. These movements saw their end in 1991 with the disintegration of the Soviet Union, then in China in 1978 with the rise of Deng Xiaoping (a pragmatist who saw what was best to produce value, opting for capitalism in the economic sphere with dictatorship in the political sphere). The installation of free trade zones and the transition to a market economy is coming.

In Latin America, starting in 1990 and instigated by a call (Castro and Lula) to relaunch socialism-communism as a movement opposed to neoliberalism (¨cause of poverty and originator of inequality¨), there are very similar processes that make them called its authors as living examples of socialism (21st Century Socialism). Additionally, there are other processes of slow development, but some of their members are calling to accelerate the revolution as if there existed underneath a process underway that we had not requested, for which we had not voted, but that is going to be carried out. .

Doctrine: Set of ideas, teachings or basic principles defended and in which that certain interest groups create and that systematically guide their actions.

These ideas may be based on the analysis of reality and experience, or on historical facts, or on the Should Be, or they are simply utopias.

Utopias and some overly sublime ideals, even though they are inspired by the best intentions, when they become doctrines and in the hands of messianic-megalomaniacal leaders have proven to be the greatest mass murderers and genocidaires in history (This applies both to the right and to the left).

Political constitution (16): one of the greatest achievements of the French Revolution is to guarantee in the constitution the rights to class equality and freedom. The constitution of a country is what guarantees the freedom of individuals from the irresistible power of the state, which is the holder (in the sense that it owns what is not its own) of legal violence and weapons. Freedom can be acquired before a state through the establishment of rights and the division of powers.

Equal Classes (17): Marxism offers the elimination of classes and with this the elimination of exploitation. In several countries, socialism occurred, as did the suppression of important parts of the population (very high cost). However, the promise was believed; This was not fulfilled. It could not be fulfilled! There is an implicit credibility in the formulation of the proposal, but there is also a hidden trap: its dialectical structure that does not go beyond launching the promise without supporting the how, does not show its drawbacks or its contradictions - there is a fundamental difference between describing a fact that is happening to another ideal; They are different methodologies in which the description of the action, that is, of the events that are happening in a process in reality have their own weight, in this case negative and right there we can see their shortcomings. However, the seductive, charming short proposal suffers from all this. They are not comparable.

Political Power (18): the elimination of political power refers to that stage of socialism in which the state disappears, because inequality disappears and a later stage called communism follows. In this writing the two words become synonymous because this final event of disappearance never occurred and we believe it to be totally improbable. The use in much of this book of the words together, that is, socialism-communism, is to avoid the fallacy of distraction that is normally carried out to distance the discussion that socialism has never worked, reformulating the premise that communism never existed. had given. As of this writing, both are the same.

Production (19): according to historical materialism, production relations determine social, cultural, moral and even religious relations between individuals.

Antonio Gramsci (20): Italy (1891-1937). Philosopher, sociologist, politician, anthropologist, and Marxist theorist. Founder of the Communist Party of Italy in 1921. Books: Notebooks from prison.

Postmodernist current (21): postmodernism is an entire philosophical current that occurred from the late sixties to the nineties of writers, sociologists, anthropologists, politicians, economists, with extensive experience and depth in their studies, which are functional to the left because they see Socialism as its ultimate goal, however, they offer different paths to Marxism-Leninism, which sought the fall of the capitalist economic system through armed revolution and the direct attack on the coercive oppressive systems of Liberal Democracy, and then eliminate private property, changing all the values of Society to values functional to a planned and single-direction economy. In that order.

Postmodernism provided new ideological tools, apparently very disjointed, but at the right level and given the circumstances, they are very effective in - first and then a cultural hegemony (indoctrination) - deconstructing all values, and the morality of a society until reaching the pillars and bases of the system by relaxing its entire imaginary of ideas and beliefs, unleashing the small intermediate forces hidden and contained in the contradictions of society.

A postmodernist does not talk or argue about his ideas; For them any discussion is about power and to convince me. Then, it is implicit in their philosophy to deny the discussion because it has no logic for them: two classes do not reach an agreement because the discussion is part of a game of oppression.

Some authors that we could include in this current are: Antonio Gramsci (although he died a little earlier), Mitchel Foucault, Louis Althusser, Jacques Derrida, Jean Paul Sartre, Simone de Beauvoir, Jean Francois Lyotard, Jean Baudrillard, Gilles Deleuze, among others.

Deconstruct (22): undo the structures of a concept after an intellectual analysis to give it a new meaning. It was initially used by Jacques Derrida to deconstruct texts, and by extension, the movement has used it to deconstruct all the concepts, values, and pillars of society in its desire to tear it down to give a new meaning in accordance with its intentions. His sin: under firm human redesign, he destroys (deconstructs) social and moral concepts that have taken humanity thousands of years to develop. Its final effects on civilization are unknown.

Khaos (23): it is used with K in this writing to separate it from the word with C. When we use it with K, it is in its meaning of disorder and induced confusion.
Directed Khaos has the potential that the confusion it generates diverts general attention from the clear and precise objectives of destroying the system. In addition to that, it relaxes the morality and the value system, in a way that allows more risky adventures seeking to break the rule of law, the laws and the prevailing legislation, while all disciplinary codes are subverted, formal and informal institutions are broken. in charge of some way of maintaining order. This confusion and disorder is induced by multiple liberations of revolutionary power that have the small contradictions (differences that collide with each other and were settled with a code of discipline or with formal and informal institutions such as prison or patriarchy) of society, which now They have broken free and are colluding with Khaos.

Non-instinctive norms (24): non-instinctive norms are the aspects of behavior that talk about those elements that are learned that the person accepts spontaneously by imitating them, in which there is no agreement - the acceptance to use them is given in those conditions because they are convenient for the development of civilization. These elements can form instinctual-based institutions such as the family, as well as expanded -non-instinctive- institutions such as those that allow commerce in the extensive order of society. The normal course is to be part of the uses and customs, which can later become laws or formal and informal institutions. Finally, they are all part of the rule of law, which is what allows social, economic, and political relations to occur with order and transparency. The above makes trade possible; makes civilization possible.

The strong instinctive order – such as filial love and love for children – makes the family possible; But the rest of the things that allow two groups that do not know each other to negotiate are non-instinctive relationships, learned by the force of their goodness and in which one accepts that it is beneficial for these types of regulations to exist.

Marxist historical materialism (25): historical materialism is the way in which Marxists interpret the economic history of societies; In other words, they explain that the behavior of a society is due to the type of economic relationships they have. We explain: in the feudal era, land ownership generated all the other series of formal and non-formal relationships and institutions so that that type of economic relationship of ownership over the land occurred, which is the only thing that produced value and wealth at that time. In capitalist society, it is the private production goods that recreate a whole series of institutions, fictions, laws, the mechanism of language, the family, culture, etc., all so that this production system can occur and reproduce.

Progressivism (26): (ChatGPT OpenAI). Progressivism seeks to promote social and political change with the aim of moving towards a more equal and just society. Features that may vary according to the country:

Private and state ownership of productive goods: they accept private property as necessary and seek state ownership in issues such as public services, health, education, etc.

Social justice: Progressivism is concerned with addressing social and economic inequalities, seeking to promote policies that reduce the gap between rich and poor. This may include the implementation of social welfare programs, seeking a deep redistribution of income, that is, of income through taxes and the institutions of a welfare state, increase in the minimum wage, gender equality, rights of the workers and social protection.

Civil and human rights: Progressives typically defend and promote civil and human rights for all individuals, regardless of race, gender, sexual orientation, religion, or any other characteristic. This means supporting equal marriage, gender equality, protecting minority rights and fighting discrimination.

Sustainability and the environment: Progressivism tends to value sustainability and environmental protection. It seeks to address climate change, promote renewable energy, reduce pollution, and preserve natural resources for future generations.

Education and equal access: Progressives generally support quality public education and equal access to education. This may include the expansion of preschool education programs, access to affordable higher education, and the promotion of educational opportunities for all citizens.

Inclusive policies and social integration: Progressivism seeks to promote social inclusion and the integration of all people in society. This may involve promoting more open migration policies, recognizing, and respecting diverse cultural identities, and fighting discrimination and racism.

Slavery (27): we are going to obtain several definitions - free of naivety and as much as possible adjusted to the time - because they all suit the objective of this writing. The beginnings of slavery date back to ancient times and were born from a way of using defeated labor in battles, instead of execution. The slave had to be coerced, forced under the threat of death and all rights taken away to be able to subject them to total defenselessness against their subsequent master and new owner of their existence. This practice became the basis of the economy of most nations of the Ancient World, moving from uses and customs to written law; then forced by the power of the state's weapons. Slavery as such gave way to servitude in which the servant acquired some rights but remained tied to the land.

Currently, there is a modern concept of slavery related to a tax burden such that it does not allow you to have the fruit of your work. In this book we will not touch on the racial slavery so widely implemented by the colonial powers in the New World.

Feudalism, its uses, customs, and legal issues around property (28): the Ancient Age brings to the Middle Ages the issue of land ownership (the only source of value and wealth creation at the time) headed by the kings. and the nobility; you had to belong to that social class to have property; that was the law. When the discovery of America occurred with large expanses of untamed lands, the English, Spanish and Portuguese crowns faced the challenge of transferring an entire scheme of administration and property to the new world: the English crown failed again and again by pretending that the colonists of the empire return to vassalage and servitude in North America, an America without gold and with an aggressive indigenous population (this ended with the extermination of almost the entire indigenous population and the acquisition of black slave labor in Africa). The English crown (Virginia Company) solved the problem by granting land to the colonists, without titles of nobility (and an act outside the prevailing law), making them landowners and then requiring them to pay tributes and taxes to the crown; It was already too late, they acquired weapons to defend themselves.

In South America, the Spanish and Portuguese crowns managed to transfer the entire feudal administration to their new colonies, giving noble titles to the expeditionary conquerors (now they could have lands in the name of royalty); Unlike North America, there was a lot of gold and they managed to dominate the indigenous people by subduing them as indentured labor.

Immense tanks (29): The indigenous people did not know gunpowder, nor the horses that were the "tanks" of that time; The Indians fled in terror at such a presence. It is not an apology against the Spanish, nor against their race, which we will have something in our blood. It is rather something about the "Laws of War" normally the human being, after a conquest, exterminates, subjugates, enslaves, or makes the defeated pay the costs of war.

Mita and the encomienda (30): two systems of servitude, not to mention slavery, that the Crown had to force the indigenous people, defeated in war, to give away their work in the mines (Mita) or to the owners of the land (Encomienda). Isabel la Católica (tormented soul on the verge of death) in a death rattle and seeking to save her soul, recognizes ¼ of a soul in the aborigines, which is why they had to be evangelized.

Feudal System (31): In the original feudal system, only Nobles were owners, so it was necessary to issue them Noble Titles so that they could own, manage, and inherit in the name of the Spanish crown.

Mestizos and (Pernada Rights) right of first step (32): mestizaje is the mixture of two races, in this case the white one with the indigenous one. In the Colony, if you could demonstrate a certain degree of white blood, that is, mestizo, you left slavery, you left the Mita and the Encomienda. (it was very important to deny indigenous blood). The miscegenation occurred due to the confluence of several aspects. The first Spain had been influenced by Jewish migrations and for eight centuries they were occupied by the Moors, so that sporadic cases of mixing were quietly accepted. The second, the Spanish did not exterminate (as the Anglo-Saxons did in the USA) the indigenous people who submitted. The third, The Right of Pernada, is that the Nobleman had the first sexual right over the daughters of his servants who reached the age of merit; This explains the reason why it occurred so widely in the conquered territories. The result of this medieval (feudal) custom, that is, these illegitimate children of bastard blood (Royal and Plebe) did not inherit titles or possessions. Finally, Queen Isabel La Católica, on her Death Bed and to redeem her soul, had recognized some soul in the aborigines (blacks were never recognized with souls until independence).

Indians (33): Could this be the reason why people today deny their indigenous ancestry? Is the Servility to which they were subjected so deeply rooted in our Collective Unconscious that we still, after 300 years, continue to use the denial of our race as a defense mechanism? If the indigenous people could demonstrate that they were a mixture, that is, mestizos, they could escape the power of the encomendero and achieve their freedom. They had more soul...
Many of the mestizos and even clearly indigenous people, especially in the Cundiboyacense highlands, call themselves white and in fact when they are reproached about their race, they do not know that they are indigenous or mestizos.

Hard work (3 4): He was considered impure and lower class.

Gini coefficient (35): Gini coefficient where 0 is perfect equality (everyone has the same income) and 1 is perfect inequality (one person has all the income and the others have none).

In rich countries it measures inequality in wealth (none has a negative income). In poor countries it measures income inequality (it does not include wealth, that is, it does not consider savings represented in real estate, which is what happens in societies that deny access to banking systems).

Global Gini coefficient 0.63 the income of the richest 20% of people in the world is 28.7 times higher than that of the poorest 20%.

According to the United Nations, a Gini coefficient greater than 0.40 is alarming, since this indicates a reality of polarization between rich and poor, being a breeding ground for antagonism between different social classes, which can lead to discontent or social unrest.

Socialism and Communism (36): they are used in this writing as synonyms, although for Marx socialism was a previous and momentary stage in which the State had to disappear to move on to communism and now everyone would be free and happy. The word socialism followed by communism is used extensively, basically because it is easier for the unsuspecting reader to identify them and to avoid the explanatory fallacy and their difference to divert the discussion from the central topic.

WORLD BANK REPORTS DATED APRIL 10, 2014 AND OCTOBER 5, 2022 (37):

GROWTH IS NOT ENOUGH TO END POVERTY, ACCORDING TO THE WORLD BANK GROUP

WASHINGTON, April 10, 2014. According to a report released today by the World Bank, economic growth, while essential to reducing poverty, has limits. Countries must complement efforts to increase growth with policies that allow more resources to be allocated to the extremely poor. These resources can be distributed through the growth process itself, by promoting more inclusive growth, or through public programs, such as conditional and direct cash transfers.

The report also notes that while it is imperative that people escape extreme poverty, it is also important to ensure that, in the long term, they do not stagnate at a level slightly above the extreme poverty line due to who lack the opportunities that would allow them to achieve a better life.

"Economic growth has been instrumental in reducing extreme poverty and improving the living conditions of many poor people," said World Bank Group President Jim Yong Kim. "However, even if all countries grew at the same rate as they have done over the last 20 years, and even if income distribution did not change, global poverty would only be reduced by 10% by 2030, from 17, 7% in 2010. This is simply not enough. To end extreme poverty, we must place special emphasis on achieving more inclusive growth and increasing the number of programs aimed at aiding the poor directly."

"To put an end to extreme poverty, it would be necessary for 50 million people every year, until 2030, to stop making up the vast number of the poorest, those who earn less than US$1.25 a day. This means that 1 million people should be lifted out of poverty every week for the next 16 years. Although the work will be extraordinarily difficult, I am convinced that we can achieve it. This generation has the chance to end extreme poverty," added Mr. Kim.

According to the report, growth alone is unlikely to end extreme poverty by 2030, since as poverty decreases, growth tends to lift fewer people out of poverty. This is because, upon reaching this stage, many of the people who still live in extreme poverty find themselves in a situation in which it is extremely difficult to improve their living conditions.

Likewise, it is noted that the increase in income inequality can mitigate the impact of growth on poverty reduction. Inequality, in addition to being a problem, has other consequences: in countries where income inequality increased, the effect of growth on poverty was smaller or even reversed. On the contrary, research indicates that, in countries where inequality decreased, the reduction in poverty corresponding to a given growth rate was greater. Even if there are no changes in inequality, the power of economic growth to reduce poverty is lower in countries where there is initially greater inequality. Thus, the World Bank Group's goals of ending extreme poverty and promoting shared prosperity are closely linked: sustained progress in the fight against extreme poverty also requires continued attention to what happens to the poorest 40% of the population.

"It is sad to note that in our prosperous world more than one billion people live in extreme poverty, and it is encouraging that the World Bank Group has called not only to alleviate poverty but also to eradicate it and promote a more equitable world. To achieve this we will need determination, as well as ideas and innovation, since the paths of the economy are unpredictable," he stated. Kaushik Basu, First Vice President, and Economist of the World Bank.

The shared prosperity goal established by the World Bank, and ratified by shareholders in 2013, provides a means to understand inequality of income and opportunity. Although great strides have been made in lifting people out of extreme poverty, many are still poor, often due to a lack of opportunity. Focusing attention on the poorest 40% of the population can help ensure that these people also reap the full benefits of the economic progress of the country in which they live.

To aid the poorest 40% of the population, it is essential to know their characteristics, which vary from country to country.

In Rwanda, for example, 63% of the population lives in extreme poverty; that is, a percentage greater than the entire segment of the 40% with the lowest income. In Colombia, on the contrary, 8% of the population lives in extreme poverty, and in Turkey this has fallen to an irreducible level, since, according to international standards, only 1.3% of the population is extremely poor.

In Bangladesh, two-thirds of the poorest 40% of the population live in rural areas, while in Brazil the percentage drops to 23%. In Rwanda, 11% of the lowest-income 40% received secondary education, while in Turkey the percentage rises to 55%. In terms of employment, in the Philippines 63% of the poorest 40% of the population work in the agricultural sector, while in Jordan the percentage drops to 11%.

"The complexities linked to identifying the poorest 40% of inhabitants in each country highlight the challenges that arise when formulating policies according to the country's circumstances to reach them effectively," said Jos. Verbeek, lead author of the report and senior economist in the World Bank's Development Prospects Analysis Group.

To reduce poverty, it is necessary to know where the greatest number of poor people live and, at the same time, focus on places where living conditions are most difficult. This involves concerted efforts in the countries where many of the planet's 1.2 billion poor live. The top five countries, in terms of the number of poor, are India (with 33% of the world's poor), China

(13%), Nigeria (7%), Bangladesh (6%) and the Democratic Republic of the Congo (5%), which together house almost 760 million of the planet's poor. If five other countries were added—Indonesia, Pakistan, Tanzania, Ethiopia, and Kenya—the figure would rise to almost 80% of the extremely poor. The report points out, therefore, that to end extreme poverty it will be essential to dedicate special attention to these countries.

However, in many smaller countries, the proportion of people living below the poverty line is much higher. In 16 countries, more than half of the population lives in extreme poverty. The top five countries, in terms of poverty density, are the Democratic Republic of the Congo (where 88% of the population lives below the poverty line), Liberia (84%), Burundi and Madagascar (81%, respectively). and Zambia (75%). Reducing poverty in these places is as important as making progress in countries where the absolute number of poor is much higher.

To achieve both goals, the World Bank Group will need to tailor its support to each nation's level of urbanization, the magnitude of its energy needs, levels of basic services, the human capabilities of each citizen, and the capabilities of its governments. Success will depend on the broad implementation of transformative solutions, which could include programs to improve sanitation services in thriving cities, projects to ensure more efficient use of water for agriculture and other purposes, expanding health coverage for lower-income people or expanding welfare-to-employment transition programs in places with high levels of youth unemployment.

Likewise, progress to improve the living conditions of the poor will not be sustainable if the environmental consequences of economic development are not considered. To sustain economic development, it is important to ensure that the use of resources in growth processes is more efficient and that these processes are less polluting and have a greater capacity for adaptation without necessarily entailing a reduction in their pace.

GLOBAL PROGRESS IN THE REDUCTION OF EXTREME POVERTY IS SLOWED
BY 2030, ALMOST 600 MILLION PEOPLE WILL NEED TO SUVIST ON LESS THAN USD 2.15 A DAY

WASHINGTON CITY, October 5, 2022. According to a new study by the World Bank, the goal of ending extreme poverty worldwide by 2030 is unlikely to be achieved if economic growth does not show historically unprecedented rates for the rest of this decade. The study concludes that COVID -19 represented the biggest setback to global poverty reduction efforts since 1990, and that the war in Ukraine threatens to worsen the situation.

The new edition of the World Bank report, *Poverty and Shared Prosperity* , presents the first comprehensive picture of poverty around the world following the extraordinary series of shocks to the global economy in recent years. The pandemic is estimated to have pushed some 70 million people into extreme poverty in 2020, the largest single-year increase since tracking these numbers began in 1990 . As a result, an estimated 719 million people were subsisting on less than $2.15 a day at the end of 2020.

"Progress in reducing extreme poverty has basically stopped, compounded by weak growth in the global economy," said David Malpass, president of the World Bank Group . "Our mission is concerned about the rise in extreme poverty and the decline in shared prosperity caused by inflation, the depreciation of various currencies and broader overlapping development crises. This spells a bleak outlook for billions of people around the world. It is necessary to introduce adjustments in macroeconomic policies to improve the allocation of global capital, promote monetary stability, reduce inflation, and reactivate the increase in median income. The alternative is the current situation: slowing global growth, higher interest rates, greater risk aversion and fragility in many developing countries."

The report states that 2020 marked a historic turning point: the era of global income convergence gave way to divergence. Most of the cost of the pandemic fell on the poorest: among the sectors that are located in the lowest 40% of the distribution, income losses reached an average of 4%, that is, double that among the 20 % richer. As a result, global inequality rose for the first time in decades.

The application of solid fiscal policy measures made a notable difference, as it allowed us to mitigate the impact of the COVID -19 pandemic on poverty. In fact, the average poverty rate in developing economies would have been 2.4 percentage points higher if there had been no fiscal response. However, public spending was much more useful for poverty reduction in richer countries, which generally managed to *fully offset* the impact of COVID -19 through fiscal policies and other emergency support measures. Developing economies had fewer resources and therefore spent less and achieved less: upper-middle-income economies offset only 50% of the impact on poverty, while low- and lower-middle-income economies barely a quarter.

"Over the next decade, it will be crucial for developing economies to invest in improving health conditions and education, given the severe learning loss and health-related setbacks they suffered during the pandemic," said Indermit Gill, Chief Economist and Senior Vice President for Development Economics at the World Bank. "In a time of record debt and scarce fiscal resources, this will not be easy. Governments should concentrate their resources on developing human capital and maximizing growth."

The new report provides for the first time current and historical data on the new global extreme poverty line , which has been raised to $2.15 a day to reflect the most recent purchasing power parity data , from 2017. Poverty extreme decreased dramatically worldwide between 1990 and 2019, the last year for which official data is available. But progress slowed after 2014, and policymakers now face a more complex context, as extreme poverty is concentrated in the areas of the world where it will be most difficult to eradicate: sub-Saharan Africa, conflict-affected areas and rural.

Today, sub-Saharan Africa is home to 60% of all people living in extreme poverty – 389 million, more than any other region. Here the poverty rate is close to 35%, the highest in the world. To achieve the poverty reduction target set for 2030, each country in the region would need to achieve per capita gross domestic product (GDP) growth of 9% per year for the remainder of the current decade. This represents an exceptionally difficult goal for countries whose GDP per capita grew, on average, 1.2% in the 10 years before the COVID -19 pandemic.

Governments must act without delay on three fronts:

- *Avoid blanket subsidies and increase targeted cash transfers:* In low- and middle-income economies, half of all spending on energy subsidies benefits the richest 20% of the population, who consume the most energy. Cash transfers are a much more effective mechanism to support the poor and vulnerable groups.

- *Emphasis on long-term growth:* High-return investments in education, research and development, and infrastructure projects need to be made without delay. In times of scarce resources, more efficient spending and better preparation for the next crisis will be key.

- *Mobilize domestic revenue without harming the poor:* Property and carbon taxes can help increase tax revenue without harming the poorest. The same can be said for expanding the tax base for personal and corporate income tax. If it is necessary to raise sales and excise taxes, governments should minimize economic distortions and harmful distributional effects by simultaneously implementing targeted monetary transfers that offset the effects of such taxes on the most vulnerable households.

More inclusive growth (38): OpenAI ChatGPT response: For the World Bank, inclusive growth It means that economic growth must be sustainable, equitable and benefit all members of society, including the poorest and most vulnerable. This is an approach that seeks to ensure that economic growth is not only measured by the increase in GDP, but also by its ability to reduce poverty, create jobs, improve living conditions, and reduce inequality.

In this sense, the World Bank promotes policies and programs that seek to improve people's access to economic and social opportunities, promote financial inclusion, reduce barriers to entry into the labor market, improve education and training, and support the development of small and medium enterprises. All of this to promote more equitable and sustainable economic growth that benefits all members of society.

conditional and direct cash transfers (39): OpenAI ChatGPT response: Conditional cash transfers (CCT) and direct cash transfers (DCT) are two forms of financial assistance

that the World Bank promotes in some of its development programs.
Conditional monetary transfers refer to the delivery of an amount of money to the poorest and most vulnerable families, but its delivery is subject to the fulfillment of certain conditions. These conditions may include requirements for education, health care, nutrition, and other basic services, which families are expected to meet in order to receive the money. The objective is for families to use the money to improve their quality of life and that of their children, and thus reduce poverty.

On the other hand, direct monetary transfers are deliveries of money to people without specific conditions. These transfers are used in emergency situations, such as humanitarian crises, natural disasters, or armed conflict, to provide immediate financial assistance to affected people.

Overall, both conditional and direct cash transfers are important tools for the World Bank in fighting poverty and promoting economic and social development. However, the World Bank also recognizes that these transfers are only part of a broader approach to addressing development challenges and that they need to be combined with other policies and programs to achieve sustainable and long-lasting results.

Human design in the economy (40): It is crucial to clarify this point because part of our mixed economy proposal is a mixture of human design and free enterprise. The new technological and innovation companies mostly arose from someone's creative spontaneity and with determination they managed to carry out their dream and their idea. The state companies that socialism promotes are of human design - they are born completely procedural; What makes it state is public investment, administration under public laws and the protected market - it is something that human beings already know how to do and have done before, such as public services, the large food industry, industrial production, etc. Human design is also often called constructivist rationalism or socialism; This current again and again fails to create new value and wealth. Contrary to the constructivist rationalists, nature, or the spontaneous order, I create a system that does work in creating value and wealth but that is based on the natural individualistic selfishness of the human being when pursuing his own interest and not on the very good obligation of the socialists. All wealth created in the individual spontaneous order becomes private property. On the other hand, there are sectors of human design that become part of the private sector: these sectors are created under laws (most of the parafiscal taxes) and that can be regulated and processed under the same laws, however, they will be part of private capital and managed by private parties and regulated by the free market (what is sought here is the administration of a vital service in private hands because it is considered better administration"). The health sector, professional risks, layoffs, pensions, etc. operate in this field. There is an example in which it is not a vital service, but it can be regulated by limiting the direct participation of the interested parties and allowing a third party to mediate, profit and establish the connection that the market needs; In some states of the United States there is this regulation that leaves only intermediaries joining the parties of those who need houses and those who offer them (the advantages in the real estate market are debatable, as well as the need itself and the costs that increase it to the process).

However, we consider that without human design this process of creating the vital umbrella in basic services around the companies of ordinary people (families, micros, and enterprises in general), would not be possible. This will not happen spontaneously in the time it is needed.

Neo communists (41): in some cases, we will call them Neo-Marxists; understand the same. In this book we use the words socialism and communism interchangeably for the same effect; We do not enter the fallacy of discussing the order they have or whether the chicken or the egg came first. Finally, we use the word neo communists to give the appropriate meaning to the indirect strategy. Gramscian postmodernist; After all this analysis, we have removed the masks to discover who is behind it and their real intentions.

Serious Marxist error in economics (42): many of Marx's errors (we will mention some that have not been explained in this book and on which much remains to be done) are the subject of analysis by revisionists; The so-called post-Marxists - of whom there are many bad guys - the majority consider that the path was wrong, but not the end. That failed to consider key aspects:

-Like that the rising human being only works for himself and his family, or that the human being who barely achieves something, no matter how little, values it very much, so much so that he will face (surround, ignore or finally emigrate) any law or policy that takes him away from his dreams. The reader notices that this idea (original from Milton Friedman) is developed in this book suggesting that the person in the process of acquiring private property and seeking their well-being is not fertile to the ideas of socialization or collectivization.

-His predictions regarding the disparity in the distribution of wealth, which placed the rich in two opposite poles against a large majority of the poor... did not occur; In fact, the opposite happened since after lifting large masses out of poverty, the free market substantially improved the well-being of the vast majority of the population, turning them into the middle and upper middle class (in developed societies). For the reader it is clear that the lower classes (without property) accept subsidies; The rising social classes, that is, the middle and upper classes, will defend any property acquired.

-That the forced violent path that Marx himself proposed was taken due to the expropriating actions, the violence that coercive policies to reduce inequality bring; that this path is only possible under an iron dictatorship that brought tyrannies that overshadowed any good initial design. That the expropriatory path only led to scarcity and great famines. We must clarify that, if Democracy is preserved, the people in a free election will always choose their well-being (even if it is unequal), removing any possibility of equalizing society. Democracy is only compatible with freedom.

-**Gramscian postmodernism** took the wrong path again, since they only changed the order of the recipe - the strategy of taking power is a winner, but socialism proved to destroy value, not create it - now, if there is not enough wealth created, they will face the same problems as the pure Marxist recipe. Returning to what was said in this paragraph, we realize that the postmodernists have had an advantage over Marx because their analyzes are based on past events and not on supposed utopian futures as was the case with Marx; They simply ignored reality, doctrine preceded them.

-After the predictions, when time brings calm to many actions taken on the ground, we find that the progress of some of the redistribution policies, as well as the consolidation of them in what the welfare state represents, have been given in the richest societies (Europe and the United States itself) where consensus has been key; never imposition or coercion as we traditionally know these policies.

-It seems that contrary to what Marx thought, his ideas are more accepted and agreed upon in developed and rich societies, where they consent to a reduction in their well-being in pursuit of the tranquility of society.

This book is written in the hope that we will not abandon the paths of freedom to their fate.

www.ingramcontent.com/pod-product-compliance
Lightning Source LLC
Chambersburg PA
CBHW070818250726
48662CB00003B/1006